The Case for Identity Politics

RACE, ETHNICITY, AND POLITICS

Luis Ricardo Fraga and Paula D. McClain, Editors

The Case for Identity Politics

POLARIZATION, DEMOGRAPHIC CHANGE, AND RACIAL APPEALS

Christopher T. Stout

University of Virginia Press
CHARLOTTESVILLE AND LONDON

University of Virginia Press

Printed in the United States of America on acid-free paper

First published 2020

ISBN 978-0-8139-4498-2 (hardcover)
ISBN 978-0-8139-4499-9 (ebook)

9 8 7 6 5 4 3 2 1

Library of Congress Cataloging-in-Publication Data is available for this title.

This book is dedicated to Calvin and Parker Stout.

You are my inspiration.

Contents

Contents

Foreword

The publication of *The Case for Identity Politics* is timely. The work explores a subject that is as relevant today as it was fifty years ago, when I coauthored the book *Black Power: The Politics of Liberation* with Kwame Toure (formerly Stokely Carmichael).

The term "identity politics" is relatively new in electoral discourse. But it is not new in practice in the United States and other nations, such as South Africa. Identity politics have been practiced in the United States since the founding of the new nation in 1776. The Preamble to the Constitution states: "We the People . . . in Order to form a more perfect Union . . . establish Justice . . . and secure the Blessings of Liberty to ourselves and our Posterity." That is to say, for the posterity of the kin, kith, and kind of Anglo-Saxon males, who were in effect "the People," beneficiaries of this new "more perfect Union."

Over time this goal and the more democratic definition of "the People" has been altered through a long and protracted process, constitutional amendments, a civil war, and other sociopolitical events. Early identity politics changed as new groups were assured rights and gained the franchise. The pundits or politicians did not call this process "identity politics." But it was definitely that. Fast-forward to the twentieth century: women got the right to vote on August 18, 1920, and Native Americans in 1924. Black males had a postslavery Reconstruction franchise (the Fifteenth Amendment of 1870), but this was not enforced with teeth until the necessary Voting Rights Act of 1965. And even today blacks and other minorities still face voter-suppression activities.

The term "identity politics" took center stage during the 2016 presidential election when Hillary Clinton lost to Donald Trump, some say because she made vigorous appeals to certain identifiable electoral groups, namely, women, blacks, and Latinos. She was criticized for pandering to these groups. Trump, the victor, too was criticized for pandering (to put it mildly) to whites whose identity with a putative white America was being threatened. And thus, the discourse was changed. Identity politics became viewed as something negative. Nonsense I say.

The negatives associated with asserting group identity—which I would state more aptly as "identity consciousness"—are not new. I and my late coauthor Kwame Toure started it all—or as some would say, inflamed it all—with the publication of *Black Power* in 1967. The book invoked identity consciousness, specifically a powerful racial consciousness. We attacked, among other things, institutional racism (a term we introduced) and emphasized the need for racially conscious policies, in contrast to the race-neutral policies that had united white liberals, blacks, and others. What caused the greatest controversy was our calling for blacks to "close ranks" in order to more effectively pursue their racially conscious political and policy objectives. This alienated whites that had worked with blacks in the civil rights movement. What was misunderstood in the original edition of *Black Power*—which I corrected in the 1992 Afterword—was that "closing ranks" and pushing for race-conscious policies were needed so that black interests would not be ignored when their organizations entered into broader coalitions. Case in point: while black organizations enthusiastically supported the Social Security Act of 1935, black domestic and farm workers were locked out of its benefits. The same later held with discrimination against blacks in other federal programs, especially those administered by states and local governments, especially in the South. The reason for closing ranks and raising black voices for racially conscious policies was to get a respected seat at the table of coalition politics. Black power was needed as a precursor for coalition politics, learned and earned the hard way through experience.

I see the spirit of "closed ranks" in the identity-conscious groups today in that they push vigorously for identity-conscious objectives in the areas of racial justice, women's rights, LGBTQ rights, criminal justice, religious rights, and both sides of the immigration and border security debates. I suggest there should be more emphasis on these previously overlooked groups. These identity-conscious groups should heighten their participation in U.S. politics (i.e., law-abiding participation, as *Black Power* proposed nothing illegal). They should be proud of their identity: proud to be black, Latino, Native American, women, and LGBTQ, as much as Irish Catholics, Italian Americans, and Polish Americans, and yes, a genuinely patriotic and law-abiding white American identity, have been and continue to be proud of theirs.

But Americans should not only rely on their identity. They must bring that identity into the electoral process. Alone they cannot function effectively. They must push for their seat at the table of coalitions, confident, secure, and from a position of strength. It has to be understood that ultimately coalitions will have to be based not on their identities, but rather on their shared interests. Not one or few groups are going to rule in the future. Those that will must of necessity turn identity into common interest, form coalitions, learn how and when to organize and to compromise. For too long Americans have used its multiracial, multiethnic, multigender, multicultural political process to divide and rule. They must now use identity for a more positive goal.

Charles V. Hamilton

Acknowledgments

This book would not have been written but for three important conferences around deracialization as an electoral strategy. The first was "Black Politics in a 'Colour-Blind' Era: Re-Examining Deracialisation," which was hosted by Nuffield College, University of Oxford, and organized by Desmond King and Richard Johnson. It was through the discussions at this conference that I thought more critically about deracialization as campaign tool. Following this, I attended "*Black Power* at 50," a conference hosted by Columbia University and organized by Frederick Harris and Kimberly Johnson celebrating the fiftieth anniversary of the book *Black Power: The Politics of Liberation in America*, which was cowritten by Charles V. Hamilton and the late Kwame Toure (Stokely Carmichael). In preparation for this conference, I wrote a chapter in which I compared my previous work to Hamilton's seminal work on deracialization. This ten-page manuscript has been expanded to become this book. Finally, I fleshed out many of the ideas that appear in this book at the conference "Black Politics after Obama" hosted by the James Weldon Johnson Institute at Emory University and organized by Andra Gillespie. I can say with certainty that without these opportunities to be around wonderful scholars doing amazing research on the campaign strategies of underrepresented groups I would not have pursued or completed this project. I am grateful for all of the organizers for putting these important conferences together and for including me. This book is a testament to their hard work and generosity.

I am grateful for Charles V. Hamilton being willing to write the foreword for this book. His foundational work on black politics has inspired many careers in political science. My own career is no exception. His creation and discussion of the concept of deracialization motivated this project. As is evident by the foreword, he remains actively engaged and continues to provide insightful commentary about the state of race in American politics. I would also like to thank Delecia Forbes for aiding with the foreword.

I am also grateful to my colleagues and the students that I have had the good fortune to work with at Oregon State University. It was discussions with students in my "Civil Rights Politics and Policies" course in Winter 2017 and in Dwaine Plaza and Marilyn Stewart's course on "Black Resistance in the Era of Trump" that really helped me think critically about this book in its early stages.

Rebecca Warner also kept me on track in the production of this book. I set a deadline to finish the manuscript, and she checked in on me to make sure I was keeping pace. I am thankful for her help as well as her comments on the project. I would also like to thank my colleagues Alison Johnston, Rorie Solberg, Brett Burkhardt, Esther Matthews, Jon Stoll, Brent Steel, Hua-Yu Li, Sarah Henderson, Erika Wolters, Keith Baker, Ana Spalding, Hilary Boudet, Andrew Valls, Elizabeth Schroeder, Amy Below, and Paul Thompson for their comments and support during the time I was completing this project.

I am eternally indebted to all of the formal and informal mentors who have played a significant role in my career thus far. In particular, I would like to thank Martin Johnson and Paula McClain. The former was an informal undergraduate advisor whose selflessness and dedication to educating the next generation of scholars is something I work hard to emulate every day. The latter provided me my first opportunity to learn how to conduct political science research at the Ralph Bunche Summer Institute. It was my experience in this wonderful program that led me to pursue a career in political science.

This work is an extension (albeit a far-removed one) of the work that I completed as a graduate student at the University of California, Irvine. Without the guidance and suggestions of my advisors Katherine Tate, Louis DeSipio, Carole Uhlaner, and Bernie Grofman, I would not have had the confidence or skills to complete this project. I am extremely proud to have had the opportunity to be an Anteater and receive the guidance of these amazing scholars.

While not an exhaustive list of scholars who have been shaped my career and my thinking around this topic, I would like to thank coauthors, friends, and other scholars who have been supportive of this work, including Jennifer R. Garcia, Gregory Leslie, Maneesh Arora, Natalie Masuoka, Kristine Coulter, Peter Miller, Reuben Kline, Michael Tesler, Lorrie Frasure-Yokley, Danvy Le, Kathy Rim, Leah Ruppanner, LaGina Gause, Matt Baretto, Nadia Brown, Neil Chaturvedi, Steve Weldon, Catherine Corrigall-Brown, Danielle Lemi, Scott McClurg, Dante Jackson, David Jackson, Dana Jackson, Tobin Grant, Randy Burnside, Christina Greer, Kenn Ghaffarian, Megan Ming-Francis, and Eric Juenke, for all of their advice and assistance. I would also like to thank the two anonymous reviewers on this book. Their careful reading of the manuscript and comments and suggestions have vastly improved this study.

This is my second book with the University of Virginia Press. I have been very lucky to work with this wonderful organization and be a part of the "Racial and Ethnic Politics" series. The editors and series editors have always been very supportive of my work. I would like to first thank Dick Holway, who played an instrumental role in my development as a book author. Dick was very enthusiastic when I first presented this project to him. I was very appreciative of his passion for this project and comments on early drafts. I would also like to thank Nadine Zimmerli who served as my editor when Dick retired. Nadine showed the same excitement for this project and worked extremely hard in shaping the book in the final stages. She was also very involved in making sure the project was published in a timely manner.

I am forever indebted to my parents, Theresa and Timothy Stout, who have been amazing role models whom I continue to look up to. Their hard work and sacrifice is the sole reason that I am in the position I am in today. Their generosity as caregivers continues as grandparents. They are both very active in my children's life, which has given me more time to work on research. In this way, they continue to open doors for me.

My sister, Vanessa Stout, is not only a fantastic sibling, but also an innovative scholar whom I have had the pleasure to coauthor with. Conversations and advice from her have been important in the development of this project.

I am fortunate to be married to Kelsy Kretschmer, a fellow social scientist. I cannot imagine my life or my career without her. At every step of the way, Kelsy's advice has been invaluable. She is my inspiration to be a better person and scholar. She is the best partner a person could have, and all of my accomplishments would not have been possible without her.

Finally, I became a much better person after the birth of my children Calvin and Parker. At the University of California, Irvine, Katherine Tate once told me that having kids makes you a better scholar. I did not understand this until they were born. I work harder, more efficiently, and smarter because of them. The opportunity to spend time with them is pure bliss and is my motivation to stay focused during work hours. They are brilliant and full of joy. I am hopeful that I can provide them all of the opportunities that I enjoyed. I also am hopeful that the future will be bright for them and their generation.

The Case for Identity Politics

INTRODUCTION

The End of Identity Politics?

The 2016 U.S. presidential election was unique and important in many ways. Hillary Clinton became the first woman ever to represent a major political party as the nominee for president. The Republican nominee, Donald Trump, was a true political outsider with no experience in government. In an era of growing political polarization, both candidates had record low favorability ratings (Enten 2016). In addition to the unique nature of their bids for the White House, both candidates made overt identity-based appeals to their base. These campaign strategies were starkly different from the tactics used by most modern presidential candidates.

On the one hand, Trump made numerous appeals to white working-class and rural voters. His campaign slogan, "Make America Great Again," has been associated with a period of time when working-class and rural individuals could make a good living without having a college degree. Moreover, many argued that Trump's campaign played to whites' fears that the changing demographics of the nation would displace white voters and damage the country. On the other hand, Clinton appealed to the growing number of racial and ethnic minorities in the United States, and to women. Her campaign slogan, "Stronger Together," has been characterized as celebrating diversity. Moreover, Clinton's campaign website had a specific section on racial justice in which she made numerous appeals to both Latinos and African Americans.

Clinton's campaign was praised as being much more organized compared to the campaign of Trump (Sides, Tesler, and Vavreck 2019). Moreover, many expected that Clinton was almost a lock to become the next president of the United States because the Obama coalition had grown over the past four years. Most preelection polls and political pundits corroborated this expectation. On the day of the election, *FiveThirtyEight* gave Trump just a 28.6 percent chance of winning. Trump even told a crowd in Wisconsin in December 2016 that he had expected to lose on election night (McCaskill 2016; Barnett 2018).

In spite of these expectations, Trump surprised many political experts and prognosticators and upset Clinton. The day after the election, pundits and the Democratic Party worked hard to find answers for their stunning defeat. Some argued that Clinton's ties to the business community made it difficult for her to attract the support of working-class voters (Allen and Parnes 2017). Others pointed to her lack of campaigning in the critical Midwestern states of Michigan and Wisconsin (Dovere 2016). However, one of the most consistent criticisms of Hillary Clinton's campaign was that it had focused too much on identity politics.

Within days of Clinton's defeat, the *New York Times* published an article by Columbia University historian Mark Lilla (2016) titled "The End of Identity Politics." In the article, Lilla (2016) argued that the Democratic Party's focus on the plight of underrepresented groups alienated white voters. Moreover, he argued that if the Democratic Party does not abandon this strategy it will lead to more failure in the future. "One of the many lessons of the recent presidential election campaign and its repugnant outcome is that the age of identity liberalism must be brought to an end." Lilla was not alone in his condemnation of identity politics. Writing for the *Denver Post*, Froma Harrop (2016) argued that Clinton's focus on underrepresented groups obscured her economic message and doomed her campaign: "Clinton's fervent messaging to Latinos, African-Americans, Asians, Muslims, the LGBT community and women went beyond the usual targeting. It drowned out her economic platform, which would have done so much more for the struggling white workers who chose Donald Trump."

The calls for ending identity politics did not stop there. Since the election, opinion editorials titled "The End of Identity Politics" or slight variations of this have been published by RealClearPolitics, *Daily KOS*, the *National Review*, and the *New York Times* (see Casey 2017; Hanson 2017; Lilla 2016; Williamson 2016). Each article made a similar argument: The Democratic Party spent too much time tailoring appeals to underrepresented groups and sacrificed the white working class as a result. The takeaway from these articles is clear: If the Democratic Party wants to win again, it must focus on a liberal economic agenda and distance itself from identity politics.

The argument that the Democratic Party should abandon identity politics is not new. After repeat defeats of the party's presidential candidates in 1968 and 1972, many advocated that the Democratic Party move away from its focus on civil rights. Strategists argued that the party should run a campaign devoid of racial appeals, also known as a deracialized campaign. Supporters of the deracialized strategy argued that the party's focus on race made it difficult for Democrats to appeal to working-class whites and southerners who were at one time key members of the Democratic Party's New Deal coalition. Following these suggestions, presidential and statewide candidates adopted a deracialized strategy—with some success. The advantages of the deracialized strategy were exemplified by the election of Jimmy Carter in 1976, Bill Clinton in 1992 and 1996, and Barack Obama in 2008 and 2012.

However, a lot has changed with regard to race relations since Obama's reelection to the White House in 2012. A number of high-profile police shootings and acquittals, increasing evidence of growing racial economic disparities, retrenchments on voting rights, and the growth of racial hate groups have made race a more salient issue in American politics. Moreover, demographic changes in the United States have made racial/ethnic minorities a more influential voting bloc. For example, Obama in 2012 received less support from whites than Michael Dukakis did in 1988 but won 221 more electoral votes. Obama's success demonstrates the growing significance that racial/ethnic minorities play in American politics.

While a deracialized strategy has been successful for the Democratic Party in the past, the question remains whether it is still the most advantageous strategy in the current political context. One of the chief strategists behind the call for deracialization in the 1970s, Columbia University professor Charles V. Hamilton (1977, 3) argued that the political context should determine when the deracialization strategy is most applicable: "A deracialized strategy makes certain assumptions about the American electoral political arena. . . . It assumes, likewise, that the political participants realize that elections in this system are not *for all time* but occur from *time to time*. The latter assumption means, of course, that a strategy adopted for one election in a particular context is not written in stone, but is precisely a strategy used at that time to maximize the possibility of achieving certain goals."

While a significant amount of work has explored whether deracialization strategies work well in contexts that are majority black or white (see, e.g., Gillespie 2012; H. Perry 1991) and whether some voters are more supportive of a deracialized approach than others, no work has explored how the national political context shapes the efficacy of a deracialized campaign approach. Controversies over the Democratic Party's focus on racial appeals in 2016, along with the unique political context in which it occurred, provide a great opportunity to assess whether the Democratic Party distancing itself from identity politics is a prudent strategy.

The Case for Identity Politics explores whether racial appeals improve the electability of candidates from the Democratic Party in the current political context. In doing so, this book provides information about *when* a racialized approach is most effective. The early chapters of the book describe the current racial and political context. I then analyze whether voters of different races/ethnicities and political parties have shifting views about race relations in a period where activism around racial issues has increased. Subsequently, I explore why whites, and in particular white Democrats, may be more supportive of a racially progressive agenda using a variety of public opinion polls and whether whites of different partisanships are more or less likely to support candidates who make racial appeals or appear racially progressive.

The book then shifts to focus on the political preferences of African Americans and Latinos. In these chapters, I analyze whether the current political context has increased blacks' and Latinos' levels of "linked fate," a measure of racial solidarity. Moreover, I explore whether blacks and Latinos, who in the past have supported deracialized candidates, are developing a stronger devotion to candidates who make racial appeals. The final section of the book uses the results from previous chapters to investigate whether the use of racial appeals is enhanced by the growing number of racial/ethnic minorities in the United States. Through this analysis, I hope to not only answer questions about whether the use of racial appeals was and will be problematic for the Democratic Party from 2016 going forward, but also to further our understanding of how the political climate shapes voters' reactions to politicians using identity politics.

Defining Deracialization

As noted above, in 1977 Charles V. Hamilton outlined a campaign strategy to help the Democratic Party craft a plan to build a multiracial coalition, arguing the party should avoid appeals to race. Hamilton recognized that the Republican Party was using the Democratic Party's stances on civil rights issues to mobilize unsympathetic whites and break apart the New Deal coalition of blue-collar workers, union members, racial/ethnic minorities, and white southerners. To combat this strategy, Hamilton (1977) argued that the Democratic Party may benefit from focusing on color-blind, class-based policies, designed to benefit *all* poor people, such as universal employment, expansions in healthcare, and income maintenance programs. He also argued that this new strategy, a deracialized campaign strategy, should avoid targeted appeals to underrepresented racial groups. In essence, the deracialized campaign style was meant to revive the New Deal coalition that created a bond between blacks, whites, and other groups by focusing on class interests rather than racial interests.

By focusing on class over race, Hamilton (1977) argued, the Democratic Party would still advance black political interests without turning off racially conservative voters. For example, blacks were (and still are) disproportionately unemployed and uninsured at the time Hamilton was writing. As a result, a campaign strategy that could address the problems faced by many blacks without explicitly discussing race could help the Democratic Party engage economically liberal but racially conservative whites while at the same time helping the black community.

Moreover, many have argued that a focus on class over race may produce better outcomes for a broader swath of the black population. William Julius Wilson (1987), in his study *The Truly Disadvantaged*, argued that race-based policies generally expand opportunities for wealthier blacks and fail to address problems faced by poorer blacks. Similarly, Reed (2013) argued that even if racially targeted policies could erase class disparities between blacks and whites, a society in which the top 1 percent of income earners has so much more wealth and opportunity than the bottom 99 percent is immoral. As a result, shifting focus to class rather than race not only presents an electorally advantageous strategy, but it appears most beneficial to racial/ethnic minorities. This focus on class-based appeals versus race-based appeals is at the heart of the deracialization strategy.

After his strategy was applied successfully in the 1976 election, Hamilton (1977) outlined the deracialization framework in a three-page article "Deracialization: Examination of a Political Strategy," which was published in the *First World Journal* in March 1977. The article had an immediate and widespread impact on American politics. The framework was used by several Democratic presidential candidates, including Bill Clinton and Barack Obama. Moreover, it was used to advance the political opportunities of countless black candidates who, before the strategy had been widely implemented, were largely confined to representing majority-minority electorates.

The success of the strategy was perhaps most evident with the Black Tuesday candidates, who expanded black representation in numerous majority white cities and states. On November 7, 1989, a number of black officials were elected to majority white cities, including New Haven, Connecticut; Seattle, Washington; and Cleveland, Ohio. Moreover, it was on this day that L. Douglas Wilder became the first African American to be elected governor of any state (Virginia). Most political commentators and scholars attributed the success of these candidates to their ability to focus on centrist political issues like taxes and crime and to distance themselves from racial or racially tinged issues like welfare, affirmative action, and busing.

In addition to inspiring a generation of politicians, Hamilton's deracialization framework also inspired a large number of social scientists, who explored the effectiveness of the strategy in great detail (Gillespie 2010; Johnson 2015; Liu 2003; McCormick and Jones 1993; Orey and Ricks 2007; Reeves

1997; Stout 2015). One of the seminal works on this topic is "The Conceptualization of Deracialization" by Joseph McCormick and Charles E. Jones (1993). In this study, the authors provided a formal definition of a deracialized campaign as one conducted "in a stylistic fashion that defuses the polarizing effects of race by avoiding explicit reference to race-specific issues, while at the same time emphasizing those issues that are perceived as racially transcendent, thus mobilizing a broad segment of the electorate for purposes of capturing or maintaining public office" (76). McCormick and Jones (1993) also provided examples of what a deracialized campaign should look like in practice. According to these authors, a deracialized candidate will avoid discussing racial policies such as affirmative action, voting rights, civil rights, and immigration. Additionally, a deracialized candidate may work to distance themselves from racial/ethnic minorities by avoiding public appearances with prominent blacks and/or Latinos.

Why a Deracialized Campaign Can Be Useful

There are a number of reasons why a deracialized campaign was necessary for left-leaning candidates to succeed, particularly during the 1980s and 1990s. First, there was fear that white voters would not support candidates who appeared to be engaging in minority racial favoritism. Minority racial favoritism is the idea that left-leaning candidates, regardless of their race, will redistribute resources and opportunities to blacks and Latinos at the expense of whites. For example, whites have long been opposed to affirmative action as a policy because many see it as unfairly benefiting blacks to the detriment of whites (Swim and Miller 1999). If left-leaning candidates hope to win in elections in majority-white settings, they have to demonstrate that they will not engage in minority racial favoritism, given that some whites are turned off by racially progressive political stances. This may be particularly important for the Democratic Party given that their white base supports its economic policies but is often turned off by their discussion of racial issues. As a result, a deracialized strategy can remove the cross-pressures white Democrats face and boost their levels of support for liberal candidates.

Additionally, proponents of a deracialized approach argue that Republican candidates will exploit left-leaning candidates' stances on racial issues to drive a wedge between racial/ethnic minorities and working-class voters who have traditionally been part of the Democratic Party's base. As Hamilton (1977, 3) pointed out, "A political party not likely to obtain a significant share of a particular group's votes would find it advantageous to attempt to isolate that group by making overt and covert appeals to more receptive groups." There are several examples of this. First, in the 1988 presidential election, the

George H. W. Bush campaign exploited Michael Dukakis's policy as governor to allow weekend furloughs for inmates. In addition to painting Dukakis as soft on crime, they used the image of a black man named Willie Horton and discussed his murder and rape of a white couple to attract white voters (Mendelberg 2001). The advertisement played on fears that left-leaning candidates were too weak on criminals so as to protect racial/ethnic minorities, all at the cost of the public safety of whites (Mendelberg 2001). Along the same lines, in a 1990 North Carolina U.S. Senate race, Republican Jesse Helms attacked his Democratic opponent Harvey Gantt's support of affirmative action in an advertisement that showed a white male losing out on a job because they "gave it to a minority."

More recently, a 2010 television advertisement by Nevada U.S. Senate candidate Sharon Angle portrayed Latinos as gang members to incite fears among whites that the growth of the Latino population in the United States would lead to increased levels of crime (Parker 2017). She connected the growing Latino population in the United States to her opponent Harry Reid's liberal positions on immigration reform. Two years later, Republican presidential candidate Mitt Romney ran a campaign advertisement that argued that his opponent Barack Obama was weakening the 1996 Welfare Reform Act to make it easier for people to get welfare without working. The ad appeared to be exploiting fears among whites that left-leaning candidates unfairly provide social services to minorities (Nteta and Tarsi 2016).

In combination, these attacks use liberal candidates' support for racial policies as a way to demonize them with otherwise sympathetic centrist white voters. A deracialized campaign approach is effective because it removes these tools from Republicans. Moreover, if Republicans use these racially aggressive tactics without much basis, they run the risk of appearing as racist, which has been shown to decrease support for them (Mendelberg 2001).

Finally, there is some research to suggest that racial/ethnic minority voters may be more receptive to deracialized campaigns in recent years. The main argument for this is that young black and Latinos are less likely to perceive the same levels of discrimination as their predecessors (Cose 2011). As a result, they tend to believe that candidates who focus on race are pandering to their demographic by playing on racial/ethnic divisions that no longer exist. This is in part aided by the fact that many black and Latino leaders have moved to the political center as they hope to advance within the Democratic Party (see Gonzalez Juenke and Sampaio 2010; Tate 2010). Blacks and Latinos in the electorate adopt these more centrist racial attitudes because they follow the lead of coracial/ethnic political leaders. In sum, many argue that a deracialized campaign may help left-leaning candidates maximize their vote.

Deracialization in Practice

Following the success of the Black Tuesday candidates and later the success of Barack Obama, numerous studies have been conducted to try to determine whether deracialization truly enhances the opportunities of left-leaning candidates. The earliest work on this topic identified both the benefits and problems of a deracialized approach. For the former, several studies noted that white voters were more supportive of deracialized candidates, particularly if these candidates were African American. For example, Jeffries (1999) and Frederick and Jeffries (2009) demonstrated that white voters were much more supportive of deracialized candidates than they were of candidates who made some racial appeals.

In addition to attracting white voters, left-leaning white and black candidates have successfully used a deracialized approach to put together multiracial coalitions. Canon, Schousen, and Sellers (1996) demonstrate that black candidates who use deracialized campaigns in diverse districts often perform better than their deracialized counterparts because they are able to win a sizable amount of the black vote and capture the lion's share of the white vote. Gillespie (2010, 2012) arrives at a similar conclusion in her analysis of Cory Booker's campaign to become mayor of Newark, New Jersey. Moreover, some have argued that a deracialized approach may improve candidates' standing with black voters. McIlwain and Caliendo (2011) used experimental methods to demonstrate that when all else is equal, black and white voters prefer deracialized candidates to their racialized counterparts.

Potential Pitfalls of Deracialization

However, it is important to note the deracialization is not without its critics. In particular, several studies demonstrate the limits of a deracialized campaign strategy. The most identified shortcoming of deracialization is that it demobilizes black and Latino turnout. This may be particularly problematic for deracialized racial/ethnic minority politicians who largely rely on the support of coracial or coethnic voters to succeed. For example, Citrin, Reingold, and Green (1990), Orey (2006), Pierannunzi and Hutcheson (1996), and Wright Austin and Middleton (2001) in separate studies show that blacks and Latinos are less likely to turn out to support candidates who run deracialized campaigns. This made a huge difference in elections that were decided by a few percentage points. For example, Citrin et al. (1990) argue that California gubernatorial candidate Tom Bradley's deracialized approach led to lower levels of black turnout at the polls, which could have made the difference in an election where Bradley and his opponent were only separated by 2 percentage points. Along the same lines, I've demonstrated that black candidates who do not make racial appeals experience a decline in black political support (Stout 2015). My previous book argues that racial/ethnic minority candidates who distance themselves too much from race appear as unsympathetic and squander their goodwill with coracial voters.

Additionally, myself and others have suggested that a deracialized campaign approach may not actually lead to large gains among whites (Johnson 2015; Stout 2015). For example, Lewis, Dowe, and Franklin (2012) demonstrate that in spite of Obama's deracialized campaign in 2012, he received just 40 percent of the white vote (see also Sinclair-Chapman and Price 2008). Moreover, in previous work I also show that whites are statistically as likely to support black racialized candidates as they are black deracialized candidates (Stout 2015). I argue that this is driven by the fact that regardless of whether black candidates racialize or not, they are perceived as making race-based appeals (see also Block 2011). Additionally, my previous work suggests that racialized candidates also receive less electoral support from Latinos and blacks (Stout 2015).

When candidates make conscious efforts to disassociate from minority communities, many may feel that the candidates are just taking their vote for granted and may be less willing to turnout or support them on Election Day (McCormick and Jones 1993; H. Perry 1991). This may be particularly bad for racial/ethnic minority candidates as they may be perceived as particularly uncaring when they fail to discuss the issues that concern those who share their race/ethnicity. Blacks and Latinos may feel demoralized by candidates/elected officials who do not speak about issues that concern them and become less engaged as a result, in turn hurting black and Latino candidates because they are expected to advance the political interests of those in their racial/ethnic community.

Context and Deracialization

One of the difficult things about the deracialization literature is that, depending on the case, there tend to be conflicting results. In some cases, a deracialized campaign advances a candidates' ability to succeed (McCormick and Jones 1993; Price 2016; Reeves 1997) but in others it appears to be counterproductive (Gillespie 2012; Johnson 2015; Stout 2015). The inconsistent results demonstrate the necessity for further theorizing about the efficacy of deracialization. Clues to better understanding this puzzle may come from Hamilton's early writing on the topic. Here, as mentioned above, the political context may help us understand when candidates should make identity-based appeals. Hamilton (1977, 5) noted: "The deracialization document was addressed to a strategy applicable to electoral politics in the presidential contest of 1976. It is not a strategy to be pursued *at all times in all places*. Whether it would (or should) apply in a local election with a majority black electorate remains to be calculated. How it should be applied in conjunction with protest and pressure-group politics remains to be calculated. *But at all times calculation is the key*" (my emphasis).

Most previous research on deracialization has focused on the racial composition of the electorate as the predominant predictor of when a race-neutral campaign might succeed (Hamilton 1977; Liu 2003; McCormick and Jones 1993). Put simply, scholars argue that when the electorate is majority white, candidates should ignore race-based appeals to attract white voters. When the electorate is majority-minority, then the candidate should focus on identity politics to maximize their support.

However, this assumes that white voters will always be opposed to racial appeals and minority voters will always be supportive of this outreach. Instead, it is highly likely that the significance of race in society largely shapes when the white, black, and Latino electorates will be most receptive to policies aimed at ending racial inequality. Moreover, political strategies are largely contingent on who decides elections, which has shifted significantly over the last forty years since Hamilton's original proposal for a deracialized campaign strategy. By taking contextual factors more seriously, we may better understand when a deracialized approach is the most effective. Moreover, we may gain insight into whether voters in the current political context will reward or punish candidates for making racial appeals.

The New Civil Rights Movement

A significant amount of research demonstrates that context shapes political opinion and voting behavior. For example, Egan and Mullin (2012) demonstrated that individuals who are exposed to extreme weather patterns are more likely to support action being taken on climate change. Along the same lines, attitudes about social welfare and crime policy are driven by the salience of crime and the employment rate of the country (see Kinder and Kiewiet 1979; Marschall 2004). In combination, when individuals are presented with new information, and particularly information that they can personally sympathize with, they are more likely to shift their attitudes.

Previous studies have found that shifts in attitudes about race can also occur under the right context. In his seminal work on the civil rights movement, McAdam (1999) demonstrated that northern whites became more supportive of the government taking action to address racial inequality following a number of high-profile protests. McAdam (1999) describes how a confluence of contextual factors made the 1964 Civil Rights Act and the 1965 Voting Rights Act possible in a country that was majority-white and long opposed to supporting the government taking action on race relations. One of the biggest developments was that changes in technology made it possible for individuals to view some of the horrific obstacles that blacks in the South had to overcome to accomplish mundane activities like voting or riding a bus.

For example, public opinion about racial inequality shifted dramatically after civil rights protestors marched from Selma to Montgomery in Alabama to demand that black Alabamans have the right to register and vote. On March 7, 1965, protestors faced a significant amount of violence from the police as they arrived in Montgomery and were ultimately beaten back across the Edmund Pettis Bridge. The image of peaceful protesters being unable to vote simply because of the color of their skin was a poignant one for many Americans. Following the event, whites sided with the protestors over the police by a more than 2-to-1 margin (Kohut 2015). The spectacle became known as Bloody Sunday and led to a large shift in public opinion about the needs for a voting rights bill. For these and other reasons, including the importance of blacks as a swing vote and the rising black middle class, politicians were encouraged rather than discouraged to take bold steps to address racial inequality. As a result, numerous policies were passed to address the concerns of the black community.

There is good reason to believe that the current political context provides incentives for politicians to advance a racially progressive agenda. For example, there has been a heightened awareness among whites that racial discrimination constitutes a serious barrier to normalcy for blacks and Latinos. As in the civil rights movement, a new technology, the smartphone, has allowed the public to easily view examples of discrimination leading to the unwarranted shootings of African Americans. Moreover, the Black Lives Matter movement has made Americans more aware of the tangible consequences of racial discrimination. These changes have been correlated with a shift in white public opinion supporting more action to ensure racial equality. For example, in a 2015 Pew Research Center poll a majority of white respondents (~53%) agreed with the statement that more changes needed to be made so that blacks can enjoy equal rights with whites (Kohut 2015). As was seen during the civil rights movement, the public's support for addressing racial inequality may change how individuals react to racial appeals.

Whites are not the only ones who have become more supportive of changes being made to the political system to advance racial equality in recent years. In *The End of Anger*, Ellis Cose (2011) showed how black millennials don't harbor the same levels of black group consciousness as their parents. Many younger blacks pointed to the success of Barack Obama as evidence that with hard work and playing by the rules, blacks could succeed in this country. However, just five years after the publication of *The End of Anger*, these same black millennials were some of the most active members of Black Lives Matter movement, and a recent Pew poll of black millennials demonstrated that over 80 percent of them supported the movement (Horowitz and Livingston 2016). While black millennials are just one part of the black community, the late Obama years saw a resurgence in black group consciousness and black activism. For example, more blacks in 2016 displayed the highest levels of linked fate captured in any survey dating back to the 1980s (see chapter 5 for more details).

Given blacks' increased levels of consciousness in the current political context, politicians who run deracialized campaigns may face a significant backlash from the black community. Hamilton (1977) suggested a deracialized campaign must be met with pressure among blacks to ensure that government officials are responsive. He notes that "the real burden of a deracialized strategy, in fact, is not to lay one's self open to having been coopted, but require continued diligent political mobilization to be able to reward and punish" (4). Hamilton's prophetic statements may be playing out in practice if blacks are more likely to punish elected officials whom they perceive as ignoring the plight of the black community.

Most previous research on deracialization has focused on black and whites (see Gonzalez Juenke and Sampaio 2010; Wright Austin and Middleton 2004; see also Stout 2015 as an exception). However, Latinos' responsiveness to racial appeals may also be influenced by the current racial climate. Having surpassed blacks as the largest racial/ethnic minority group, Latinos have also faced increased levels of discrimination in the form of racist rhetoric. Moreover, their panethnic group has been the target of restrictive policies, including punitive immigration legislation and voter identification laws. This increase in discrimination may lead Latinos, like blacks, to find an increased sense of group consciousness. In addition, it may lead them to be more supportive of candidates who address racial/ethnic inequality in their campaigns. Even in the 2016 election, the perception that Hillary Clinton cared for Latinos was a strong predictor of whether they supported her or not (Barreto 2017). In summary, the current racial context may increase the interest of whites, blacks, and Latinos in racialized appeals.

Polarization and the Increasing Efficacy of Racialized Politics

Several recent studies have demonstrated that Americans have become more ideologically sorted by their partisanship (see, e.g., Levendusky 2009).

In particular, liberals are much more likely to identify with the Democratic Party and conservatives are much more likely to identify with the Republican Party (Levendusky 2009). Along these lines, Americans have become more sorted with regard to their views of African Americans and Latinos (Tesler 2016). In 1976, when Hamilton first wrote about deracialization as a strategy, there were no significant differences in black "feeling thermometer" scores (i.e., scores that measure how well-liked or disliked an individual/group is) between white Democrats and white Republicans according to the American National Election Studies (ANES). This was largely driven by the fact that many white Democrats during this period had negative views of the black community. According to the 1976 ANES, 43 percent of white Democrats rated blacks at 50 points or lower on the 0 (cold) to 100 (warm) feeling thermometer scale.

Since that time, many of these individuals have left the Democratic Party, and those who remain tend to be more progressive on racial issues. For example, in the 2012 ANES there were significant differences between white Democrats and white Republicans, and less than a third of white Democrats rated blacks as 50 points or lower on the feeling thermometer scale. While Democrats have become more racially liberal, Republicans have moved in the opposite direction. In fact, the proportion of Republicans who rate blacks at 50 points or lower on the feeling thermometer scale actually increased by about 3 percent between 1976 and 2012. Taken in combination, individuals are becoming more sorted by their racial attitudes into one of the two major parties.

These changes in racial polarization have direct consequences for racialized politics. As voters sort based on their opinions about race, fewer liberal politicians have to worry about appealing to a group of individuals who are ideologically consistent on some issues but are weary of racially progressive politics. For example, when Jimmy Carter campaigned for president in 1976, there was a sizable number of white Democrats who supported his economic policies but were opposed to any legislation that expanded opportunities for blacks. These cross-pressured voters were exemplified by people like Mississippi Democratic U.S. senator John C. Stennis, who endorsed numerous liberal policies such as advocating for public works spending and limiting the United States' role in the Vietnam War. However, Stennis was a staunch supporter of racial segregation. He and many southern Democrats like him were willing to support the Democratic Party, but not if they supported racially progressive policies. As a result, it was strategic for Democratic candidates to not overemphasize progressive racial politics so as to appeal to these individuals.

Today, there are fewer individuals who identify as liberal who also are antagonistic to racial policies. As a result, Democratic candidates who want to appeal to copartisans worry less about whether their positions on racial issues will alienate a segment of their supporters. In fact, several studies demonstrate that many progressive Democrats prefer candidates who advance black's and Latino's political interests (Tesler and Sears 2010; Stout 2015). As a result of ideological sorting, politicians don't face the same challenges of having to appear as liberal on some issues while ignoring racial issues to be elected. As voters become more sorted by partisanship and racial attitudes, it is unlikely that Democratic politicians' positions on racial issues alone will be what drives copartisans or ideologically similar independents away. Politicians in this era may no longer pay the same penalty for discussing racial issues.

Changing Demographics and a Changing Electorate

In 1968, the poor performance of Democratic presidential nominee and civil rights advocate Hubert Humphrey in the reliably Democratic states of Louisiana, Georgia, and Mississippi exposed problems for the Democratic Party. Many southern whites were unhappy with the party's growing support for a progressive civil rights agenda. Richard Nixon was able to exploit these problems in 1968 and 1972 by focusing on a "Law and Order" campaign that played to whites' negative stereotypes about blacks (McCombs and Shaw 1972). The strategy was widely successful as Nixon won in a landslide in 1972 and did well in the South, traditionally a Democratic stronghold. This was extremely problematic for the Democratic Party at the time because they were not consistently winning states like New York or California. As a result, the Democratic Party desperately needed to perform well in southern states to win the White House.

The necessity of the Democratic Party appealing to southern white voters is evident from the fact that between 1964 and 2004, the only Democrats to win the White House had connections to the South (Lyndon B. Johnson, Jimmy Carter, and Bill Clinton). To win at the national level, Democrats would largely have to appeal to white southerners who might be weary of supporting a candidate who professed a racially progressive agenda. This is exactly what made a deracialized approach so necessary during this period.

However, the political landscape has changed in two fundamental ways since then, which may limit the importance of the white vote in the South for the Democratic Party. The first is that the electoral map has changed, with states like California, Illinois, and New York, which at times had gone with the Republican Party, now safely Democratic. This change makes the Democratic Party less reliant on southern white support. For example, in 2004 Democratic presidential candidate John Kerry famously made the statement that he could win the presidency without winning a single southern state (Guillory 2012). Kerry ultimately lost the presidential election, but had he carried Ohio, he would have indeed won the White House without winning a single state in the South.

More importantly, changes in the demographics in the United States have made it so that elected officials, and in particular Democratic elected officials, must appeal to racial/ethnic minorities to win elected office. During the time of Hamilton's writing of the "Deracialization Strategy," Latinos made up less than 5 percent of the population. As noted above, they now are the largest minority group in the United States and account for 15 percent of the nation. At the same time, blacks are exceeding expectations with regard to participation given that they tend to be disproportionately poorer and less educated. These traits are often are associated with lower levels of turnout (Philpot, Shaw, and McGowen 2009; Tate 2003. In combination, minority voters are making up an increasingly important part of the electorate. In fact, census estimates suggest that the country will become majority-minority by the year 2043 (Haynes, Merolla, and Ramakrishnan 2016).

These changing demographics provide strong incentives for politicians to appeal to racial/ethnic minorities. This is best illustrated by the multiracial coalition that led to Obama's victories in 2008 and 2012. In 2012, Obama lost the white vote by 20 points. This margin was the largest by which any Democratic presidential candidate had lost in the previous twenty-eight years (Walter Mondale lost by a wider margin in 1984). Obama did particularly poorly among white southerners, who in the past had been a crucial swing vote. In fact, Obama received less than 30 percent support from white voters in the South according to exit polls (Scala, Johnson, and Rogers 2015).

So how did Obama succeed without the winning the southern white vote? He did so by putting together a coalition of liberal whites, African American voters, and Latinos (Lewis-Beck and Nadeau 2009). Black and Latino voters were particularly mobilized by the historic nature of his campaign. Obama proved that candidates can succeed in national elections if they are able to mobilize liberal whites, blacks, and Latinos. This will become a more fruitful strategy in the future as these groups grow as a percentage of the electorate. In sum, the combination of democratic dominance of more populous states, the Democratic Party's systematic decline in southern states, and changing demographics presents a new context where a racialized campaign may be more advantageous than a deracialized one.

A Note on Terminology

Together with "deracialization," which I defined earlier in this introduction, I also use the terms "racial appeal" and "racialization" throughout this book. I define "racial appeal" as any form of outreach that is targeted specifically at members of underrepresented groups. When candidates discuss reparations for slavery, recognize black history month, address racial/ethnic income equality, or speak in Spanish they are making a racial appeal. Similarly, when I use "racialization," I am arguing that a candidate is using racial appeals meant to advance the interests of racial/ethnic minorities. This is an important distinction to make because previous work has tied racialization to both liberal and conservative racial policies. While this term could be tied to policies meant to inhibit or advance the interests of racial/ethnic minorities, in this book racialization refers only to politicians making attractive appeals to blacks and Latinos.

Additionally, when I mention "racialized campaigns," I am not only speaking about campaigns that are solely or mostly based on racial appeals. Instead, I generally speak of racialized campaigns as campaigns that make some racial outreach as part of their appeals to voters. This type of a racialized campaign is much more common given that there are few campaigns that are built solely to focus on race. As a result, I use a broad definition of racialization when I use this term. For example, 2020 U.S. presidential candidate Elizabeth Warren would be described as running a racialized campaign in my definition because of her appeals to racial/ethnic minorities. A quick perusal of her website reveals that while her campaign does not ignore race, it is not solely focused on racial issues. For example, in her "Plan" section of the website (as of September 27, 2019), she has forty-five different issues listed. However, only about five are explicitly tied to racial groups, including "Valuing the Work of Women of Color" and "Leveling the Playing Field for Entrepreneurs of Color," among others. While some may disagree with my definition of this term, for the purposes of this book I use a broader definition of racialization, which includes individuals who make at least some appeals to people of color.

Chapter Outline

The Case for Identity Politics explores whether and how different racial/ethnic groups' racial attitudes have changed over time, and how these shifts in public opinion may lead blacks, Latinos, and liberal whites to be more supportive of Democratic candidates who use racial appeals in the current political context. Chapter 1 explores how race became more salient after the election of Barack Obama in 2008. Here I focus on how the Tea Party movement, sparked by Obama's election to the White House, increased concerns about racial discrimination in society. I explore how this, in combination with the high-profile police shootings of people of color, the Black Lives Matter movement, and Donald Trump's nomination to the White House, led to dramatic changes in American's attitudes about racial issues.

Dramatic shifts in the racial context of the United States have an important impact on public opinion. I discuss this in chapter 2 by focusing on how changes in the racial context influence whites' attitudes about racial/ethnic minorities and racial policies. I demonstrate that America's growing interest with race combined with growing political polarization is leading white Democrats to express more progressive racial attitudes now than in the recent past. Conversely, it has led Republicans to become slightly more conservative on these issues. In combination, the results of this chapter show that gaps in racial attitudes among white Democrats and white Republicans have grown substantially in the last ten years and that much of this growing division is driven by the increasingly racially liberal attitudes of white Democrats.

Much of the change described in chapter 2 has been driven by partisan realignment, which is explored in chapter 3. In this chapter, I assess how growing divisions in partisanship and voting behavior among working-class whites with high or low levels of racial resentment may reshape how parties work to appeal to this electorate. The analysis in this chapter demonstrates that white working-class voters, a group that was originally the target of deracialized campaigns, are severely fragmented around issues of race. As a result, a one-size-fits-all policy around deracialization may no longer work to attract this group of voters. Moreover, as these voters have moved stronger toward one political party, labeling them as "swing voters" may no longer be accurate.

This substantial shift in polarization and partisanship raises questions about whether abstaining from racial appeals is still an effective strategy to attract white support. In chapter 4, I analyze how white Democrats, Republicans, and independents respond to candidates who appear racially progressive through the use of a survey experiment and survey data. For the latter, I use the ANES and Pew Research Center polls to explore whether Democratic presidential candidates from 1980 to 2016 were punished for appearing as racially progressive. The results demonstrate that unlike previous elections, perceptions of racial progressivism in 2016 did not lead whites to be less supportive of Hillary Clinton. Instead, white Democrats who perceived Clinton as racially progressive were more likely to vote, boosting her chances of success. The results of the Pew analysis demonstrate that whites did not become more or less supportive of Obama after he made a public appeal to Latinos in the form of expanding protections for the undocumented parents of American citizens. The results of an experimental analysis show that white respondents, regardless of partisanship, were equally supportive and enthusiastic for a hypothetical Democratic candidate who focused on racial issues as they were for the same candidate when they focused on liberal economic issues. In combination, the results demonstrate that racial appeals may not lead to less support for Democratic politicians, and, in some cases, it may actually mobilize supportive white voters.

While attracting white support is essential for election to most offices in the United States, discussions about race are especially significant for members of underrepresented groups. Chapters 5 and 6 focus on African Americans' reaction to the changing racial climate in the United States and their responses to racial appeals. In chapter 5, I discuss why the high-profile police shootings of blacks, the Black Lives Matter movement, and the perceived poor treatment of Obama by whites has led to a heightened sense of black linked fate. I then show that this change in levels of linked fate among blacks overlaps with their greater support for racially progressive policies.

Using the ANES, a Pew poll, and an online experiment, in chapter 6 I show that this change in racial policy preferences and group consciousness among blacks translates into greater levels of support for racially liberal Democratic candidates. I find that blacks are more supportive of racially liberal candidates in both the ANES and the experiment in primary elections, but partisanship washes away the influence of racial progressivism in general elections. I also find that blacks are more mobilized and enthusiastic for Democratic candidates who are perceived as more likely to address racial inequality. However, I find little evidence that blacks respond to appeals to the Latino community. Overall, the results from chapters 5 and 6 demonstrate that blacks reward candidates who engage in political outreach to their community.

Modern racial appeals must take into account the reaction from not just blacks and whites but also the growing Latino population in the United States. Chapter 7 explores whether the racial context in the United States has increased Latinos' levels of group consciousness and whether Latinos have become more liberal on racial issues in recent years. The results demonstrate that Latinos have increased in their levels of panethnic linked fate and hold more racially liberal attitudes now than in the recent past. In chapter 8, I show that this change in ethnic consciousness among Latinos leads them to respond positively to racially progressive candidates. Latinos are more supportive of these candidates in the primaries and are more mobilized and enthusiastic for these candidates in the presidential election. I also find that Obama's approval ratings increased substantially among Latinos after his announcement to protect more undocumented individuals from deportation. The combined results demonstrate that racial/ethnic minorities respond positively to racially progressive candidates. Moreover, they demonstrate that the efficacy of appealing to these groups through discussions about race is greater now than in the past.

The efficacy of racial appeals is also largely be affected by changes to the demographic patterns in the United States. In chapter 9, I assess how the results from the previous chapters in combination with the growing political power of racial/ethnic minorities may make racial appeals more fruitful as time progresses. I examine the effectiveness of these appeals at different levels of government by exploring whether racially liberal candidates at the top of the ballot have the ability to improve perceptions of the party overall. The results show that blacks', Latinos', and white Democrats' perceptions of a racially progressive president lead to more positive feelings for the Democratic Party. However, the same racially progressive candidates lead white Republicans to view the Democratic Party more negatively.

The conclusion synthesizes the analysis in this project to summarize how candidates should use racial appeals to maximize their chances of success. In particular, I argue that in the current political climate Democratic candidates should not shy away from racial appeals because polarization makes mobilization a more effective strategy compared to attempting to persuade unmovable voters. I also argue that the Democratic Party should engage in multiracial outreach that does not minimize their appeals to white working-class voters. While I show that racial appeals improve the Democratic Party's standing with the electorate, I argue that a campaign that is solely focused on racial/ethnic minorities is likely to be equally exclusionary and ineffective as a deracialized campaign that subjugates the interest of blacks and Latinos. Overall, the analysis in *The Case for Identity Politics* demonstrates that, under the right conditions, appeals to underrepresented groups can boost political organizations' chances of success by engaging racial/ethnic minorities and mobilizing sympathetic whites.

1
The Increasing Significance of Race

On November 4, 2008, Barack Obama became the first African American to be elected president of the United States. To some, Obama's election signified an end to race as a social problem in the country. Obama was the realization of the hope that with hard work blacks too could share in the American Dream (Stout and Le 2012). One black Virginian discussing the election of Obama noted, "This is the first time, to me, that it truly represents 'we the people.' Finally, equal rights, not being judged on the color of your skin but the character—that's what this whole thing means to me" (Montagne 2008). The then future first lady Michelle Obama stated that the support her husband received on the campaign trail made her proud of her country (Hayden 2017). The election of Barack Obama promised growing opportunities for many racial/ethnic minorities.

This moment had been predicted by sociologist William Julius Wilson in his important book *The Declining Significance of Race*. Wilson (1980) argued that over time expanding opportunities for wealthier blacks combined with changing opportunities for poorer blacks would make race less salient in society. As a result, race would recede as an important identity and Americans would become sorted based on class. This change would lead to more of a focus on economic differences among politicians as race would no longer be the major cleavage in American politics.

However, Obama's election to the White House symbolized a loss of power to some whites. This fear may have been amplified by the media's focus on identity in the 2008 Democratic primaries in which the two frontrunner candidates were a female (Hillary Clinton) and an African American (Barack Obama). The display of these two untraditional candidates vying for the highest position in the country led the media to focus heavily on the historic nature of their candidacies and what it meant for American politics. Moreover, the groundbreaking nature of Clinton's and Obama's candidacies and the lack of attention that the white male candidate (John Edwards) received may have increased whites' fear of losing their political dominance.

In the month of Obama's inauguration, the *Atlantic* published an article entitled "The End of White America" by Hua Hsu. Hsu (2009) argued that the 2008 election in combination with demographic change had made it so that whites felt like they were losing their political hegemony. One interviewee in Hsu's article summed up the sentiment that some whites were feeling: "But people are stressed out about [changing demographic patterns]. 'We used to be in control! We're losing control!'" (Hsu 2009). This fear of a changing America gave rise to political movements that were hostile to minority interests and Obama in particular.

The backlash to Obama and the 2008 presidential election made it hard to deny that racism still existed in the United States. This became even more evident with a slew of killings of minority men and women by police officers in 2015 and 2016, many of which were video recorded. These incidents created a countermovement in 2014 to the growing racial conservatism in the United States known as Black Lives Matter. Black Lives Matter hoped to shed light on the fact that racism was still a significant barrier to normalcy for people of color. While the election of Obama was supposed to make race less salient, it did the opposite. The competing narratives about race in the United States moved it from being a "post-racial" society to, as Tesler (2016) put it, a "most-racial" society.

This chapter explores the varied ways that Obama's campaign and election revealed the underlying effects of race, ethnicity, and class identity in the United States. I will first discuss how the combination of the 2008 presidential election and the growing number of blacks, Latinos, and Asian Americans in the United States spurred greater levels of racial conservatism among whites and their elected representatives. I will then look at how the success of these racially resentful political movements led to a curtailing of rights among racial/ethnic minorities. This in turn made discussions of racial discrimination more prevalent in the media and the public. I will also discuss how both the rising expectations of people of color following Obama's successful presidential campaign and continuing police brutality led to the formation of Black Lives Matter, whose activism made race and racial discrimination more salient. The growing salience of race and recognition of discrimination in the United States is demonstrated using data from Lexis-Nexis, Access World News, and Google Trends. Following this, I will show that the growing salience of race has led white Democrats, blacks, and Latinos to become more aware of racial biases in contemporary society. The chapter concludes by discussing how the greater recognition of racial prejudice may make individuals more supportive of policies that address racial inequality. This in turn may benefit candidates who do not shy away from racial issues in their campaigns.

White Backlash

Due to higher levels of births among Latinos and blacks and the growing number of Asian American and Latino immigrants, the United States is projected to become a majority-minority nation in the near future. Moreover, there are some estimates that the majority of those under eighteen will be black, Latino, or Asian American by the year 2019 (Roberts 2008). The rapid changes to the demography of the United States are also playing out at the state level. For example, in 2000 California became a majority-minority state and in 2015 Latinos outnumbered whites in the state. Similarly, in 2010 both Texas and New Mexico became majority-minority.

As is true in all periods, changing demographics increase levels of resentment and fear among those in the majority. The growth of Irish Catholics in the United States during the 1850s, for example, led to counterpolitical movements and even a political party known as the Know Nothings. The increase of Asian immigrants in the American west in the latter half of the nineteenth century resulted in the Chinese Exclusion Act of 1882 and violence against Asian Americans. Today, changing demographic patterns have produced the same levels of anxiety and fear among some whites. Abrajano and Hajnal (2015) and Parker and Barreto (2013) have demonstrated that the growing number of racial/ethnic minorities in the United States has increased levels of anxiety about the future for some white Americans.

This anxiety often creates a sense of an in-group versus out-group rivalry that permeates into politics (Jardina 2019). Craig and Richeson (2014) have demonstrated that when individuals are presented information that whites will no longer be in the majority by 2050, they tend to endorse racially conservative policies and became more likely to identify with the Republican Party. Similarly, Outten et al. (2012) have shown that when presented information about the growing minority population in the United States, a significant portion of whites became angrier and more fearful of racial/ethnic minorities, as well as more supportive of those who share their race.

These lab experiments also played out in the real world and were exacerbated by Obama's election to the White House. The reports indicating that racial/ethnic minorities would soon make up the majority of the nation in combination with the outcome of the 2008 presidential election symbolized a real-world shift in the political power of whites. These two factors gave rise in 2009 to a political movement known as the Tea Party that was very hostile to President Obama (Parker and Barreto 2013). For example, supporters of the Tea Party were significantly more likely to question Obama's legitimacy to serve as president by arguing (falsely) that he was not born in the United States. Williamson, Skocpol, and Coggin (2011) engaged in a participant observation of Tea Party groups in Boston and noted that they viewed racial/ethnic minorities as receiving an unfair amount of government subsidies and advocated for ending programs that aided the poor.

The Success of the Tea Party and Growing Awareness of Racial Discrimination

The rise of the Tea Party was to many the first sign that racial biases were alive and well during the Obama administration. The origins of the Tea Party are in some ways debated, but many argue the group began with an impassioned speech by CNBC correspondent Rick Santelli in which he argued that average people were becoming frustrated with having to bail out their neighbors who responded recklessly during the housing boom of the mid-2000s (Williamson, Skocpol, and Coggin 2011). The first protests associated with the Tea Party occurred on February 16, 2009, in Seattle. On Tax Day 2009, Tea Party protests were held in over seven hundred cities across the United States (Williamson, Skocpol, and Coggin 2011).

While ostensibly the Tea Party's aim was to end what they perceived as wasteful spending in Washington, many viewed the movement as being fueled by racism and anxiety about changing demographic patterns (Parker and Barreto 2013). This perception was fueled by claims by black legislators that they had been harassed by Tea Party members in Washington, DC. Civil rights icon and Georgia U.S. House representative John Lewis claimed to have been called the n-word when leaving his congressional office by members of the Tea Party. Witnesses say that Missouri congressman Emanuel Cleaver was spat on. Additionally, several studies were produced demonstrating that the Tea Party was in part fueled by racial biases and fear about change. This was most extensively done in Parker and Barreto's (2013) book *Change They Can't Believe In: The Tea Party and Reactionary Politics in America*. The authors used national-level data to demonstrate that Tea Party members and sympathizers are more likely to be motivated by the fear of changing demographics in the United States.

For these reasons, the Tea Party was viewed by a large percentage of the population as being motivated by racial animus, which was sparked by Obama's election to the White House. An ABC News/*Washington Post* poll conducted in early 2010 showed that a majority (57%) of Americans viewed the Tea Party as being fueled by racist sentiment (Parker and Barreto 2013). Perceptions of the Tea Party as harboring racial prejudice combined with the size of the movement raised questions about whether racism had declined.

The movement's success and the policies that followed would further cement awareness of racial prejudice being prominent in the United States.

The Tea Party was able to flex its political muscle in 2010, the first election after its inception. The energized political movement played a large part in the Republican Party's ability to pick up sixty-three seats in the U.S. House. The movement enjoyed similar levels of success at the state level, where Republicans took almost a dozen governors' offices from Democrats and seventeen state legislative chambers switched from Democratic to Republican. The large changes in control, particularly at the state level, gave Republicans a significant opportunity to enact many of the policies that had been advocated by the Tea Party.

The movement was later aided by loosening restrictions on voter protections, which came as result of *Shelby County v. Holder.* On June 25, 2013, the U.S. Supreme Court decided on the constitutionality of Section 4(b) of the Voting Rights Act of 1965, which contains the formula to determine which jurisdictions are subject to have their voting laws precleared by the Justice Department. Shelby County sued the federal government arguing that the formula put in place in Section 4(b) was unjust because the renewal of the Voting Rights Act (which was a stipulation written into the law) never addressed the original formula put forth in 1965. As a result, extensions of the Voting Rights Act put an unfair burden on counties like Shelby that may have improved over the almost fifty years since the passage of the influential voting rights legislation. The Supreme Court sided with Shelby County in a 5-to-4 decision and argued that Congress had to reassess the formula for preclearance—a task that has not been taken up as of 2020.

Armed with the political victories of 2010 and the severe weakening of the Voting Rights Act, many states passed legislation that made it harder for racial/ethnic minorities to vote. One of the most controversial of these policies was the introduction of voter identification laws. While these laws seem innocuous in that they simply require individuals to present some form of voter identification before they vote, several research studies have demonstrated that these laws disproportionately make it harder for young people and racial/ethnic minorities to vote (Hajnal, Lajevardi, and Nielson 2017). For example, a 2014 U.S. Government Accountability Office report found that 20 percent of blacks did not have the proper identification to vote in their state. Moreover, Hajnal, Lajevardi, and Nielson (2017) found that Latino turnout declined by about 7 percent in strict voter identification states.

Questions about voter identification laws intended to discriminate against minorities became even more salient when pundits noticed large discrepancies in how these laws were being applied. In Texas, for example, a license to carry a gun could be used as a form of identification, but a student identification card could not. The former tends to be held by conservative whites, while the latter is often held by a more racially diverse group of individuals who are more likely to vote for the Democratic Party. In North Carolina, the Republican-controlled general assembly asked for voting records and then rewrote voting laws to make it harder for people of color to vote. A judicial panel who ruled against the updated voting laws said that the legislation was written to exclude people of color with "almost surgical precision" (Ingraham 2016). For these reasons, it is not uncommon for discussions around voter identification laws to be tied to words like "discrimination" and "bias." For example, based on an Access World News search of all newspaper articles that include "Voter ID laws" or "Voter Identification Laws" in the title, the words "discrimination" and "bias" appeared in about 20 percent of the cases. These laws raised awareness that racial discrimination had not disappeared in the age of Obama.

In addition to voter identification laws, many attributed Obama's treatment from the right as being driven in part by racism. This was particularly true around the "Birther" movement that accused Obama of being born outside of the United States and suggested that in spite of his high-profile membership in Chicago's Trinity United Church of Christ that he was in fact a Muslim. Moreover, many attribute Congress's lack of support for Obama's policy as being driven by racial animus (see, e.g., Garcia and Stout 2019). Tesler (2013), for example, demonstrates that congressional districts in which the average constituent had high levels of racial resentment were significantly less supportive of the Affordable Care Act of 2010. Along the same lines, Senator Jay Rockefeller (D-W. VA) argued that he felt that racism was at least partially to blame for opposition to Obama in an interview: "It's very important to take a long view at what's going on here. And I'll be able to dig up some emails that make part of the Affordable Care Act that doesn't look good, especially from people who have made up their mind that they don't want it to work. Because they don't like the president, maybe he's of the wrong color" (quoted in Waldman 2014).

Even President Obama acknowledged that racism may influence how others were assessing his presidency. In an interview with *New Yorker* columnist David Remnick (2014), Obama argued that an individual's race shapes evaluations of his presidency. "There's no doubt that there's some folks who just really dislike me because they don't like the idea of a black president." In combination with the rise of the Tea Party and voter identification laws, the impact of claims of racism against the president made voters more aware that racial biases had not disappeared as a result of Obama's election.

Black Lives Matter

While the treatment of Obama and the rise of the Tea Party made people more cognizant of racial discrimination, a political movement known as Black Lives Matter demonstrated that this discrimination had tangible impacts on racial/ethnic minorities. Black Lives Matter was founded by three black women, Alicia Garza, Opal Tometi, and Patrisse Cullors in 2013, in response to George Zimmerman's acquittal after he shot and killed Trayvon Martin, a black teenager. The Martin case received national attention because Zimmerman had made phone calls to the police telling them he was following the black teenager, which he continued to do in spite of the fact that the police dispatcher asked him to stop. The salience of the case led Obama to respond, mentioning that Trayvon Martin could have been his son (Krishna 2019). While Black Lives Matter originated as a result of the Martin shooting and the acquittal of Zimmerman, it gained significant attention after the police shooting of another African American teenager, Michael Brown, by Darren Wilson in Ferguson, Missouri, in 2014. The primary mode of communication that Black Lives Matter uses is Twitter. In the three weeks after Brown's death, the hashtag #BlackLivesMatter grew from about 200,000 tweets to over 12 million tweets (Freelon, McIlwain, and Clark 2016). In all, the hashtag has amassed over 41 million tweets since its inception.

While the goals of Black Lives Matter are diverse and include support for the transgender movement, fights to limit globalism, and ageism, the hashtag is primarily associated with holding killers of racial/ethnic minorities accountable. The movement uses Twitter and other social media platforms to disseminate cell phone camera footage and bring attention to the poor treatment of people of color, primarily by law enforcement. Some of the most notable cases demonstrate blacks being harassed and shot with little justification. For example, in 2014 Cleveland police officers shot and killed a twelve-year-old boy named Tamir Rice who was described as brandishing a weapon to dispatchers. Video later showed that police officers shot the child within seconds of arriving on the scene, and the "weapon" Rice was holding turned out to be a toy gun. A year later, a Charleston, South Carolina, police officer was caught on video shooting an unarmed black male, Walter Scott, and dropping a weapon near him. In 2016, cellphone video footage emerged of the black mental health care worker Charles Kinsey being shot by police officers in Miami, despite having his arms up. These are just a few of the dozens of cases that drew significant media attention.

Black Lives Matter was not only successful in bringing the issue of police brutality to light, it also made a large impact on the political discourse by demonstrating the tangible implications of racism on public safety. The movement's achievements in this area and the growing perceptions of racial bias that came after Obama's election to the White House created a greater recognition of racial prejudice in the United States. It is under this context that we move from a "postracial" society to one where there is a much greater awareness that race influences individuals' social and political well-being.

The Rise of Trump

It was also under this context that a political outsider with a shaky history of race relations was able to rise to the White House. Several scholars argue that the rise of Donald Trump is the culmination of the growing racial divide in the United States (Sides, Vavreck, and Tesler 2018). Trump differed from many previous politicians in that he was much more explicitly hostile to racial/ethnic minorities. For example, in his campaign launch speech Trump stated, "When Mexico sends its people, they're not sending their best. . . . They're sending people that have lots of problems, and they're bringing those problems with us. They're bringing drugs. They're bringing crime. They're rapists" (quoted in Huber 2016). In 2017, as president, he stated that there were good people among the white supremacists who marched in Charlottesville, Virginia, in a protest to keep Confederate statues in the city (S. Perry 2018). He also reportedly stated that America was accepting too many immigrants from "shithole" countries, implying that America was allowing too many immigrants from African and Latin American nations (McCluskey 2019).

In the past, research had demonstrated that such explicit racial appeals were detrimental to a candidate (see Mendelberg 2001). However, Trump's ability to make such comments and be elected demonstrates the growing acceptance of racial discrimination among some Americans (Valentino, Neuner, and Vandenbroek 2018). As a result, many Americans have become more cognizant of the racial discrimination that racial/ethnic minorities face in the United States. This is particularly true of Latinos who appear as targets of much of Trump's rhetoric. From arguing for a border wall along Mexico to labeling Mexican immigrants as rapists to supporting and pardoning controversial Arizona sheriff Joe Arpaio, Trump's rhetoric has served to increase perceptions of the amount of discrimination Latinos face in the United States.

Media and Discrimination

If the salience of racial discrimination increased in the Obama era, we might find evidence for this in the media coverage of racial bias and the use of internet search engines to find topics related to these issues. For the former, there is much research that demonstrates that media outlets both shape and follow trends in society (Kerbel 2000). As a result, higher levels of interest in racial discrimination as a social problem should manifest in greater news coverage about the topic.

As the media and politicians speak out more about racial issues, the public too may become more concerned and interested in the topic of race. This may be manifested in individuals seeking out more information on this topic through Google searches. Recent research has demonstrated the efficacy of analyzing Google searches to better understand trends in the United States (Carneiro and Mylonakis 2009). From predicting where the flu is coming to vote choice, Google searches have become a bellwether for where America is heading (Carneiro and Mylonakis 2009; Stephens-Davidowitz 2014). Thus, if there is greater awareness and interest in racial discrimination in recent years, we should observe an increase in Google searches about topics related to racial bias. Moreover, the Google searches may indicate that many Americans were unaware or not thinking much about racial issues until recently. When individuals use search engines like Google, they are demonstrating that they want to become better informed about the salience of race in the particular political context they are living in.

To test these possibilities, I examine the complete universe of newspapers that are available on Access World News, which collects newspapers articles from over six thousand different newspapers across all fifty states. I also examine the headlines of news transcripts from Lexis-Nexis, which collects data on news segments from ABC News, American Public Media, CBS News, CNBC News, CNN, CTV Television, Fox News Network, and MSNBC. The vast majority of Americans who get news from television get their news from one of these stations. Finally, I use data from Google Trends to see whether Americans have been searching for information related to racial discrimination in recent years. Google Trends keeps the volume of searches about any particular topic and scores them based on how salient they are. Google Trends scores are calculated by taking the number of searches for the word divided by the total number of searches. It then standardizes this number by examining the relative frequency of this term over time.

Results

Figure 1.1 presents information about the frequency in which (A) U.S. newspapers, (B) major network television stations, and (C) Google searches discussed racism or some related term between 2004 and 2016. I start my analysis in 2004 because that is the first year for which Google Trends data are available. I consider the following terms as being related to

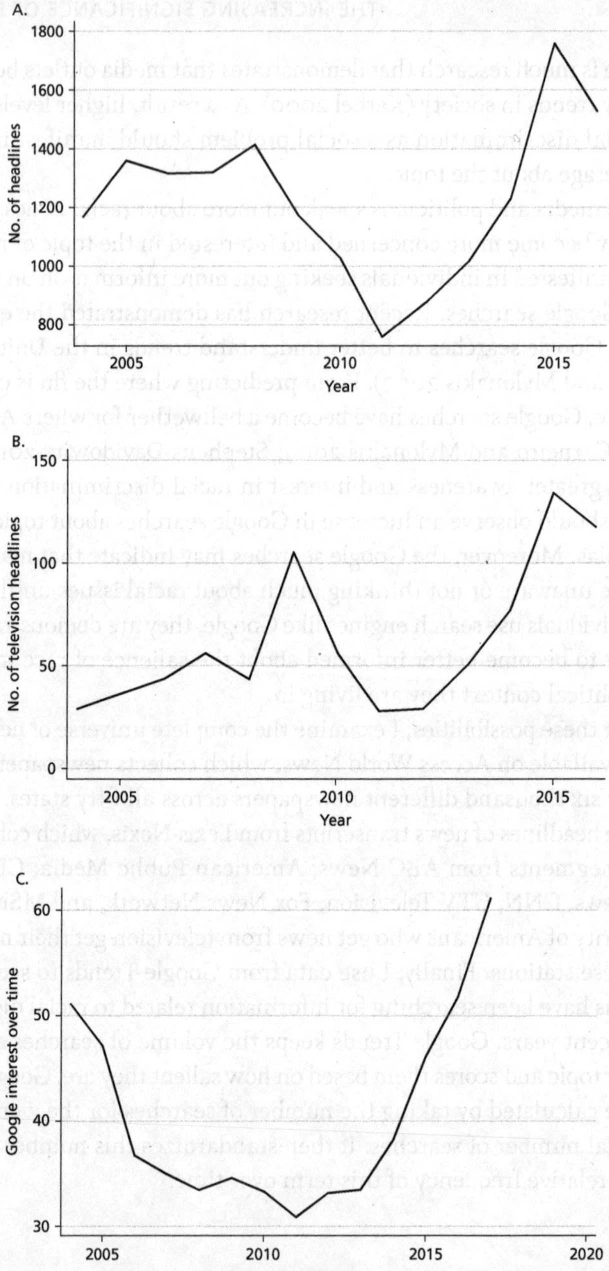

FIGURE 1.1. Discussions of racism or related words in A: U.S. newspaper headlines, B: U.S. television news transcripts, and C: Google searches (the numbers on the y-axis represent the search interest relative to the highest point on the chart for the selected region and time)

Source: A: Access World News; B: Lexis-Nexis; C: Google Trends.

racism: "Racial Prejudice," "Racial Inequality," "Racial Discrimination," "Racism," and "Racial Bias." I examined the frequency of these words in the headlines of U.S. newspapers and the headlines of transcripts for major news agencies to ensure that the story was centered on this issue. For Google Trends searches, I examined the trends' weighted average for the combination of these search terms.

The results in figure 1.1 demonstrate that coverage of racial inequality in the media has grown substantially during the Black Lives Matter era. Figure 1.1A presents the number of headlines that use one or more of the following terms "Racial Prejudice," "Racial Inequality," "Racial Discrimination," "Racism," and "Racial Bias" between 2004 and 2016. There was a substantial decline in the number of media sources discussing racism in the headlines during the first few years after Obama's election to the White House. This is consistent with the expectation outlined above that recognition of discrimination was low immediately following the election of Obama in 2008. For example, between 2008 and 2011, the number of headlines that include one of the racism-related terms declines by over six hundred. However, after the rise of the Tea Party, the high-profile police shootings, and the Black Lives Matter movement, there has been a substantial increase in the number of newspaper headlines that discuss discrimination. For example, there were a thousand more articles discussing racial discrimination in the headline in 2015 than in 2011. Moreover, the largest amount of discussion in newspapers around discrimination occurred in 2015 and 2016.

We see a similar pattern when we examine mentions of racism-related words in headlines of major news networks (figure 1.1B). Similar to the newspaper data, we see an early peak in discussions about racism during the 2008 presidential election. However, consistent with expectations, there is a steep decline in news stories focusing on racial discrimination in the first few years after Obama's election. In fact, in the twelve-year period examined in figure 1.1B, 2011 had the fewest number of news stories centered on racial discrimination. There has been a recent increase in the number of television news stories that focus on racism, however. In both 2015 and 2016 there were more stories on this topic than in any of the previous years analyzed in my time frame. In fact, there were about thirty more segments on racial discrimination in 2015 than there were in 2008, the year Obama's campaign for presidency made race and racism in the electorate a popular story.

The discussion of racial discrimination in the media appears to seep into the public consciousness according to the Google Trends data presented in figure 1.1C. However, there appear to be some discrepancies between interest around racial discrimination in the media and on the internet. While there was a spike in interest in discrimination in 2008 by the media, the public was less likely to seek out information about this topic on Google. Between 2004 and 2012, there was relatively little interest in racism and racial discrimination based on the volume of Google searches. However, starting in 2013 and continuing through 2016 there was a large spike in the average number of searches about topics related to racial discrimination. The highest volume of searches relative to other years again can be seen in 2015 and 2016. Figures 1.1A–C together present substantial evidence that in recent years individuals and the media have been much more interested in racial discrimination.

Does This Matter?

The previous section demonstrated that the media has been increasingly focusing on racial discrimination and that the public has been searching for more information about this topic in recent years. However, whether this translates to anything more than curiosity is still unknown. The argument that candidates may benefit from making race-based appeals in the contemporary United States hinges on the assumption that greater levels of awareness of racial bias are related to greater levels of acceptance that racial discrimination is a problem. Moreover, this greater recognition should also translate into greater levels of sympathy for racial/ethnic minorities. To test whether attitudes toward racial/ethnic minorities have changed in recent years, I turn to the General Social Survey (GSS) and the Pew Research Center's political polls.

The GSS asked respondents in 1977, 1985, 1986, and each year between 1988 and 2016 the following question: "On the average (Negroes/Blacks/African Americans) have worse jobs, income, and housing than white people. Do you think these differences are due to A) Discrimination, B) Inborn Disability, C) Lack of Education, or D) Lack of Will?" If changes in discussions about racial discrimination in society are influencing attitudes about the causes of racial disparities, we should see more individuals attributing differences in racial inequality to discrimination. The Pew poll more recently began asking respondents to decide which of the following was truer: "Our country has made the changes needed to give blacks equal rights with whites" or "Our country needs to continue making changes to give blacks equal rights with whites." Again, if greater coverage of discrimination is influencing the population, there should be an increasing number of individuals agreeing with the statement that more work is necessary to erase racial inequality in the United States after 2014, which is the year Black Lives Matter gained a significant amount of attention. Additionally, Pew asked respondents in 2009, 2013, 2015, and 2017 whether Hispanics face a lot, some, a little, or no discrimination. By examining this question, we can get a sense of whether Americans became more cognizant of Latino discrimination.

It is important to note that I do not expect everyone in the electorate to be equally influenced by increased claims of discrimination. In fact, it is possible that a large segment of the population may view increased coverage of racial inequality quite skeptically. I expect that white Democrats, blacks, and Latinos would be the most responsive to claims that racial inequality is driven by discrimination. This is in part due to these groups' general belief that societal factors influence individuals' opportunities (Hopkins 2009). Moreover, these groups also tend to be more willing to alter their attitudes in the face of claims of racial discrimination (Nelson, Sanbonmatsu, and McClerking 2007). Conversely, conservatives may feel more defensive about claims of discrimination given their general belief that individual life outcomes are based more on individual effort (Hopkins 2009). They may also feel that claims of racial discrimination will be used to advance minority rights at the expense of their own interests (Parker and Barreto 2013). Given that I expect that an individual's race and partisanship will shape how individuals respond to the changing climate about race relations in the United States, the analysis in the next section disaggregates voters by their partisanship and race/ethnicity. I provide descriptive statistics separately for white Democrats and white Republicans, and white independents along with information about blacks' and Latinos' racial attitudes.

Figure 1.2 presents the average number of white Democrats, white Republicans, and white independents who believe that racial discrimination was the main cause of racial inequality in the United States from 1977 to 2016. The results provide substantial evidence that the increase discussion of racial inequality in the media and in internet activity has led white Democrats to become much more cognizant of racial discrimination. Between 1977 and 2012, a minority of white Democrats believed that discrimination was to blame for blacks' poor social standing. In fact, in most years between 40 percent and 45 percent of white Democrats attributed racial inequality to something other than discrimination. However, in 2016 a majority of white Democrats, about 56 percent, believed that racial discrimination was to blame for racial disparities in the United States. In the same year a higher percentage of white Democrats agreed that discrimination was the main cause for racial inequality than in any other year. This suggests that changes in the racial climate driven by the aggressiveness of the Tea Party, the emergence of the Black Lives Matter movement, and high-profile instances of police brutality

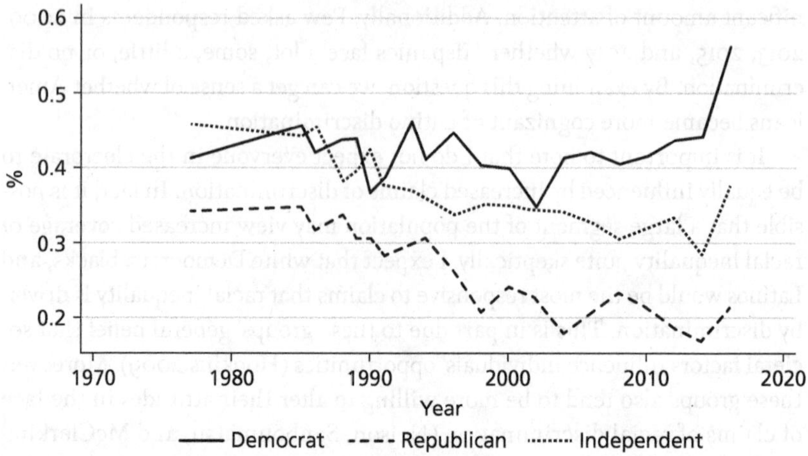

FIGURE 1.2. Percentage of white Democrats, white independents and white Republicans who agree that discrimination is main cause of inequality (1977–2016)
Source: GSS.

have led to a greater awareness among whites Democrats that racial discrimination presents a significant barrier to normalcy for blacks.

We observe a much weaker change in white Republicans' and white independents' perceptions of the causes of racial discrimination over time. While white conservatives have always been skeptical of discrimination as the main cause of racial inequality, the number who believed it was declined significantly during the 1990s and 2000s. So much so that in 2012 fewer than 20 percent of white Republicans agreed that racial discrimination was the main cause of blacks' poor performance relative to whites. The current racial climate appears to have led to a small reversal in this trend in 2016, but overall white Republicans appear to be on average very skeptical that racism is the main culprit for racial disparities in the United States.

White independents appear to follow a similar pattern. Like Republicans, whites who describe themselves as political independents appear to be increasingly more skeptical that racial discrimination explains racial inequality in the United States over the period examined in this analysis. White independents appear to have been the most skeptical of this link in 2012, but the number reversed slightly in 2016. Overall, the results in figure 1.2 suggest that white Republicans and independents became slightly more likely to attribute racial disparities to discrimination in 2016. In contrast, white Democrats have become much more aware of racial discrimination in recent years.

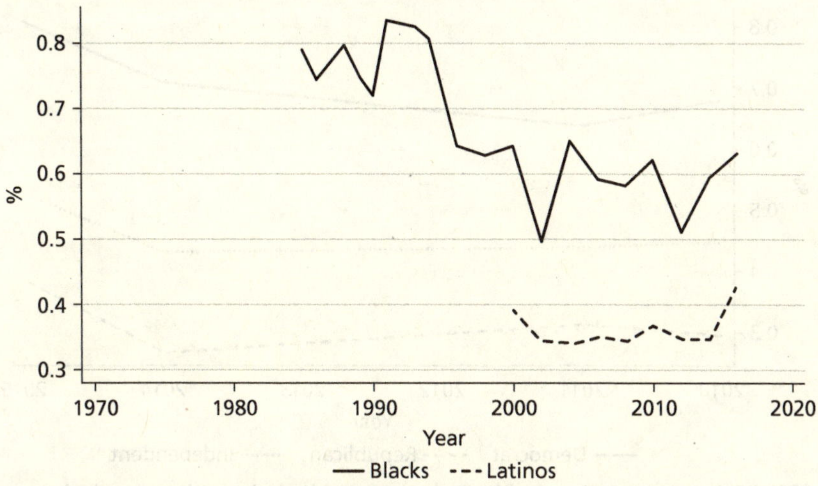

FIGURE 1.3. Percentage of blacks and Latinos who agree that discrimination is main cause of inequality (1977–2016)
Source: GSS.

Figure 1.3 presents blacks' and Latinos' attitudes about whether racial discrimination may explain continuing racial disparities in the United States. The results indicate that Latinos follow a pattern that is similar to white Democrats. In all years between 2000 and 2012, fewer than 40 percent of Latinos attributed blacks' poor social standing relative to whites to racial discrimination. However, in 2016 this number increased to 43 percent, which represents a 9 percent increase in just four years. Like white Democrats, more Latinos attributed racial inequality to discrimination against blacks in 2016 than in any other year in this analysis.

Surprisingly, blacks as a group have become more skeptical that racial discrimination is the main cause of racial inequality in the past twenty-five years. In 1990, for example, over 80 percent of blacks attributed their position in society to discrimination. However, by 2000 fewer than half of blacks took the same position. While fewer blacks agreed that discrimination was a primary problem in 2016 compared to 1990, there were significantly more blacks who agreed that discrimination was the cause of racial disparities in 2016 than in 2012. In 2016, almost two-thirds of blacks agreed that racial discrimination was the cause of racial inequality compared to just 51 percent of blacks in 2012. While figure 1.3 presents mixed results for blacks, it does demonstrate that blacks as a group remain highly cognizant of the role that racial discrimination plays in creating unequal outcomes in society.

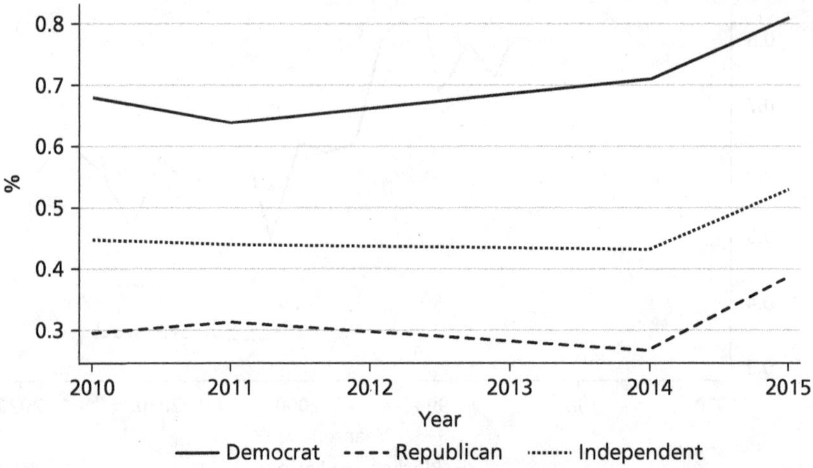

FIGURE 1.4. Percentage of white Democrats, white independents, and white Republicans who agree that more needs to change to give blacks equal rights (2010–15)
Source: Pew Research Center.

The results in figure 1.4 provide more evidence that the public is responding to growing interest in racial discrimination. The figure shows that the average number of respondents who agree with "Our country needs to continue making changes to give blacks equal rights with whites" more than "Our country has made the changes needed to give blacks equal rights with whites." The data is again disaggregated by white Democrats, white Republicans, and white independents.

It appears that partisanship is a strong predictor of respondents' attitudes about racial discrimination. White Democrats consistently agree that more work is necessary to ensure that blacks obtain equal rights with their white counterparts. In 2011, about 60 percent of white Democrats agreed that blacks had not yet achieved equal rights. However, by 2015 this figure has increased nearly 20 percent. In that year, 78 percent, a large majority of white Democrats, agreed that more work was necessary to achieve equal rights for blacks and whites. White independents follow a similar pattern. Before 2015, a minority of white independents (~40%) believed that the country has a substantial amount of work to do to achieve racial equality. However, by 2015 more than half (52%) agreed that more work was necessary. Even white Republicans, who are much more likely to agree that enough work has been done already to achieve equality between the races, have been slightly more likely to agree that more work was necessary in recent years. In early 2014, for ex-

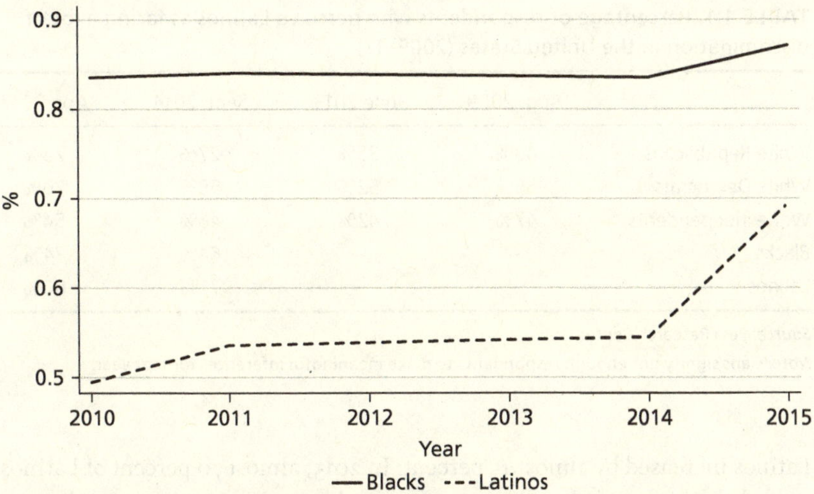

FIGURE 1.5. Percentage of blacks and Latinos who agree that more needs to change to give blacks equal rights (2010–15)
Source: Pew Research Center.

ample, only 25 percent of white Republicans thought that more work was necessary for blacks to achieve equality. However, just one year later this figure had grown by 13 percent. While I disaggregated this Pew poll to compare differences by partisanship, it is also important to note that in 2015 a majority of all whites (53%) agreed that not enough work had been done to ensure equality between blacks and whites.

Figure 1.5 presents the percentage of blacks and Latinos who agree with the statement "Our country needs to continue making changes to give blacks equal rights with whites." Similar to whites, both blacks and Latinos have become more likely in recent years to agree that more racial progress is necessary to minimize the differences between racial groups. Over 80 percent of blacks agreed that more needs to be done to address racial inequality for every year this data was collected. However, in 2015 this figure grew by about 4 percent in just one year after the Black Lives Matter Movement gained significant attention after the shooting of Michael Brown. As of 2015, over 87 percent of blacks agreed that more changes were necessary for this country to erase racial disparities.

Latinos follow a similar pattern as whites and blacks. In all years, a majority of Latinos believed that more work needs to be done to address black-white disparities in society. However, in just one year, between 2014 and 2015, support for more aggressive actions to be taken to end racial inequality among

TABLE 1.1. Percentage of respondents who perceive Latinos as facing a lot of discrimination in the United States (2009–17)

	Aug. 2009	June 2013	Sept. 2014	Apr. 2017
White Republicans	43%	35%	27%	23%
White Democrats	55%	52%	58%	70%
White independents	47%	42%	46%	54%
Blacks	–	–	64%	74%
Latinos	–	–	71%	80%

Source: Pew Research Center.

Note: Gaps signify not enough respondents to make meaningful inferences for that year.

Latinos increased by almost 15 percent. In 2015, almost 70 percent of Latinos agreed that more work was necessary to address continuing racial disparities. In summary, all racial groups in 2015 were more likely to agree that the United States needs to make more progress to end racial inequality.

Table 1.1 presents the percentage of white Democrats, white Republicans, white independents, blacks, and Latinos who agreed that Latinos faced "a lot" of discrimination. The table was constructed by combining Pew polls taken in August 2009, June 2013, September 2014, and April 2017. The question that Pew asked respondents in those years was "Please tell me how much discrimination there is against each of these groups in our society today. How about . . . Hispanic Americans? Would you say there is a lot of discrimination, some, only a little, or none at all?" Unfortunately, there were too few black and Latino respondents in the 2009 and 2013 polls to draw meaningful inferences about these populations, so information for these years was excluded.

As with discrimination against African Americans, there appears to be a growing recognition among white Democrats and white independents that Latinos face "a lot" of discrimination. This was particularly true after the campaign and election of Donald Trump in 2016. In April 2017, 70 percent of white Democrats viewed Latinos as facing a lot of discrimination. Moreover, 12 percent more white Democrats believed that Latinos faced a lot of discrimination in the United States in the 2017 Pew poll than in the 2014 Pew poll. Similarly, white independents were more likely to perceive Latinos as facing a lot of discrimination in 2017 than in the past. In 2017, a majority of white independents (54%) stated that Latinos face a lot of discrimination, an 8 percent increase from three years earlier.

The only group of whites who have become more skeptical of Latinos facing a lot of discrimination is white Republicans. In the 2017 poll, only

23 percent of white Republicans thought that Latinos faced a lot of discrimination. This represents a 4 percent decline from 2014 and a 200 percent decrease from 2009. The rise of Trump within the Republican Party and growing fears about whites losing their numerical majority may have spurred white Republicans to be less concerned about Latino discrimination. Moreover, some may fear that recognizing Latino discrimination may divert resources from their racial group.

Both blacks and Latinos became more likely to perceive Latinos as facing a lot of discrimination in 2017. That year, about three-quarters of blacks and 80 percent of Latinos believed that Latinos faced a lot of discrimination in the United States. For both groups this represents about a 10 percent increase from 2014. Moreover, the combination of results in table 1.1 demonstrates that the vast majority of white Democrats, blacks, and Latinos are cognizant of racial discrimination among Latinos.

Conclusion

Numerous polls at the end of Obama's presidency presented evidence that most Americans believed that race relations had worsened in the United States after 2008. For example, 54 percent of Americans in a 2016 CNN/ORC poll said race relations were worse under Obama's watch. Obama surprised many when he said that in spite of these polls race relations were getting better and would continue to improve in an interview with ABC journalist George Stephanopoulos. Obama noted that he was "absolutely convinced that race relations on the whole are actually better now than they were 20 years (ago)," to which Stephanopoulos replied incredulously, "Better now?" Obama responded, "Yes," [because] we have greater awareness of where we're falling short than we used to" (Wilson 2019). Similarly, former secretary of state Condoleezza Rice recently stated that she feels the country has made a lot of progress over the past fifty years in spite of the rise of hate crimes under the Trump presidency. Secretary Rice argued that while hate crimes are on the rise, at least there were more punishments now for offenders than when she was a child in Alabama. Moreover, there were greater opportunities for African Americans (Wilson 2019).

As this chapter has shown, however, as a result of Obama's presidency racial inequality, which had been swept under the rug during the pre-Obama years, came to the fore as a result of the Tea Party, police brutality, the Black Lives Matter movement, and Trump's presidential campaign. In combination, they led to a greater awareness that we were far from entering into a postracial society. Instead, Obama's election indicated to most that more work was necessary if we hoped to address racial inequality.

The analyses in this chapter demonstrate that Obama's election led to the rise of racially conservative politicians who, through their treatment of Obama and the legislation that they supported, made people more aware that racial discrimination existed. This increased after the emergence of the Black Lives Matter movement and technology that made it easier for the population to view egregious cases of racial discrimination. These incidents increased media attention about racial discrimination in the United States, demonstrated by the fact that there were more stories in both newspapers and television that were centered on racism in 2015 and 2016 than in any year dating back to 2004. At the same time, all racial groups displayed a greater belief that more work was necessary to address racial inequality. Notably, whites and in particular white Democrats have become much more cognizant of racial discrimination in the past few years according to data from the GSS and the Pew Research Center. In combination, Obama's claim that the increasing racial rhetoric may indicate improvements for race relations rather than detriments seems to play out empirically.

However, whether greater levels of recognition of discrimination improve perceptions of racially discriminated groups or alter policy preferences to address inequality remains to be seen. In chapter 2, I will explore whether whites, disaggregated by partisanship, are becoming more racially progressive in this context. If whites are becoming more racially progressive, then it makes sense that politicians may be rewarded rather than punished for making race-based appeals in their campaigns.

2

Stability and Change

HOW THE GROWING RACIAL LIBERALISM OF WHITE DEMOCRATS INFLUENCES RACIAL POLARIZATION

Hillary Clinton's and Donald Trump's 2016 presidential campaign slogans summed up American's diverging responses to changing demographic patterns. Trump's slogan, "Make America Great Again," was charged by many as being an appeal to white working-class males. Kristen Weir (2017) wrote in a feature article in the American Psychological Association's *Monitor on Psychology* that the slogan was especially appealing to white males who felt that the country's increasing focus on the plight of women and racial/ethnic minorities came at the expense of their well-being during a period of growing income inequality and higher levels of mortality among poor whites." Along the same lines, *New York Times* columnist George Packer (2016) wrote, "When [Trump] vows to 'make America great again,' he is talking about and to white America, especially the less well off."

In contrast, Clinton's campaign slogan was "Better Together." It celebrated diversity in terms of partisanship, ideology, gender, sexuality, race, and ethnicity. Clinton summed up this idea in an October 9, 2016, tweet: "We are going to respect each other, lift each other up, and celebrate our diversity. #Debate #StrongerTogether" (Clinton 2016). *Washington Post* opinion writer Paul Waldman (2016) argued that "stronger together" stood in direct contrast to Trump's campaign, which took more aggressive positions to racial/ethnic and religious minorities: "[The slogan] is a response to Donald Trump's divisive ethno-nationalist campaign, his argument to white voters that their problems can be blamed on immigrants and Muslims and foreigners. Clinton will no doubt be taking every opportunity she can to remind non-white voters . . . of Trump's hostility toward them." Clinton's slogan was meant to appeal more to the growing number of racial/ethnic minorities who make up the core of the Democratic Party.

The two presidential campaign slogans tell a tale of growing divisions in whites' responses to the changing racial/ethnic patterns in the United States. The Democratic Party has enjoyed extremely high levels of support from racial/ethnic minorities. Conversely, the Republican Party has done increasingly well with white working-class voters, who were the cornerstone of the New Deal coalition. As demographics and party allegiances shift and America becomes more polarized, it is possible that white voters within these parties are becoming more divided on racial issues. White Democrats may increasingly perceive blacks and Latinos as their allies and may become more supportive of policies that address racial/ethnic inequality. White Republicans, meanwhile, may view these growing demographic groups as competitors for political power and may have worsening views of these individuals. Additionally, the issue of race and racial discrimination is becoming much more difficult to avoid for politicians. As politicians adopt divergent views about race relations, then we may see even greater levels of polarization in public opinion on racial/ethnic minorities.

However, unlike other areas of disagreement between Democrats and Republicans, which others have shown has been driven by Republicans becoming more conservative in recent years, it is possible that growing polarization on racial issues may be in part driven by growing liberalism among white Democrats (Grossman and Hopkins 2016; Mann and Ornstein 2017). This in part may be attributed to Democratic leaders taking more liberal positions on race relations in recent years, along with the influence of social movements like Black Lives Matter on public opinion. Moreover, as white Democrats increasingly view blacks and Latinos as a key part of their political coalition, they may shift to be more approving of racially liberal policies.

In this chapter, I will explore how greater levels of political polarization around racial issues have occurred in recent years. It begins by exploring the causes of political polarization in modern America to explain the growing levels of partisan divergence on views of race. I will then use the American National Election Studies (ANES) and the General Social Survey (GSS) to determine whether whites' attitudes about racial/ethnic minorities have become more divided based on partisanship. The results suggest that white Democrats have not only become more favorable toward racial/ethnic minorities in recent years, they have also become more interested in supporting programs that address racial inequality.

Contrary to expectations, in 2016 white Republicans too had shifted toward becoming more sympathetic to racial/ethnic minorities in many areas compared to the 2012 data. However, this shift is much smaller and still represents a steep decline in sympathy compared to white Republicans in the 1980s. This work provides more nuance to previous research on growing polarization. With regard to racial issues, it appears that growing polarization is being driven by Democrats becoming more liberal while white Republicans largely remain stable in their position on these issues. In combination, the results suggest that much of the partisan polarization around racial issues among whites is driven by Democrats expressing more sympathetic views toward minorities in recent years. The shifting attitudes of white Democrats to support more racially liberal policies is significant because it incentivizes liberal candidates to make race-based appeals.

The Growing Political Divide

By many accounts, America has become more divided along party lines in recent years. From attitudes about health care, the minimum wage, and abortion to less political factors such as wine preferences, where we shop, and what movies we watch, our political party is becoming a more salient factor in our preferences (McCarty, Poole, and Rosenthal 2016). Why are we more divided now than we have been in the past? Political scientists have identified several factors, including gerrymandering, an increase of money in American politics, southern realignment, narrowcasting, and growing divisions among political elites as potential causes of increased polarization. It is this last factor that may be most relevant to our discussion on growing levels of racial polarization among white voters (Fiorina and Abrams 2008; Levendusky 2010; McCarty, Poole, and Rosenthal 2009, 2016).

Levendusky (2009) demonstrated that Americans were becoming more ideologically consistent with their political parties (see also Lenz 2009; Tesler 2016). What this means is that liberals are much more likely to identify with the Democratic Party and conservatives are much more likely to identify with the Republican Party. This seems self-evident, but for much of the latter half of the twentieth century there were many conservative Democrats, who largely resided in the southern portion of the United States, and a large number of liberal Republicans, who mostly lived in the Northeast. This historical legacy led voters of both parties to get in some ways inconsistent messages from their representatives. The best example of this may be the position held by southern Democrats before the passing of the 1964 Civil Rights Act. They advocated for expanding social welfare programs (appearing liberal) but were against advancing civil rights for blacks (appearing conservative).

Because of a series of changes in the electorate, including unions working to improve relations with blacks, the growth of racial progressives within the Democratic Party, and the Republican Party's appeal to disaffected racially conservative white voters, voters began to select politicians who were much more ideologically consistent (Brady, Han, and Pope 2007). This ideological consistency grew as parties began to take the strategy that the best way to win when with the minorities was to be more of an opposition party rather than compromise with the majority (Lee 2016).

The growth in these ideologically pure politicians spread to the electorate as voters began to adopt the positions of their preferred politicians (Lenz 2009; Levendusky 2009). This feedback loop between ideologically pure politicians and ideologically pure voters makes any compromise by politicians dangerous as both the media and ambitious competitors will highlight compromise as a reason for replacement. Thus, if the opposing party takes one position on an issue, the best strategy for reelection may not be to find a middle ground, but to counter that party's position.

Given that parties are expected to take positions on salient issues, both parties and their political leaders have staked claims about racial policies as they have become more salient. Tesler (2016) and Parker and Barreto (2013) note that because of Obama's election to the White House, political parties have become more polarized on racial issues. Moreover, as was discussed in more detail in chapter 1, the Republican Party was urged by the Tea Party to introduce several policies that disproportionately diminished opportunities for racial/ethnic minorities. As Republican politicians pushed for voter identification laws, crackdowns on undocumented immigrants, travel bans, and greater scrutiny for Muslims, more minorities viewed the Republican Party as being too hostile to be their preferred party (see Philpot 2009, 2017; Stout and Garcia 2015). Along the same lines, Trump's campaign, which highlighted crimes by Latinos and argued that "politically correct" protections for minorities infringe on the rights of whites, led Republicans to view minorities more poorly.

Moreover, when the Black Lives Matter movement began in 2013, the Republican Party was less responsive and receptive to the movement than the Democrats. In fact, greater levels of support for police officers were voiced by Republican elected officials. This may be best exemplified by a speech by David Clarke, the sheriff of Milwaukee County, Wisconsin, at the 2016 Republican National Convention in which he argued that groups like Black Lives Matter violate basic codes of decency in society and advocate for anarchy. Clarke also initiated a chant of "Blue Lives Matter," arguing that more attention needs to be paid to violence against police (Biesecker 2017). Blue Lives Matter opposes itself to the Black Lives Matter movement by implicitly stating that concessions to Black Lives Matter come at the expense of the safety of police officers. As Republicans stake out their ground on these issues, so do their voters. Tesler (2016) demonstrated that levels of racial resentment, support for Affirmative Action, and opposition to interracial dating all became stronger predictors of Republican partisanship during the Obama years.

Conversely, the Democratic Party has increasingly become perceived as a home for racial progressives. Obama, as the head of the Democratic Party, signified to many that the party valued diversity (Stout and Garcia 2015). This is evident in the ANES, which shows that voters were more likely to believe that Obama worked to advance racial equality more than previous presidential candidates. The Democratic Party also worked to overturn policies that limited opportunities for racial/ethnic minorities. The most salient of these areas were voter identification laws and immigration reform. Democratic politicians were much more likely to speak out against voter identification laws and to vote against them in state legislatures (Hajnal, Lajevardi, and Nielson 2017). Moreover, they were more vocal in their support for providing legal status to undocumented immigrants who reside in the United States. This is best exemplified by President Obama's Deferred Action for Childhood Arrivals policy, which was launched in 2012 and provided protections for some undocumented immigrants.

Additionally, the Democratic Party has embraced the Black Lives Matter movement more than their Republican counterparts. A July 26, 2016, *Los Angeles Times* story was headlined "Black Lives Matter Playing a Prominent Role at Democratic Convention" (Memoli 2016). Indeed, the Mothers of the Movement, a group of mothers who lost their sons to police brutality and which is deeply tied to the Black Lives Matter movement, was given a prime-time spot at the Democratic National Convention. Hillary Clinton also met with these women several times during her presidential campaign. The Democratic Party's greater embrace of the Black Lives Matter movement, protection for undocumented immigrants, and their opposition to policies that would disproportionately disadvantage minorities sent a clear signal to the Democratic electorate that the party cared about racial/ethnic minorities. If Lenz (2009) and Levendusky (2013) are correct, Democratic voters tend to adopt the same racially progressive positions as elected officials within their party. Moreover, individuals who oppose these positions may leave the Democratic Party, leaving it much more consistent on support for racially progressive policies.

Political Polarization: The Role of Racial/Ethnic Divisions in the Electorate

In addition to differences about message, perceptions of political parties play a large role in how individuals may view different racial/ethnic groups. Philpot (2009), for example, found using both qualitative and quantitative data that blacks as a group were largely skeptical of the Republican Party because they saw it as being less representative of people like themselves (see also Stout and Garcia 2015). Tesler (2016) notes that many whites viewed the Democratic Party as less hospitable to individuals who share their race after

Obama was elected. If party image matters, it is possible that whites' attitudes about racial/ethnic minorities may also change as race becomes more associated with these political organizations.

The two major parties in the United States are becoming increasingly divided by race and gender. Blacks, Latinos, Asian Americans, and women have become more supportive of the Democratic Party over time. In contrast, white males, evangelicals, and southerners have become the strongest supporters of the Republican Party (Pew Research Center 2015). While blacks have long been supportive of the Democratic Party, there was a resurgence in black Democratic partisanship during the Obama years (Stout and Garcia 2015).

The same pattern seems to hold for Latinos. Based on National Election Pool data, 44 percent of Latinos sided with the Republican nominee George W. Bush in the 2004 presidential election. In both 2012 and 2016, however, the Republican nominee failed to get even 30 percent of Latino voters. Moreover, some suggest that the estimates in 2016 were too high due to methodological issues of the sampling design in the National Election Pool. Analysis by Latino Decisions suggests that almost 80 percent of Latinos supported Clinton in 2016, the largest level of support a Democratic candidate has ever received from Latino voters. The growing levels of support for the Democratic Party from racial/ethnic minorities may lead white voters within the Democratic Party to be more supportive of these groups as they may be perceived as political allies.

Republicans, meanwhile, are performing increasingly well with white male voters. For example, according to the ANES about 32 percent of white males identified as members of the Republican Party in 2008, but this number had grown by 6 percent in 2016. In part, this was driven by some Republican politicians making the argument that changing demographics in the United States have decreased the number of blue-collar jobs available to whites. As a result, it would not be surprising to find that the views of whites who are members of the Republican Party toward racial/ethnic minorities have soured.

Data

Democrats' views of blacks and Latinos have improved substantially in recent years. This has been driven by numerous factors, including greater awareness of racial discrimination (see chapter 1), stronger rhetoric in support of racial/ethnic minorities by Democratic politicians, and feelings of political closeness among Democratic whites. Republicans, meanwhile, have viewed racial/ethnic minorities more negatively in recent years as Republican politicians have taken more hostile stands on minority interests/rights, portraying minorities as competitors for jobs and political power.

To support these statements, I now turn to the ANES and examine three key variables to measure whether polarization in politics has translated into diverging levels of support for racial/ethnic minorities. The first two measures are part of the "feeling thermometer" survey tool in which respondents are asked to rate groups on a 0 to 100 scale; a score of 0 indicates that the individual feels coldly or negatively toward the group, whereas a score of 100 indicates a high level of support for the group. The groups examined in figure 2.1 include blacks and Latinos.

To ensure that individuals were not universally positive or negative about all racial/ethnic groups, I standardized levels of positivity by subtracting each individual's favorability rating toward blacks and Latinos from their favorability ratings of whites (see Kam and Kinder 2012 and Wilcox, Sigelman, and Cook 1989 for a similar approach). Given that individuals generally have strong preference for those who share their race (Casellas and Wallace 2015; Tate 2003), we should expect that most individuals will have negative scores on these differences. I calculated the average difference between the racial/ethnic minority feeling thermometer and the white feeling thermometer for whites from each major political party in the United States and political independents for all presidential election years between 1984 and 2016.

Feeling Thermometer Scores

Figure 2.1 presents the average differences in feeling thermometer scores for (A) blacks relative to whites and (B) Latinos relative whites. Higher values indicate greater levels of support for racial/ethnic minorities relative to whites. The graphs are divided by partisanship (i.e., Democratic, Republican, and independent) and only include white respondents. Figure 2.1A demonstrates that the two major political parties are indeed taking divergent paths with their views of blacks. For most of the 1980s and 1990s there were not large differences between Democrats and Republicans in their views of blacks relative to whites. In fact, as recently as 2004, only 2 points separated white Democrats and white Republicans in their views of blacks relative to whites. However, by 2008 partisan differences in attitudes toward blacks began to increase. In 2008, the black-white feeling thermometer gap for Democrats and Republicans was close to 3.5 points. By 2016 this partisan gap had grown to 9 points. This difference is statistically significant ($p < .05$) based on a two-sample *t*-test.

The growing disparity is driven by both Democrats and Republicans. Democrats as a group have become much more approving of blacks relative to whites. In fact, on average, white Democrats in 2016 rated blacks as a group only 1.6 points worse than they rated individuals within their own racial group. While this is significant based on a paired *t*-test, this disparity was the

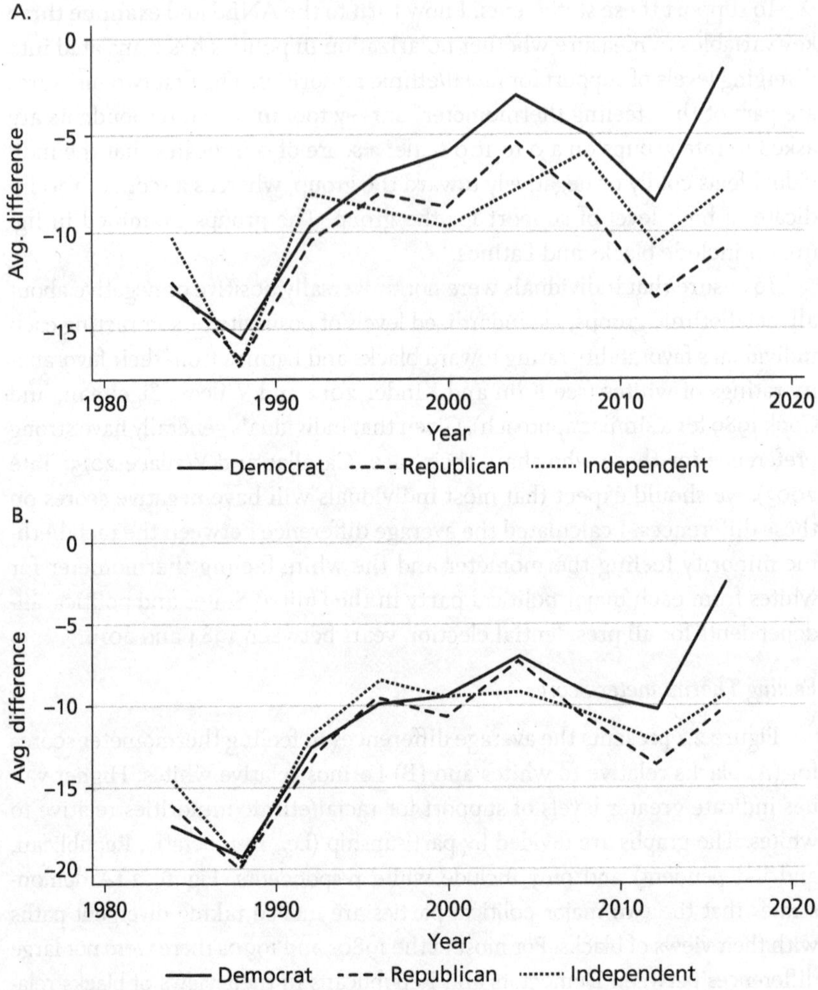

FIGURE 2.1. Whites' feeling thermometer scores for A: blacks relative to whites and B: Latinos relative to whites

Source: ANES.

Note: Scores were calculated by taking each respondent's black/Latino feeling thermometer score and subtracting their white feeling thermometer score.

smallest for any point in which the ANES collected information on racial feeling thermometer scores.

Republicans are more approving of blacks relative to whites than they have been in the past, but their attitudes about blacks relative to whites are worse in 2016 than they were in 1992. This indicates that Republicans as a group are feeling more negative about blacks relative to whites. Independents, as expected, tend to be in between Republicans and Democrats with regard to their feelings about blacks relative to whites. However, it is notable that white independents viewed blacks more favorably relative to whites in 2016 than they had in any previous year except for 2004.

We observe a similar pattern with regard to Latinos in figure 2.1B. While there were no statistically significant partisan differences before 2008 between white Democrats and white Republicans, these differences ballooned in 2016. In 2004, the difference between white Democrats and white Republicans in their assessment of Latinos relative to whites was less than a quarter of a percent and was statistically insignificant. This partisan difference grew to almost 8 points in 2016 and became significant based on a two-sample *t*-test. This growing difference in partisan attitudes about Latinos relative to whites appears to have come mostly from improving attitudes among white Democrats. White Democrats rated Latinos most closely to whites in 2016. Their attitudes about Latinos relative to whites improved by 8 points from 2012 to 2016, a difference that is statistically significant. White Republicans' attitudes toward Latinos also improved over this time but remained relatively stable between 1996 and 2016. Again, white independents fall in between white Democrats and white Republicans, and their attitudes toward Latinos relative to whites have remained stable over time.

Racial Resentment

In addition to examining partisans' explicit attitudes about different racial groups, I also explored differences in attitudes about racial resentment for white Democrats, white Republicans, and white independents over time. The racial resentment scale assesses whether individuals hold negative attitudes toward blacks (McConahay and Hough 1976). McConahay and Hough note that many individuals are unwilling to openly express their contempt for racial/ethnic minorities because of fears that they will be labeled as a racist. Additionally, Kinder and Sanders (1996) and Sears (1988) note that old fashioned racism that was based on biological difference has given way to a more socially acceptable form of prejudice in the form of cultural racism. Cultural racism is based on the idea that blacks lag behind whites in a number of social and political indicators because they don't work hard enough (Kinder and Sears 1996). Additionally, cultural racism is premised on the idea that blacks are undeserving of government aid.

The racial resentment scale uses four questions to both capture these modern forms of racism and circumvent problems of social desirability response bias. The racial resentment measure combines respondents' scores on the four questions using a five-point agree-to-disagree scale. The questions are: "Over

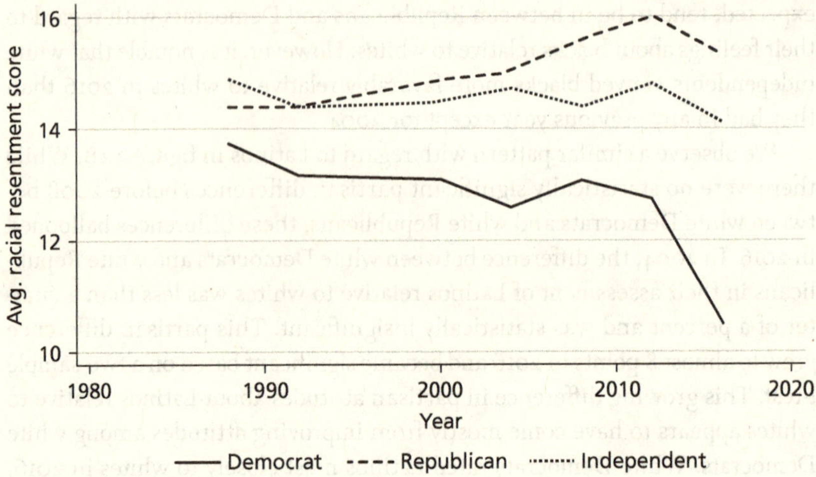

FIGURE 2.2. Whites' average racial resentment score by partisanship
Source: ANES.

the past few years, blacks have gotten less than they deserve"; "Irish, Italian, Jewish, and many other minorities overcame prejudice and worked their way up. Blacks should of the same without any special favors"; "It's really a matter of some people not trying hard enough; if blacks would only try harder they could be just as well off as whites"; "Generations of slavery and discrimination have created conditions that make it difficult for blacks to work their way out of the lower class." Those who responded to these questions in a manner that showed they felt minorities were in the position they were in because of lack of effort were coded as having high levels of racial resentment. The combined scale ranges from 4 (lowest levels of racial resentment) to 20 (highest levels of racial resentment).

Similar to the results in figure 2.1, there appears to be a dramatic change in white Democrats' levels of racial resentment in recent years (figure 2.2). White Democrats' levels of racial resentment between 2012 and 2016 declined by about 2 points on the 20-point scale. This decline is so steep that it is not only statistically significant, it is also the largest four-year change recorded by the ANES since it began using the racial resentment scale. White Democrats' levels of racial resentment were also surprisingly low in 2016. On average, white Democrats had a racial resentment score of 10.4, which means that across all four questions white Democrats were in between either not having an opinion about blacks' position in society or slightly agreeing that discrimination was the cause of all racial inequality between blacks and whites.

There does appear to be growing levels of polarization with regard to racial resentment, but this movement is mostly one-sided, with white Democrats' decline in racial resentment driving the growing disparity in these attitudes among white Democrats and Republicans. White independents and white Republicans have not changed much in their levels of racial resentment over time. Republicans had the highest levels of racial resentment in 2012 (~16 on the 20-point scale), but this number receded slightly by about a half a point in 2016. Nonetheless, this is change is statistically significant. White independents tend to have lower levels of racial resentment than white Republicans, but higher levels of racial resentment than white Democrats. Like white Democrats, they had their lowest levels of racial resentment in 2016, with an average racial resentment score of 14.8. However, this difference is only a tenth of a point lower than their previous low score in 2012, and the change over this four-year period is not statistically significant. In combination, these results indicate that growing racial polarization on implicit racial biases is being driven by changes in white Democrats' attitudes about race rather than shifting opinions among white Republicans.

Changes in Support for Racial Policies

The previous section presented strong evidence that white Democrats' attitudes about blacks and Latinos largely improved in the latter stages of Obama's presidency. Republican attitudes about these groups remained relatively stable, but in some cases, such as for blacks, they worsened slightly. While attitudes about different groups have significant implications for American politics, more needs to be done to determine whether these transformations in attitudes also coincide with changes in support or opposition for race-based programs. Given the growing awareness of racial discrimination among white Democrats (see chapter 1) and white Democrats' increasingly positive assessment of racial/ethnic minorities, we should expect that white Democrats will also be more supportive of policies that may improve racial disparities.

To test whether policy attitudes have changed for whites with different partisan attachments, I assess two measures on the ANES, a single measure on the GSS, and single measure from a series of Pew Research Center polls. For the ANES, I first examine a question that asks respondents, "Some people feel that the government in Washington should make every possible effort to improve the social and economic position of blacks. Others feel that the government should not make any special effort to help blacks because they should help themselves. Where would you place you place yourself on this [seven-point scale], or haven't you thought much about this?" A score of 1 on the scale indicates that individuals believe that blacks should help themselves without any favors while a score of 7 indicates they believe government should make a special effort to help blacks.

The second question that I examine from the ANES explores attitudes toward affirmative action. To assess public opinion on this matter, the ANES asks respondents "Some people say that because of past discrimination blacks should be given preference in hiring and promotion. Others say that such preference in hiring and promotion of blacks is wrong because it gives blacks advantages they haven't earned. What about your opinion; are you for or against preferential hiring and promotion of blacks?" This is coded simply as a dichotomous variable, with a 1 indicating support and a 0 indicating opposition to affirmative action.

Third, I use a GSS measure that asks about whether respondents believe that homeowners should be able to discriminate when selling their home. This is measured by a question that asks respondents "Suppose there is a community-wide vote on the general housing issue. There are two possible laws to vote on 1: "The Owner Decides" or 2: "Can't Discriminate Based on Race" Which law would you vote for?" I recoded this variable so that (1) is given a score of 0 and (2) is given a score of 1.

The final questions come from a series of six Pew polls conducted in 2006, 2010, 2013, 2014, 2015, and 2016. In these surveys Pew said to respondents "As I read each pair, tell me whether the first statement or the second statement comes closer to your own views—even if neither is exactly right. . . . Immigrants today strengthen our country because of their hard work and talents; immigrants today are a burden on our country because they take our jobs, housing and health care." For each year, I coded respondents as 1 if they stated that immigrants strengthened our country and as 0 if they viewed immigrants as being a burden on the country. Respondents who stated they were unsure were excluded from the analysis.

While a wide variety of questions to measure attitudes about racial policy could be selected, I analyze these questions because they are consistently asked by the same polling organizations over time. Moreover, they are asked in the same way to allow for time-series analysis. They also cover a variety of topics, including attitudes about hiring, housing, government intervention, immigration, and race.

Figure 2.3 presents the average score for each group on a seven-point scale that ranges from 1 ("Blacks help themselves") to 7 ("Government should aid blacks given previous levels of discrimination for white Democrats, white Independents, and white Republicans"). The data include all presidential election years from 1980 to 2016. The results demonstrate that white Democrats

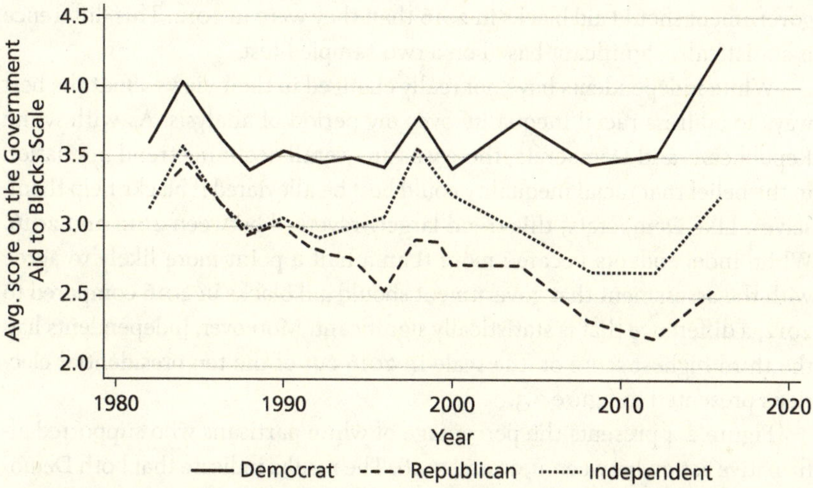

FIGURE 2.3. Whites' average attitudes about government aid for blacks by partisanship
Source: ANES.

became more progressive on racial issues in 2016. That year, the average white Democrat was closer to believing that government should aid blacks because of past discrimination than they were to believing that blacks should help themselves. White Democrats' score on this measure in 2016 (4.29) is about a quarter of a point higher than their previous high score of 4.02 in 1984. Moreover, it's more than three-quarters of a point higher than it was four years earlier. Both of these differences are statistically significant based on two-sample *t*-test. Overall, white Democrats were much more likely to endorse the idea that government should provide aid for blacks in 2016 than they were in the past.

White Republicans, meanwhile, have steadily become more likely to endorse the idea that racial inequality is driven by lack of work ethic among blacks. For example, in 1984 Republicans had a score of about 3.5 out of 7 on the scale relating to government aid for blacks. However, by 2012 this score had dropped to close to 2. While most of the polarization between Democrats and Republicans in this area has been driven by white Democrats being more likely to endorse the idea that government should aid blacks, some of the disparity is driven by white Republicans becoming more likely to endorse the idea that blacks should help themselves. Nonetheless, even white Republicans became more supportive of government helping blacks between 2012 and 2016. While still low on the seven-point scale (2.6 out of 7), Republicans were about one-third of a point closer to endorsing the idea that government should aid blacks in 2016 than they were in 2012. This difference is statistically significant based on a two-sample *t*-test.

White independents have not really changed in their views about the best ways to address racial inequality over my period of analysis. As with white Republicans and Democrats, there was an overall declining trend in relation to the belief that racial inequality could best be alleviated if blacks help themselves. Like Democrats, this trend largely reversed between 2012 and 2016. White independents became more than a half a point more likely to agree with the assessment that government should aid blacks in 2016 compared to 2012, a difference that is statistically significant. Moreover, independents had the third highest score on the scale in 2016 out of the ten presidential elections presented in figure 2.3.

Figure 2.4 presents the percentage of white partisans who supported affirmative action between 1992 and 2016. The results indicate that both Democrats and independents have grown in their levels of support for affirmative action over time. For example, in 1992 only about 18 percent of white Democrats supported affirmative action. However, by 2016 this number had grown by over 12 percent to about 30 percent. Moreover, one of the largest increases in this support for affirmative action over a four-year period occurred between 2012 and 2016. In 2012, about 21 percent of white Democrats supported affirmative action. This proportion grew by a statistically significant amount to 30 percent in 2016.

White independents followed a similar pattern as white Democrats over this period. In the early 1990s only 8.5 percent of white independents supported affirmative action. This proportion doubled to about 16 percent in 2016. This change over time is statistically significant. Moreover, support for affirmative action among independents increased by a statistically significant amount (~6 percent) over the four-year period between 2012 and 2016.

Republicans are the only group of partisans who have not become more supportive of affirmative action over time. In fact, fewer white Republicans supported affirmative action in 2016 (7.5%) than did in 1992 (10%). Again, levels of polarization around racial issues including affirmative action have increased between white Democrats and Republicans, but most of this difference stems from increased levels of racial progressiveness among white Democrats.

It is important to note that the way that the ANES frames affirmative action, using the words "preferential treatment," may lead to underestimates of support for the program (see Bacchi 2004). For example, in a March 2017 Pew poll, the organization asked the following question to assess support for affirmative action: "In general, do you think affirmative action programs de-

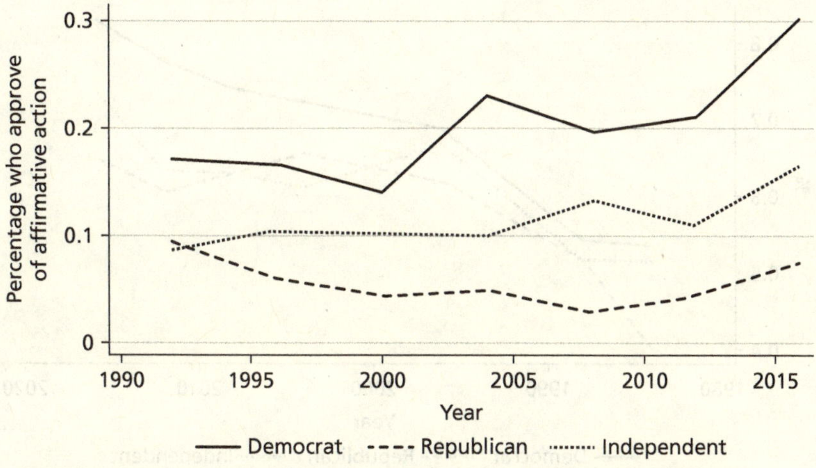

FIGURE 2.4. Whites' average levels of approval for affirmative action by partisanship
Source: ANES.

signed to increase the number of black and minority students on college campuses are a good thing or a bad thing?" Only 22 percent or respondents in this poll felt that affirmative action was a bad thing. Thus, the results presented in figure 2.4 may be conservative estimates of support for affirmative action. Nonetheless, the ANES's use of the same measure over time allows me to test whether support for the program has grown or remained stable. The results suggest that there has been a substantial increase in support for the program among white Democrats and independents in recent years.

In addition to growing levels of support for both government intervention to reduce racial inequality and affirmative action, white Democrats also became much more supportive of protections from racial discrimination with regard to housing (figure 2.5). When asked whether individuals selling their home should have the right to discriminate based on race, a majority of white Democrats have consistently preferred banning discrimination. Even in 1986, the first year this question was asked, a majority of whites believed that there are limits to how much discretion a seller should have when deciding whom to sell to. This number had grown to an overwhelming majority by 2016, with about 84 percent of white Democrats agreeing that sellers of a home should be barred from discriminating based on the race of the buyer. This represents a 4 percent increase from 2012, which is marginally statistically significant ($p < 0.10$).

Republicans too have become more supportive of prohibiting racial discrimination in selling homes over time. However, their attitudes on this topic

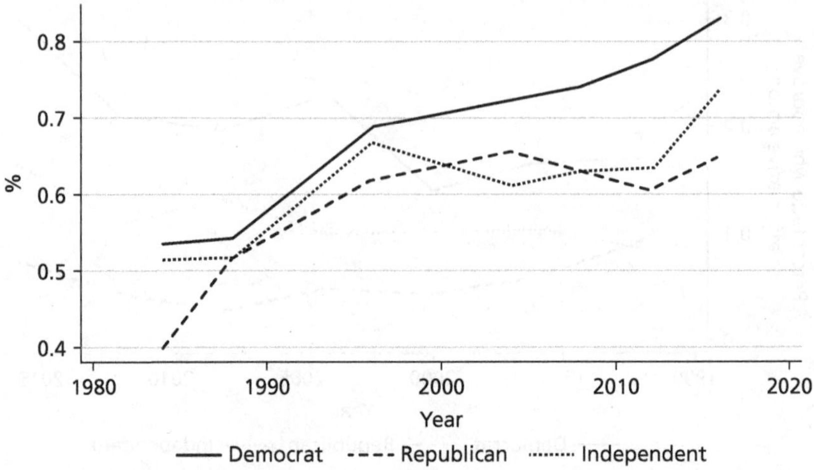

FIGURE 2.5. Percentage of whites who agree owners can't discriminate when they sell their homes by partisanship
Source: GSS.

have not changed much since 2000. In the early 1980s, most white Republicans believed that the owner should be able to decide who they sell their home to, with no restrictions. By 2004, however, a majority of white Republicans (65%) agreed that owners should have full discretion on who they sell too. This percentage remained about the same into 2016. Again, the combination of Republicans remaining fairly constant on their racial attitudes over time and white Democrats becoming more racially progressive has led to greater levels of polarization in recent years.

White independents also seem to be becoming more progressive when it comes to discrimination in real estate. In the early 1980s, independents appeared to be evenly split between allowing owners to make decisions about who they sell their home to and having protections for discrimination of homeowners. However, by 2016 the vast majority (~75%) of independents believed that owners should not be allowed to discriminate when selling their homes. As is the case with most of the analysis in this chapter, independents fall in between Democrats and Republicans in this area.

Figure 2.6 presents the percentage of white Democrats, white Republicans, and white independents who stated that they viewed immigrants as strengthening the country rather than as being a burden on it. Consistent with the other results presented in this section, White Democrats have become much more likely to believe that immigrants strengthen the nation over time. In fact, in 2016 over 80 percent of white Democrats stated that immigrants

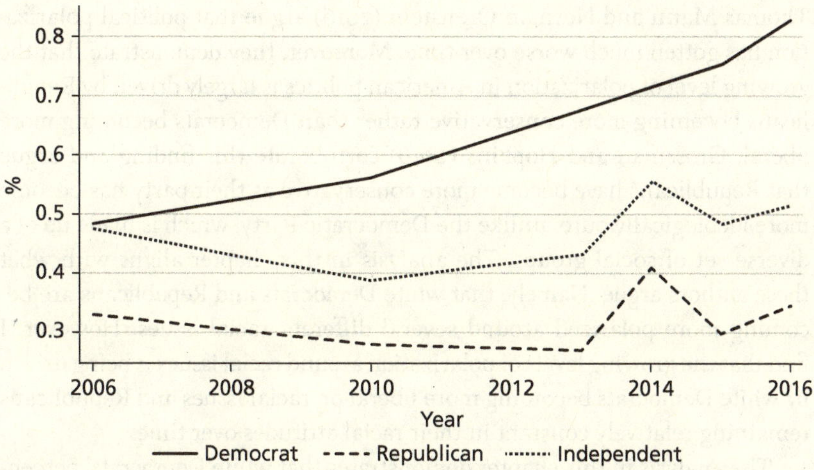

FIGURE 2.6. Percentage of whites who agree that immigrants strengthen the United States by partisanship
Source: Pew Research Center.

strengthen the nation rather than burden it. This represents a 35 percent increase in the number of white Democrats who viewed immigrants as supporting the nation from 2006 and a 15 percent increase from 2010. Both differences are statistically significant based on two-sample t-tests. In 2016, a majority (51%) of white independents also viewed immigrants as strengthening the nation rather than burdening it. However, this is a 3 percent decline from the number of white independents who viewed immigrants as strengthening the nation in 2014. Nonetheless, white independents were about 8 percent more likely to view immigrants as adding to the nation than they were in 2013.

As with other areas, white Republicans remain relatively consistent in their views of immigrants strengthening the nation versus perceiving them as a burden on the system. In almost all years from 2006 to 2016, fewer than 40 percent of white Republicans viewed immigrants as strengthening our nation. In 2016, about one-third (34%) of white Republicans viewed immigrants as improving the country. As with other areas of policy explored in this section, white Democrats appear to be displaying more liberal positions on immigration while white Republicans are largely unmoved.

Conclusion

In their *New York Times* bestselling book, *It's Even Worse Than It Looks: How the American Constitutional System Collided with the New Politics of Extremism,*

Thomas Mann and Norman Orenstein (2016) argue that political polarization has gotten much worse over time. Moreover, they demonstrate that the growing level of polarization in American politics is largely driven by Republicans becoming more conservative rather than Democrats becoming more liberal. Grossman and Hopkins (2016) corroborate this finding and argue that Republicans have become more conservative as their party has become more ideologically pure, unlike the Democratic Party, which is made up of a diverse set of social groups. The analysis in this chapter aligns with what these authors argue. Namely, that white Democrats and Republicans are becoming more polarized around several different racial issues. However, I find that the growing levels of polarization around racial issues is being driven by white Democrats becoming more liberal on racial issues and Republicans remaining relatively constant in their racial attitudes over time.

The analysis in this chapter demonstrates that white Democrats' perceptions of blacks and Latinos were more positive in 2016. Moreover, the improvements in their feeling thermometer scores for blacks and Latinos were quite dramatic. White Democrats increased their feeling thermometer score by 7–9 points for blacks and Latinos relative to whites in just four years. Moreover, their levels of racial resentment declined 15 percent over the same time period. This improvement in perceptions of racial/ethnic minorities translated into higher levels of support for government intervention to aid blacks, affirmative action, immigration, and a prohibition on housing discrimination. The combination of these results indicates that the greater awareness of racial discrimination demonstrated in chapter 1 does in fact coincide with more positive feelings about racial/ethnic minorities and is associated with greater levels of support for programs that aim to address racial inequality.

More evidence in support of this claim can be found in the fact that white Democrats differed from white Republicans in their reactions to the same racial contexts. White Republicans did not perceive higher levels of racial discrimination in chapter 1 and did not really change in their support for racially progressive policies over time. The analysis in this chapter has demonstrated that while Republicans have rated blacks more poorly in the past eight years, their attitudes about Latinos largely did not change. Moreover, while Republicans overwhelmingly oppose race-based programs, their levels of support on these issues have not shifted much over time. However, with regard to housing discrimination, they were actually more liberal in 2016 than they were in the past. In summary, polarization around racial issues is occurring, but it is driven much more by white Democrats than by white Republicans.

The above results have important implications for American politics. There is a significant amount of research that suggests that polarization leads people to see things through a partisan lens. A relevant example would be Democrats' and Republicans' divergent attitudes toward NFL quarterback Colin Kaepernick kneeling during the national anthem before a preseason game in 2016. What began as an innocuous gesture in support of racial/ethnic minorities became a national headline after Trump remarked on the issue (Schmidt et al. 2019). Following Trump's comments, partisanship largely determined where people stood on this issue, with Democrats in large part supporting Kaepernick and Republicans opposing him (Casteel 2017).

This example illustrates both the opportunities and challenges that come from the growing polarization on racial issues. White Democrats may see racial issues as something important to them and their party and become more supportive. In contrast, Republicans who remain racially conservative over time may judge racial issues as being antithetical to their interests and be oppositional to them. This makes it easier for racial/ethnic minorities to build liberal coalitions with white Democrats on racially tinged topics. However, it may also make compromise on racial issues unlikely to occur with white Republicans, who may automatically react negatively to any topic tied to race. In combination, the growing significance of race and polarization largely determining individuals' behaviors may increase gridlock where legislation meant to ameliorate problems in society are not addressed. Given the racial disparities in numerous areas, the status quo may not benefit racial/ethnic minorities.

The analyses in this chapter raise several important questions. First, how does white Democrats' becoming more liberal on racial issues influence a politician's likelihood of being rewarded or punished for making race-based appeals? The results demonstrate that higher levels of awareness of discrimination lead to more support for programs that address racial inequality. This in turn may make Democrats more receptive to race-based appeals, rather than being turned off by this form of outreach. This is a something I will explore in more detail in the following chapters. Moreover, if Democrats as a group are demonstrating lower levels of racial resentment, this could also mean that those who with high levels of racial resentment have left the party, leaving only racial progressives. If this is the case, deracializing to appeal to an already switched racially resentful voter may be a fruitless effort. In chapter 3, I will examine this possibility by focusing on how racial resentment divides working-class voters while leading to a decline in cross-pressured Democrats.

3
The Declining Significance of Class
RACIAL POLARIZATION AND WHITE WORKING-CLASS VOTERS

The former Georgia governor Richard Russell Jr. was first elected to the U.S. Senate in 1933. He was part of a Democratic wave that was a reaction to the Great Depression of 1929. Russell had a history of being an economic progressive before he joined the Senate. As governor, he had balanced the state budget without cutting salaries and worked to improve the University System in Georgia. As a senator, Russell supported New Deal legislation, introduced bills to bring electricity into rural areas, and was the architect of the National School Lunch Act of 1946, which provided low-cost or free school lunch meals to students who could not otherwise afford it. On economic issues, Russell initiated many liberal programs.

However, Russell was extremely regressive on racial issues and was an outspoken critic of the anti-lynching bills that were circulating through Congress. He participated in several filibusters to ensure that civil rights bills did not pass through the Senate. He also coauthored the Southern Manifesto with South Carolina U.S. senator and 1948 Dixiecrat presidential candidate Strom Thurmond. The Southern Manifesto argued that the South should be able to continue segregation in public areas in spite of the 1954 *Brown vs. Board of Education* Supreme Court decision.

Russell's career epitomizes the challenge that the Democratic Party faced in the twentieth century in maintaining their diverse alliance of voters known as the New Deal coalition. This political alliance made up of northern liberals, southern conservatives, union members, Catholics, and African Americans was held together by support for liberal economic principles but was sharply divided on racial issues. It was in this context that Charles V. Hamilton (1977) argued that the Democratic Party would be better served by focusing more on progressive economic policies and minimizing discussions of racial policies. It was also under this context that Jimmy Carter's and Bill Clinton's ability to combine support for liberal economic programs and racially conservative legislation helped them win the White House by appealing to working-class whites.

Many pundits and social scientists argue that it was the decline in support from white working-class voters that led to the demise of Hillary Clinton in 2016. These individuals argue that Clinton's use of identity-based appeals alienated working-class whites and drove these voters toward Trump. Columbia University professor Mark Lilla wrote in a *New York Times* editorial that Clinton "tended on the campaign trail to lose that large vision and slip into the rhetoric of diversity, calling out explicitly to African-American, Latino, L.G.B.T. and women voters at every stop. This was a strategic mistake" (Lilla 2016). Along the same lines, others argued that the Democratic Party needed to limit its focus on minority politics to regain the support of white working-class voters. For example, former Clinton advisor Mark Penn and former Manhattan Borough president Andrew Stein wrote in a *New York Times* editorial that "central to the Democrats' diminishment has been their loss of support among working-class voters, who feel abandoned by the party's shift away from moderate positions on trade and immigration. . . . They saw the party being mired too often in political correctness, transgender bathroom issues and policies offering more help to undocumented immigrants than to the heartland" (Penn and Stein 2017).

As was true in the past, many argue that racial appeals turned off working-class whites who as a group want to support the Democratic Party but are purportedly alienated by appeals to racial/ethnic minorities and other marginalized groups. If working-class white voters remained cross-pressured by their economic and social interests, then a deracialized campaign may still be the most advantageous strategy to attract these voters. If the Democratic Party deemphasized race but played up economically liberal principles, it is argued, then white working-class voters would no longer feel cross-pressured and would be more likely to join the Democratic Party.

However, as demonstrated in chapter 2, the United States is becoming more divided as a nation on racial issues. Because of this it is possible that there are far fewer cross-pressured Americans today than they were in Russell's time. Those who were not worried about racial issues and prioritized economic issues remained in the Democratic Party. At the same time, those who prioritized conservative racial issues subordinated their class identity and left the Democratic Party, further exacerbating the racial ideological divide between the parties. This shift toward ideological consistency in racial and economic issues may diminish the incentive for Democrats to appeal to racial conservatives by deracializing because their vote may no longer be easily attained. Instead, they may gain more traction by mobilizing those who are sympathetic to racially progressive policies.

In this chapter, I will explore whether racially conservative working-class voters who were key to the New Deal coalition in the past remain a significant portion of the Democratic electorate. I will begin by discussing why Democratic and minority politicians in the twentieth century benefited from minimizing their discussions about race. I will then discuss how recent changes in the political context have divided white working-class voters by levels of racial resentment. In doing so, I will show that white working-class voters are not a monolithic group who can be persuaded using the same campaign tactics. Instead, white working-class voters are politically much more like their economic elite counterparts in modern America, with both groups being divided by levels of racial resentment.

To demonstrate this, I will use the American National Election Studies (ANES) for the period 1986–2016. While I find that white economic elites' partisanship and support for Democratic presidential candidates has always been divided by levels of racial resentment, I also show that white working-class voters were until recently largely supportive of the Democratic Party regardless of their level of racial resentment. However, in recent years, such voters have diverged on this issue, and class has receded as a strong predictor of partisanship. I conclude this chapter by discussing how greater levels of consistency among white Democrats on their views toward racial/ethnic minorities removes the incentive to pursue a strategy of deracialization in order to appeal to a disappearing swing electorate of white working-class voters.

The Rise of Reagan Democrats and the Need to Deracialize

Charles V. Hamilton, the architect of the deracialization strategy, surmised that the Republican Party had been using racial issues to divide the Democratic Party following the passing of the 1964 Civil Rights Act and the 1965 Voting Rights Act: "A deracialized political strategy in the electoral political context was in my judgement a wise political strategy. It was to the advantage of the Republicans to raise issues that would have polarized the electorate and, in effect, racialized matters even more than was already the case. . . . A political party not likely to obtain a significant share of a particular group's votes would find it advantageous to attempt to isolate that group by making overt and covert appeals to more receptive groups" (Hamilton 1977, 3). This demonstrates Hamilton's fear that the Republican Party could exploit weaknesses in the New Deal coalition by making the progressive economic policies of the Democratic Party seem like handouts to racial/ethnic minorities. To combat this and to ensure that a sufficient number of whites who wanted to strengthen the social safety net would not drift away from the

Democratic Party, Hamilton (1977) advocated that candidates discuss the advantages that *all* racial groups would enjoy with the passage of programs like universal employment, universal health care, and raising the minimum wage (see also R. Perry 2011).

Using a mostly deracialized strategy, Jimmy Carter was able to recapture the White House in 1976 after eight years of Republican rule. He did this by putting together a coalition of overwhelming black support and moderate support from white southerners who did not view Carter as being excessively progressive on racial issues. It was this temporary coalition that allowed Carter to win every southern state, a feat that was necessary given that he lost large states outside of the south, including California and Illinois.

Carter hoped to extend his success going into the 1980 election, but a series of setbacks including rising gas prices, a credible primary challenge, the Iran hostage crisis, and stagflation made the electoral landscape much less favorable. Additionally, Carter's opponent, California governor Ronald Reagan, was able to successfully appeal to southern and working-class whites by exploiting the cultural rift within the Democratic Party. Reagan racialized issues like welfare and made the argument that Washington was using hardworking Americans' tax dollars to subsidize lazy racial/ethnic minorities (Gilens 1999). Reagan's campaigns in 1980 and 1984 were successful at using this tactic to draw the support of economically progressive Democrats who were also socially and racially conservative.

These individuals, who were closer to the Democratic Party in their economic policy preferences but sided with the Republicans on cultural issues, became known as Reagan Democrats. Reagan Democrats tended to be from the South and the Rust Belt, which were politically competitive areas in the 1980s and 1990s. These individuals were mostly white males who were high school educated and worked in blue-collar jobs. During the latter half of the twentieth century they comprised as much as one half of the total electorate (Borquez 2005). Given their number and that they could fit naturally with either political party depending on the message of the candidate, Reagan Democrats were the crucial swing voters in the presidential elections of the 1980s. As a result, more and more politicians crafted their campaign narratives to appeal to these voters.

Democrats tried to appeal to these voters by emphasizing their support for spending on infrastructure, unions, and protections for blue-collar workers while at the same time deemphasizing their support for controversial social issues like affirmative action, welfare, and busing (Wright Austin and Middleton 2004). In 1992, Bill Clinton appealed to economic liberals, for example, by speaking about the failures of trickledown economics for voters in

Rust Belt states. He demonstrated his independence from racial/ethnic minorities by campaigning as someone who was tough on crime and would reform welfare (Gilens 2001). Clinton also demonstrated his independence from the black community by criticizing comments made by hip-hop lyricist and black political activist Sister Souljah (Pittman 2006). This deracialized strategy helped Clinton gain the support of Reagan Democrats in the 1992 presidential election.

While Democrats worked to demonstrate their independence from black voters, Republicans attempted to appeal to Reagan Democrats by highlighting that the Democratic Party's focus on racial and ethnic minorities often came at the cost of the white working class. This was most evident in two campaign ads from the late 1980s and early 1990s. In September 1988 George H. W. Bush's campaign aired an advertisement famously known as the "Willie Horton ad," which portrayed his opponent Michael Dukakis as lenient on crime. Dukakis had vetoed a bill that would have kept prisoners with first-degree murder convictions from getting furloughs. In 1986, William Horton had been serving time for murder when he fled while on a temporary furlough from prison and committed robbery, rape, and assault. The advertisement played on racial fears that blacks, if not held in check with tough crime laws, would wreak havoc on the safety of white Americans (Mendelberg 2001). Similarly, in 1990 North Carolina U.S. senator Jesse Helms used an advertisement of a white hand crumpling up a rejection letter from a job that had been given to a minority applicant. The advertisement implied that the support of affirmative action by Helm's opponent, African American mayor Harvey Gantt, would lessen the opportunities of white working-class voters (Iyengar and McGrady 2007). In both cases, Republicans used Democrats' positions on race to attract white support for the Republican Party.

Given this landscape, it made sense for Democratic politicians to remain silent on the issue of race. It provided them the opportunity to highlight the commonalities between Reagan Democrats and the Democratic Party. Moreover, it provided protection against claims of minority racial favoritism. Taken together, in a context with many cross-pressured white voters, the deracialization strategy was a necessary compromise that Democrats would need to make to win elected office.

Why Class Is No Longer the Major Cleavage in American Politics

The vast majority of discussion around working-class whites and Reagan Democrats has treated these individuals as a monolith when it comes to electoral politics (see Bartels 2006; Teixeira and Rogers 2001). In particular, the assumption is that white working-class voters as a group tend to want to support the Democratic Party because of class interests but are deterred by the party's racial policies (Frank 2004; Teixeira and Rogers 2001). Historically and theoretically, there is good reason for this expectation.

There are numerous reasons why working-class whites have generally been averse to progressive racial policy. Historically, blacks and poor whites were pitted against each other by political and social elites (Dittmer 1980; Du Bois 1935). Elites argued that regardless of the economic position of poor whites, they were still on a higher rung in the social hierarchy because of their skin color, and this provided substantial social benefits (Du Bois 1935; Shaw et al. 2014). Additionally, elites argued that blacks were depressing wages to divide poorer blacks and whites. These same elites also used blacks to break unions during strikes to alienate blacks from labor unions (Shaw et al. 2014). These historical factors created an "us vs. them" mentality that divided blacks and poor whites in spite of their shared class status.

These perceived divisions remain today, with many working-class whites viewing blacks and increasingly Latinos as competitors for jobs, housing, and social services (Teixeira and Rogers 2001). This is often combined with perceptions that government is taking away resources from them in the form of taxes and social services and redistributing them to undeserving minorities (Gilens 2001). This overall sense of frustration with race relations in the United States and government leads working-class whites to be antagonistic toward policies that are perceived as benefiting minorities. This may be issues that are explicitly racial, such as affirmative action and busing, issues that are implicitly racial, such as welfare and crime, or even issues that are tied to the first black president, such as the Affordable Care Act of 2013 (Gilens 2001; Parker and Barreto 2013; Tesler 2016). Politicians have long been strategic and used these conflicts to garner political support. In the 1970s, Nixon used the Southern Strategy, which emphasized law and order and a crackdown on the "unruly" inner city, to appeal to working-class whites (Hamilton 1977). In the 1980s, Reagan strengthened these appeals by characterizing the Democratic Party as providing excessive social services for minority mothers who abuse the welfare system (Gilens 2001).

Anxiety about the growing political influence of racial and ethnic minorities has led to drastic changes in race relations between working-class whites and these underrepresented groups. Several studies have detailed what Barack Obama's election to the White House has done for whites' opinions about racial/ethnic minorities and their political behavior (Kinder and Dale-Riddle 2012; Tesler 2016; Tesler and Sears 2010). Fear of what Obama represents increased the salience of racial issues for whites, and in particular working-class whites, in their political decision-making process. Parker and Barreto (2013) also demonstrate that perceptions of the growing number of racial/ethnic minorities in the United States have led many whites to become more supportive of conservative political movements such as the Tea Party.

The Tea Party movement has capitalized on these feelings to their political advantage. In particular, several politicians associated with the movement have stoked fears that changing demographics will lead whites to not only lose social services, but also their political power (Parker and Barreto 2013). By appealing to white working-class voters using identity politics, the Tea Party has helped to consolidate many such voters who have been more concerned with race relations than class, thereby ending a long period of these voters being cross-pressured.

Tesler (2016) presents convincing evidence that many Reagan Democrats have left the Democratic Party and the divide in American politics is driven less by class and more by racial attitudes. Through a series of experiments and nationally representative surveys, Tesler (2016) shows that attitudes about racial resentment are a stronger predictor of vote choice than is class and even authoritarian attitudes. If negative attitudes about minorities are driving support for the Republican Party, it follows that not all working-class whites will follow the same pattern when it comes to their partisanship and vote choice. In particular, working-class whites with low levels of racial resentment may not be concerned by the Democratic Party's stances on race to the same degree as their highly racially resentful counterparts. This change may indicate that the significance of class has declined for working-class whites and that these voters are no longer cross-pressured between their economic and racial concerns.

This has important implications for politicians deciding whether to discuss racial issues. If the main impetus to distance oneself from racial issues is to appeal to white working-class voters, and these voters have already sorted themselves according to racial issues, then there would be few advantages to deracialize. White working-class voters who held negative opinions about minorities would have already shifted to the Republican Party, and there would be little hope of bringing them back without being hostile toward minority interests rather than ignoring them. Conversely, white working-class voters who do not hold negative attitudes about racial/ethnic minorities will remain drawn to the Democratic Party because of its stance on economic issues.

Is There a Divide among White Working-Class Voters?

If white working-class voters are a monolithic group when it comes to racial issues, partisanship, and voting, then the assumption about white working-class voters being universally cross-pressured between their economic and racial concerns remains valid. Moreover, if there have been large swings in their allegiance to the Democratic Party over time, this will indicate that under the right conditions their vote is up for grabs. Such a result would make a deracialized approach more appealing. I test these assumptions using the 1986–2016 ANES. Unfortunately, the ANES only began asking questions on racial resentment in 1986, which limits how far back I can go in my analysis. Moreover, they did not ask questions about racial resentment in 1996, so this year is excluded from my analysis.

To assess whether differences between low- and high-resentment whites of different socioeconomic status exist, I first divided voters by their class. I categorize working-class whites using Bartels's (2006) criteria. Bartels (2006) argues that working-class whites are those who are white, are below the thirty-third percentile for household income, and do not have a college degree. Individuals who held all three of these attributes simultaneously were categorized as working-class whites. As a comparison group, I examine elite whites. These individuals are whites who have at least one college degree and are above the sixty-sixth percentile for income in any given year (see Bartels 2006).

I then disaggregate individuals by their levels of racial resentment, using the four relevant items in the ANES to create a racial resentment measure. The questions use a five-point agree-to-disagree scale on the following statements: "Over the past few years, blacks have gotten less than they deserve"; "Irish, Italian, Jewish, and many other minorities overcame prejudice and worked their way up. Blacks should of the same without any special favors"; "It's really a matter of some people not trying hard enough; if blacks would only try harder they could be just as well off as whites"; "Generations of slavery and discrimination have created conditions that make it difficult for blacks to work their way out of the lower class."

The combined scale was recoded so that the scores range from 4 (lowest level of racial resentment) to 20 (highest level of racial resentment). I then placed those who on average had no opinion, disagreed, or strongly disagreed on each of the racial resentment questions (i.e., those with an overall racial resentment score of 12 or less) into a "low-resentment" group. Conversely, those who on average affirmatively responded to each of the racial resentment items (i.e., had an overall racial resentment score of 13 or greater) were placed in a "high-resentment" group.

What about Reagan Democrats?

Before we delve into differences between working-class whites and elite whites in their political preferences, I will present information about the

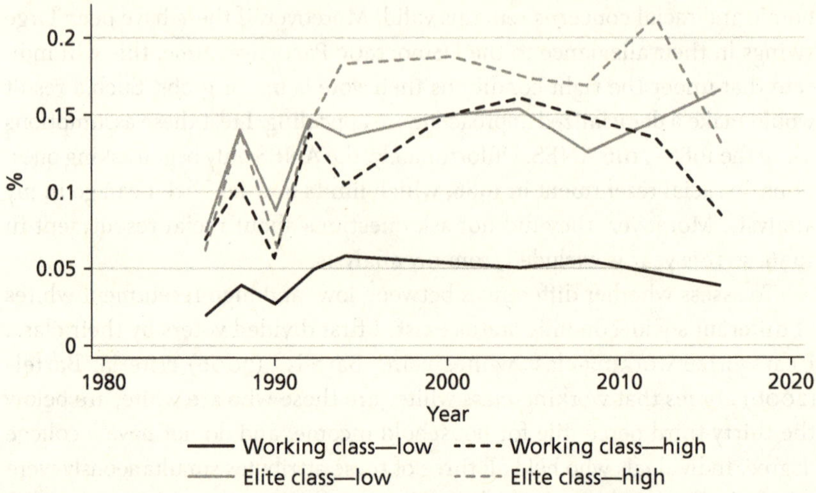

FIGURE 3.1. Percentage of elite and working-class whites with high and low levels of racial resentment
Source: ANES.

percentage of the white electorate that falls into each group. I begin by creating a total white voter population by examining the total number of whites who reported voting in the ANES. It is important to note that this number may be higher than the actual number of voters because of social desirability response bias (Silver, Anderson, and Abramson 1986). Unfortunately, because no survey that I am aware of validates voter turnout and includes racial resentment measures over a long period of time, the available data is somewhat compromised. Having established the size of the white electorate, I then divided the number of voters in each group of interest (i.e., low- and high-resentment white working-class voters and low- and high-resentment white elite voters) by the total number of white voters in the electorate for each year. This created a measure that represents the percentage of the white electorate supplied by each group as estimated by the ANES.

Figure 3.1 presents the percentage of the low-resentment working class, high-resentment working class, low-resentment elite class, and high-resentment elite class among the white electorate based on estimates by the ANES for each presidential election year between 1988 and 2016. The figure demonstrates that for the most part high-resentment whites dominate over their low-resentment counterparts. The ratio of high-resentment working-class whites to low-resentment working-class whites is generally more than 2 to 1. This is largely driven by the fact that low-resentment working-class whites routinely make up about 5 percent of the total white electorate whereas high-resentment working-class whites consistently account for 12–15 percent.

However, this difference has declined in recent elections, with high-resentment white working-class voters accounting for less than 10 percent of the white electorate in 2016. In 2016, the gap between low- and high-resentment white working-class voters was only about 4 percent. While statistically significant based on a *t*-test, this difference is the smallest in our period of interest. Several factors may be influencing this decline. First, with the growth of other racial/ethnic groups who tend to be disproportionately poor, the number of whites who are below the thirty-third percentile for income may be declining. Second, it is this group of whites who are facing the greatest levels of mortality at a younger age.

Low- and high-resentment elites tend to be more closely divided in terms of their share of the electorate. High-resentment elite whites tend to predominate, and spiked to over 20 percent in the 2012 presidential election. However, by 2016 they had declined to about 10 percent. The number of low-resentment white elites, meanwhile, has steadily climbed. By 2016, low-resentment elite whites made up the largest group in our analysis. This change in the electorate is most likely due to the declining levels of racial resentment among college-educated whites in recent years. In summary, the results in figure 3.1 demonstrate that whites with high levels of resentment make up the majority of working-class and elite white voters. However, the difference between low- and high-resentment voters in these categories is declining over time.

Figure 3.2 presents the percentage of working-class whites and elite whites who identified with the Democratic Party in the ANES from 1986 (the first year in which racial resentment data were collected) to 2016. The plot is disaggregated by working-class whites with low levels of resentment, working-class whites with high levels of resentment, elite-class whites with low resentment, and elite-class whites with high levels of resentment. The results demonstrate that a growing polarization in racial attitudes appear to be dividing working-class white voters. In the late 1980s and early 1990s there did not appear to be large differences between working class whites with high or low levels of racial resentment with regard to their Democratic identification. In 1986, for example, low-resentment working-class whites were only 3 percent more likely to identify as Democratic than high-resentment working-class whites. In 1992, high-resentment working-class whites were actually 1 percent more likely to identify with the Democratic Party than their low-resentment counterparts. Both differences are statistically insignificant based on a two-sample *t*-test.

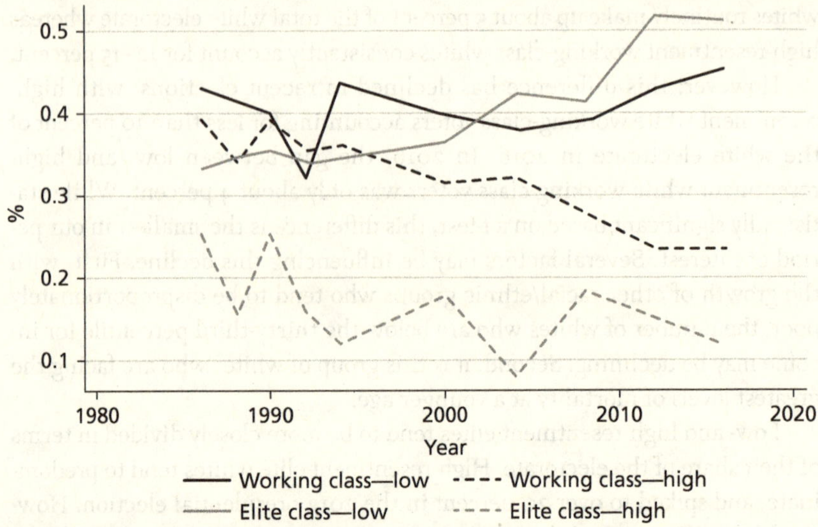

FIGURE 3.2. Percentage of whites who identify as Democrat by class and levels of racial resentment (1986–2016)
Source: ANES.

However, starting in the late 1990s, low- and high-resentment working-class whites began to diverge in their political partisanship. This division exacerbated after the 2008 presidential election, which coincided with the growth of the Tea Party movement and greater news coverage of changing demographics in the United States. In 2004, only 4 percentage points separated low- and high-resentment working-class whites in their Democratic partisanship. This difference is not significant based on a two-sample *t*-test. However, the difference grew to 11 percent in 2008, which is marginally significant based on a two-sample *t*-test ($p < 0.10$). By 2016, this difference had ballooned to 21 percent, which is statistically significant. This division was actually driven by changes in partisanship among both groups. In 2016, low-resentment whites identified with the Democratic Party at greater rates than at any point in the thirty-year period for which data are available. In spite of declining partisanship in the population, almost half (46%) of low-resentment working-class whites identified with the Democratic Party. This return to the Democratic Party may in part have been driven by greater polarization between the two parties and greater perceptions of hostility to racial/ethnic minorities. Additionally, the Republican Party's aversion to unions and to raising the minimum wage may also drive low-resentment working-class whites back to the Democratic Party.

On the other hand, high-resentment working-class whites have largely left the Democratic Party. In 1986, 39 percent of high-resentment working-class whites identified as a Democrat. After the most recent presidential election in 2016, 17 percent less individuals in this group identified with the Democratic Party. In fact, that year fewer than one in four (22%) high-resentment working-class whites identified as a Democrat. This change among high-resentment working-class whites could most likely be attributed to them perceiving the Democratic Party as favoring racial/ethnic minorities over themselves, as well as to appeals by the Republican Party specifically to this group.

Unlike white working-class voters, low- and high-resentment elite-class whites have been relatively consistent in their partisanship. Outside of the 1986 survey, where low- and high-resentment elite white voters were separated in their Democratic partisanship by 8 percent, these groups of elite whites have generally been 10 percentage points or more apart. Moreover, the difference in Democratic partisanship between these groups is statistically significant for every presidential election year included in this analysis (i.e., 1988–2016).

However, like working-class whites, low- and high-resentment white elites are also experiencing greater levels of polarization. In fact, the largest gap between low- and high-resentment elite whites occurred in 2016. While a majority of white low-resentment elites identified as a Democrat that year, only 12 percent of high-resentment elites identified as a Democrat. This almost 40 percent divide in Democratic identification has been driven by both low-resentment white elites becoming more Democratic and high-resentment white elites becoming less Democratic.

Figure 3.3 moves beyond partisanship and examines whether support for the Democratic Party's presidential nominee differs by the intersection of class status and racial resentment. The figure demonstrates that like partisanship, working-class whites with low or high levels of racial resentment have diverged in their voting preferences substantially overtime. Low-resentment white working-class voters tended to be more loyal to the Democratic presidential candidate than their high-resentment counterparts. In fact, in every presidential election between 1988 and 2016 with the exception of 2004, a majority of low-resentment working-class whites voted for the Democratic presidential nominee. Moreover, they voted at higher rates for the Democratic nominee than high-resentment working-class whites in every election in our data set except for 2004.

High-resentment working-class whites were consistently more divided in their support for the Democratic presidential nominee. For every presidential

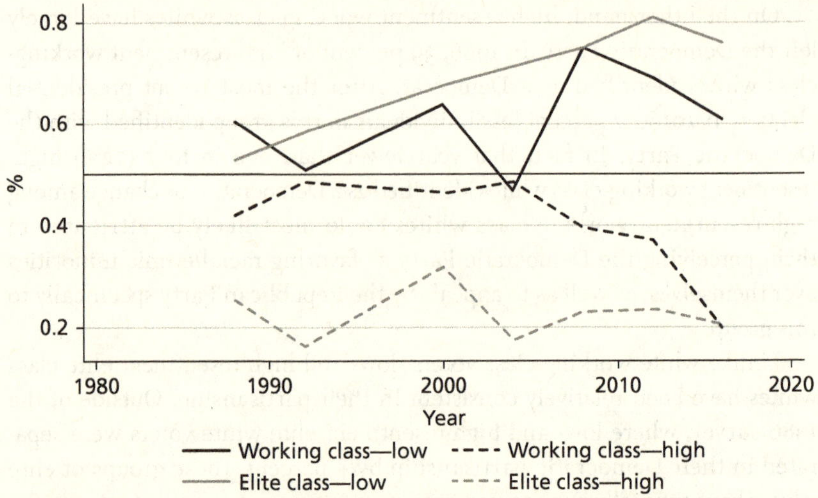

FIGURE 3.3. Percentage of white support for Democratic presidential nominee by class and level of racial resentment (1988–2016)
Source: ANES.

election between 1992 and 2004, more than 45 percent of high-resentment white working-class voters supported the Democratic presidential nominee. However, from 2008 there emerged a clearer difference between low- and high-resentment working-class whites in their voting preferences. In 2008, when Obama did surprisingly well among working-class whites, much of this difference was driven by those with low racial resentment. Three out of four (75%) working-class whites with low levels of racial resentment voted for Obama in 2008. In contrast, less than 40 percent of working-class whites with high levels of racial resentment voted for Obama in the same year. This difference is statistically significant based on a two-sample *t*-test. This indicates that Obama's strong performance with working-class whites could largely be attributed to those with low levels of racial resentment.

The gap between low- and high-resentment working-class whites remained large in both the 2012 and 2016 presidential elections. Much of this, however, was driven by high-resentment working-class whites moving away from the Democratic Party in recent years. While over 60 percent of low-resentment working-class whites supported the Democratic presidential nominee in the previous two presidential elections, less than 40 percent of high-resentment working-class whites supported the nominee in the 2012 or 2016 presidential election. In 2016, fewer than 1 in 5 high-resentment working-class whites supported Hillary Clinton.

Low- and high-resentment elite whites follow a similar pattern to working-class whites with regard to their support for Democratic presidential nominees. Low-resentment elite whites became steadily more supportive of the Democratic Party's presidential nominee between 1988 and 2016. In fact, in 2008 and 2016, more the 75 percent of low-resentment white elite voters supported either Obama or Clinton in the presidential election. High-resentment elite whites, however, have remained relatively stable in their support for the Democratic Party's presidential nominee. In only one election between 1986 and 2016 has this group of voters provided more than 25 percent support for the Democratic presidential nominee (2000). In all elections between 2004 and 2016, only about 20 percent of high-resentment white elites have supported the Democratic presidential nominee in the general election. These results suggest that elite whites, like working-class whites, are becoming more divided in their partisanship around racial resentment. However, for elite whites this is largely driven by low-resentment elites becoming more Democratic.

Class Politics or Resentment Politics?

The divergence among low- and high-resentment whites has led to a divide in American politics that appears to transcend class boundaries. Those with high levels of racial resentment differ significantly from those with low levels of racial resentment on both partisanship and support for the Democratic presidential nominee regardless of whether they are among the working class or elites. In the 1980s, the swing voters were working-class whites who largely differed from their non-working-class white counterparts. However, in recent years, the dividing line appears to be between whites with low or high levels of racial resentment.

Elite and working-class whites with high levels of resentment are becoming more similar in their political behaviors. For example, before the 2008 election there were not large differences between white working-class voters, regardless of their levels of racial resentment. However, after 2008 election this difference was growing. At the same time, high-resentment working-class whites began to look very similarly politically to elite whites with high levels of resentment. In the 2016 presidential election, less than 1 percentage point separated high-resentment white elites and working-class whites in their support for Hillary Clinton, a difference that is statistically insignificant. Moreover, the difference in partisanship between these two groups was only about 10 percent, which is not only statistically insignificant, but also substantially smaller than it was in 2004, when these groups were separated in their Democratic partisanship by about 25 percent.

Low-resentment working-class whites are also beginning to look more like white elites with the same level of resentment. For example, in 2004, only about 1 percent separated low- and high-resentment working-class whites in their support for John Kerry. At the same time, the difference between low-resentment white elites and working-class voters was over 20 percent. By 2016, the gap between low-resentment working-class and elite whites had narrowed to about 14 percent, and the gap between low-and high-resentment working-class whites had ballooned to over 40 percent. Overall, the results in figures 3.2 and 3.3 provide strong evidence that whites of any given class cannot be lumped together when it comes to their political preferences. This is particularly true for recent election cycles. Instead, the defining division among whites is less about class and more about whether they have high or low levels of racial resentment.

Conclusion

In the 1980s and early 1990s, the Democrats' path to national and even local elected offices in many places was clear: put together a coalition of racial/ethnic minorities and working-class whites. Such an approach catapulted Carter, Clinton, and Obama to the White House over the span of thirty years. Accomplishing such a task required a careful campaign strategy that did not alienate working-class whites with an agenda that was too progressive on racial issues while still finding a way to energize their racial/ethnic minority base. In today's American politics, Democratic politicians do not have to perform such a balancing act. This is largely because working-class whites are no longer politically a monolithic group. Those who are racially liberal have remained within the Democratic Party's coalition, and those who are racially conservative have largely left.

As a comparison group, I also examined white elite respondents. Unlike white working-class voters, this group has long been divided by their position on racial issues. But like white working-class voters, white elites have become increasingly divided based on racial resentment. Low-resentment white elites have become an extremely reliable part of the Democratic Party's coalition, voting for the Democratic nominee by a 3-to-1 margin in the previous two presidential elections. Conversely, high-resentment white elites are becoming much less Democratic. In fact, less than 20 percent of these voters in the previous election identified as being members of the Democratic Party.

What is most surprising about the results of this chapter is that the influence of class has appeared to wane for whites at the extremes of the socioeconomic ladder. Working-class whites with high levels of racial resentment are much closer to white elites with high levels of racial resentment in terms of partisanship and vote choice than they are to whites in their same economic class who have low levels of racial resentment. White working-class voters with low levels of racial resentment have much more in common politically with low-resentment white elites than they do with high-resentment voters in their same class. The combination of these factors means that levels of racial resentment may now be a larger divide in American politics than class.

At the same time that whites are becoming more divided based on their levels of racial resentment, the demographics of the white electorate are also shifting. White working-class voters with high levels of racial resentment comprised a smaller portion of the white electorate in 2016 than they did at any point dating all the way back to 1992. At the same time, low-resentment economic elites increased drastically in their representation in the white electorate in 2016. These shifting demographic characteristics along with a more racially divided country are changing the way that politicians appeal to the electorate. This may be particularly true for Democrats who are hoping to utilize a combination of the growing minority population and loyal white voters to build a winning coalition.

These changes in the political landscape should provide caution for those arguing that a deracialized approach will yield large advantages to the Democratic Party with white voters. As demonstrated in this chapter, white working-class voters are not a monolithic group that will uniformly return to the Democratic Party as soon as it ends its focus on marginalized groups. Moreover, such a strategy may frustrate the growing number of low-resentment white working-class and elite voters who have displayed growing concerns about racial inequality, as was demonstrated in chapter 2.

Moreover, given the growing stickiness of partisanship, Democratic candidates may gain more from mobilizing racially progressive whites who have become more closely tied to the Democratic Party rather than abandoning racial appeals to try to win back racially conservative working-class whites. Given that high-resentment whites of all classes are experiencing a decline in their overall population, Democrats may gain more leverage for engaging in race-based appeals. In the following chapter, I will test this proposition by examining whether politicians perceived as being racially progressive are punished or rewarded by whites in contemporary politics.

4

Polarization, Racialization, and White Partisan Political Behavior

History was against Barack Obama's chances for reelection in 2012. Since the end of World War II, no president had been reelected with an approval rating of less than 49 percent in March of the election year. Additionally, no president had been reelected over that same time period with an unemployment rate of greater than 7.2 percent. In March 2012, Obama's approval rating was just 46 percent according to a Gallup poll (Gallup 2012). Moreover, the unemployment rate in October that year, near the end of Obama's first term, was close to 9 percent. As the 2012 Election Day approached, a mere 18 percent of the population was satisfied with the direction of the country (Gallup 2012). Based on the fundamentals of elections, it appeared that Obama was headed for defeat.

In spite of the unfriendly political and economic context in 2012, Obama won reelection handily. Not only did he receive more than 50 percent of the popular vote, he won almost every swing state and defeated his major-party opponent Mitt Romney by over a hundred Electoral College votes. Obama's strong electoral performance was driven in large part by his ability to mobilize his base. While the country was heavily divided in their assessment of the president, Obama was able to win by ensuring that more of his voters turned out than Romney's.

Obama's reelection in 2012 provides a good example of successful strategies in modern-day campaigning. As individuals become more polarized, staying away from partisan issues to appeal to centrist voters has given way to finding the right message to mobilize the candidate's base. This change in campaigning may have important implications for the use of racial appeals. Democrats may win by not shying away from racially charged issues to appeal to voters who in large part have already left the party (see chapter 3). Instead, they may find the most success by discussing racial issues to mobilize those who are passionate about addressing racial inequality.

In this chapter, I will examine whether candidates who are perceived as being racially liberal are punished or rewarded among white voters. Moreover, I will explore whether white Democrats, white Republicans, and white independents are more likely to turn out to support or oppose presidential candidates who are perceived as using the government to address racial inequality. I will first provide a brief overview of the campaign strategies used by candidates over time and discuss why a shift to mobilization can be effective strategy. I will then explore how messages matter in mobilizing turnout and discuss how racial appeals in the current political climate may be an effective way for Democrats to mobilize their base of liberal whites.

I use both existing data from the American National Election Studies (ANES) and the Pew Research Center, along with original experimental data to help understand whether racial appeals mobilize voters of different parties. In particular, I assess perceptions of minority racial favoritism on vote choice and turnout using the 1980–2016 ANES and an online survey experiment. Analysis of ANES data demonstrates that perceptions of racial liberalism led to lower levels of white support for Barack Obama in primaries and presidential elections, but it did not affect vote choice in the 2016 election for white Democratic or white independent voters. Instead, white Democrats who viewed Hillary Clinton as using government to address racial inequality were more likely to turn out in the 2016 presidential election. Interestingly, the belief that government would aid blacks was not a mobilizer for white Democrats in any election between 1980 and 2012.

The experimental analysis demonstrates again that in the current political context the use of racial appeals does not dampen support for Democratic candidates among white Democrats or independents. While the experiment demonstrates that racialized candidates inspire high levels of intention to turn out when they appear on the ballot, this analysis demonstrates that they are not more likely to inspire higher levels of turnout than similarly situated deracialized liberals. In summary, the changes in the electoral landscape described in chapters 1–3 have made it so that candidates who use racial appeals may be rewarded with a more mobilized base without sacrificing the support of centrist voters, who in large part have already chosen a side.

Move from the Center to the Base

While written over sixty years ago, Antony Downs's (1957) *Economic Theory of Democracy* still plays a significant role in our understanding of campaign behavior. Downs theorized that there was a liberal-to-conservative axis with most voters and fewer voters at the extremes. This pattern creates an almost normal distribution. While the center may not be perfectly between the left and right axis and may shift over time, most voters occupied a space in the middle of the spectrum. This hypothesis naturally leads to the expectation that candidates who want to win must be ideologically similar to the majority in the electorate. In other words, they must be candidates who stake out centrist positions while working to label their opponents as ideological extremists (Downs 1957; Needham 2005).

Based on this research, the key to success in elections is to attract the cross-pressured or swing voter who, under the right circumstances, could vote for either party. These voters tend to be much less partisan and more often than not identified as political independents. These unaffiliated centrist voters have long been believed to be the deciding factor in any election (Bawn et al. 2012). If Democratic voters were going to support the Democratic candidate and Republican voters were going to support the Republican candidate, then whoever swing voters supported would win the election.

Based on previous research, the prized centrist voter tended to be white and racially conservative. As a result, any perceptions of minority racial favoritism could lead to lower levels of electoral support (Hamilton 1977, Gillespie 2010; Mendelberg 2001). Indeed, several studies of both black and white politicians have demonstrated that when voters, and white voters in particular, perceived candidates as favoring the black community, they were less likely to support those candidates (Gillespie 2010; Hamilton 1977; Piston 2010; Stephens-Dougan 2016). For example, as recently as 2008 Obama lost a significant amount of support from white centrists who perceived him as being too racially liberal (Lewis-Beck and Nadeau 2009; Piston 2010). Appealing to centrist voters is the primary reason why candidates shy away from race-based appeals.

The Rove Revolution

In 2000, we began to see a slight change in the strategy of appealing to the centrist voter. Instead of trying to attract swing voters whose support was unpredictable, George W. Bush's campaign manager Karl Rove theorized that Bush's best path to victory was to mobilize conservative voters and born-again Christians. Both of these groups of voters were considered strong Republicans who would certainly support Bush if they turned out to vote. Rove and the Bush campaign were largely aided by improvements in internet technology, which provided the campaign with more information about voters and allowed the campaign to send tailored messages. The plan was a success, as Bush narrowly defeated Al Gore in the presidential election.

Using tailored messages to mobilize voters was more apparent in the run-up to the 2004 presidential election, during which Bush first introduced the idea of an amendment to define marriage as being between a man and a woman. Several states followed suit by including a same-sex marriage ban referendum on their state ballots. Such actions were strategic for the Republican Party because the focus on religious issues would help mobilize evangelical voters who were sympathetic to Bush. Several studies demonstrated that this was largely effective because it increased turnout among white evangelical protestants (see, e.g., Campbell and Monson 2008). Some have even argued that the same-sex marriage ban proposition in Ohio played a large role in helping Bush win a second term (D. Smith, DeSantis, and Kassel 2006). The move from focusing on attracting moderates to mobilizing one's base has had numerous effects on campaign strategies, polarization, and turnout (Abramowitz and Stone 2006; Leighley and Nagler 2013). Moreover, the focus on mobilization may also influence the effectiveness of racial appeals.

Racial Appeals and Mobilization in a Polarized America

Based on these changes in campaign strategies, several questions arise. First, why has a shift from persuading voters to mobilizing supportive voters taken hold in campaigns? Second, can candidates' positions on issues serve as a tool to mobilize voters? Third, can a racialized approach be an effective mobilizer in contemporary American politics? Finally, can racialized appeals mobilize liberal white voters without alienating unsympathetic segments of the population?

There are several reasons why mobilization has become a more effective campaign tool in recent years. First, growing polarization in the electorate means that there are fewer centrist voters left to persuade. While the classic Downsian model assumes a unimodal distribution with most voters centered around a single mean, polarization has led to a bimodal distribution with two sets of large groups of voters at the poles of the spectrum. Additionally, these sets of voters are relatively equal in size so that no one group has a natural advantage. Candidates who move to the center risk alienating voters in their parties, with a low likelihood of altering the opinions of voters from the other side. In fact, recent research has demonstrated that partisanship matters more in opinion formation and electoral support today than it did in the past (Levendusky 2010). This research demonstrates that voters who lean toward either the Democratic Party or the Republican Party are unlikely to be persuaded by centrist campaigns.

At the same time that persuasion became a less effective campaign tool, more information arose about effective ways to mobilize voters (see Panagopoulos 2016). In recent years, social scientists and campaigns have begun engaging in numerous field experiments designed to maximize the effectiveness of mobilization efforts. These studies range from using emotions such as shame to finding the precise message to turn out reluctant voters (Gerber,

Green, and Larimer 2010; Issenberg 2012). Moreover, social science research has moved away from focusing on strategies to appeal to the centrist voter to largely concluding that mobilization is a more effective campaign tactic (Panagopoulos 2016). In combination with greater levels of polarization, the focus on mobilization is very much in vogue in contemporary political campaigns.

There is good reason to believe that macro-targeting in the form of making broader appeals to ideological congruent voters may be an effective way to increase turnout among supportive individuals. When voters feel that the candidate cares about their specific interests, they may feel that they will receive more political rewards if their candidate succeeds. Conversely, if the candidate in their preferred political party is too ideologically different from themselves, they may feel less incentive to turn out. Marcus and MacKuen (1993) demonstrated that voters are much more participatory in campaign activities when they are more enthusiastic about their party's nominee for elected office (see also Stout 2018). Along the same lines, Lefkofridi, Giger, and Gallego (2013) demonstrated that it is individuals who are on the extremes of the political spectrum who are most mobilized when they feel that the candidate is focusing on issues that they care about.

Moreover, there is research that suggests that candidates can increase enthusiasm for their campaigns by focusing on the issues that are most salient to the electorate. For example, former president George W. Bush's public appeals to religious voters through his personal narrative as a born-again Christian is argued to have inspired a significant growth in turnout among Christian voters in 2004 (Hillygus and Shields 2005). It is argued that Christian voters were more enthusiastic about Bush's candidacy because they believed he had a better understanding of the religious community. Wattenberg (2008) also found that one of the reasons for the age gap in turnout in American politics is that politicians focus on issues that disproportionately affect older voters while ignoring policies that are significant to young voters. As a result, young voters feel alienated and are much less likely to vote. In contrast, older voters feel encouraged that politicians are paying attention to their interests and are more mobilized. Overall, these studies suggest that candidates who focus on a range of messages in their campaigns may be able to mobilize more segments of the population.

Can Racial Appeals Mobilize Sympathetic Voters?

Based on previous research and my analyses in the previous chapters, I hypothesize that white Democrats will be likely to respond positively to politicians whom they perceive as being progressive on racial issues. Given that most whites who are racially conservative have now left the Democratic Party, what remains are whites who for the most part are sympathetic to the plight of racial/ethnic minorities. Moreover, as movements like Black Lives Matter gain more traction, many white liberals may display an increasing concern for ending racial inequality. As a result, they may feel compelled to turn out and support a candidate whom they perceive as addressing the issues facing underrepresented groups.

This may in part be driven by perceptions of white privilege. Individuals who perceive their race as providing them an advantage in society may display a greater interest in leveling the playing field. This often comes in the form of support for racially progressive policies (Collingwood, Pedraza, and Rush 2016; Schaffner 2011). For example, Collingwood, Pedraza, and Rush (2016) demonstrated that whites who perceive their race as providing them an advantage in society were more supportive of minority political candidates. Chudy (2017) showed that whites with this same perspective were also more likely to believe that government should aid blacks and were more supportive of affirmative action. Given this, it would not be surprising to find that some white Democrat voters may become more politically active when candidates are perceived as being racially progressive.

Moreover, given that Democratic success is largely driven by a mobilized group of liberal whites, blacks, Latinos, and Asian Americans, white Democrats may be especially interested in protecting members of their coalition. One of the major factors driving growing recognition of racial inequality is that numerous states have passed legislation that makes it disproportionately more difficult for racial/ethnic minorities to vote (see chapter 1). Given that the success of the Democratic Party is in part driven by high levels of racial/ethnic turnout, white Democrats may feel particularly protective of the voting rights of racial/ethnic minorities. As a result, they may be more enthusiastic about candidates they perceive as addressing racial issues.

It is possible, however, that any surge in turnout among white Democrats from candidates engaging in racial appeals may be met with a countermobilization of unsympathetic voters. In particular, as the Republican Party has grown in its levels of racial resentment in recent years (Tesler 2016), it would not be surprising to find that white Republicans mobilize to vote against candidates who they perceive as playing the "race card." Previous research demonstrates that one of the main drawbacks of engaging in racial appeals is that they have the potential to mobilize unsympathetic voters (Hamilton 1977; McCormick and Jones 1993; Sigelman et al. 1995). This is driven in part by fears that candidates who engage in racial favoritism will use government offices to provide benefits to racial/ethnic minorities at the expense of whites (Gillespie 2010; Piston 2011). If this is true, it is possible that white Republicans may be more mobilized to vote against a candidate whom they perceive as engaging in racialized campaigning.

Can Racial Appeals Still Be Persuasive?

In Hamilton's (1977) groundbreaking work on deracialization, he focused less on whether racial appeals could be mobilizers and more on whether racial appeals could lead cross-pressured voters to leave the Democratic Party. Indeed, McCormick and Jones (1993) in their seminal definition of deracialization identify the main goal as being focused on persuasion. In particular, they define deracialized campaigns as "campaigns conducted in a stylistic fashion that *defuses the polarizing effects of race* by avoiding explicit reference to race-specific issues, while at the same time emphasizing those issues which are racially transcendent" (76, my emphasis). However, there is some reason to believe that deracialization may not have the same polarizing effects as it has had in the past. If this is so, then the strategy to use racialized appeals may now be potentially more effective.

The first major reason why racialized appeals may no longer have the same effect as in the past is that Americans have become more polarized on racial issues. As discussed in chapter 3, even Reagan Democrats, the group the deracialized strategy was devised to appeal to, have become divided around the issue of race. Progressives will likely support a Democratic candidate regardless of if they racialize or not, and conservatives will likely support a Republican candidate regardless of how hard the Democratic candidate tries to sidestep the issue of race. For example, Obama, who is described by many as being a prototypical deracialized candidate (see Gillespie 2010; Harris 2012; Lewis, Dowe, and Franklin 2012), was still penalized by racially conservative voters (Piston 2010).

Several studies demonstrate that voters are becoming more set in their ways than before, so much so that when presented evidence that their preferred policies will not produce ideal outcomes, individuals will find ways to reason why these conclusions are incorrect rather than alter their opinion (Taber and Lodge 2006). This behavior, known as motivated reasoning, is becoming more prevalent in U.S. society (Taber and Lodge 2006). Greater levels of motivated reasoning have made it more difficult to alter individual's opinions on important issues, which in turn makes it more difficult to persuade voters, even when using wedge issues like race. In fact, recent research has demonstrated that because of "narrowcasting" and more polarized politicians, fewer individuals can be presented with evidence that will lead to lasting changes in political attitudes (Fiorina and Abrams 2008). This is particularly true for issues that are politically salient.

What about political independents and swing voters? In the past, political independents were the prize that both political parties sought. Given that these voters tended to be more centrist, their votes were generally up for grabs and could be attracted or repelled by a candidate's position. Moreover, as we saw above, these voters make up a significant portion of the electorate (Wattenberg 2009). While there is often a lot of attention paid to independent voters, recent research has demonstrated that, in spite of their political label, they are tending to act largely like their partisan counterparts (Smidt 2017). Smidt argues that as parties have taken more distinct positions, even self-identified independents have become more loyal to one party over others. Moreover, Klar and Krupnikov (2016) argue that political independents are simply partisans who are too embarrassed or frustrated with the political system to formally identify with a political party. As a result, most estimates suggest the true independent voters only make up a small percentage of the population (Smidt 2017).

Based on this, it is likely that the vast majority of independent voters respond to racial appeals similarly to Democrats and Republicans. Those who lean toward the Democratic Party may feel better about racial appeals and may be more supportive and mobilized as a result. Similarly, it is possible that conservative independents will mirror the behavior of white Republicans and reject racialized appeals from candidates at the polling booth, making them less motivated to turn out as a result. The use of racial appeals may therefore cancel out any gains or losses among independent voters.

Data

To explore the influence that perceptions of racial liberalism and racialization might have on whites, I draw on ANES data for the period 1980–2016 and an online survey experiment administered on Amazon Mechanical Turk. I use the ANES to assess the influence that perceptions of candidates' racial progressivism have on vote choice and turnout for whites of different political persuasions. First, I disaggregate whites by their partisanship and create three categories of white respondents: white Democrats, white Republicans, and white independents.

For the ANES data, my first dependent variable of interest is vote choice in the 1988, 2008, and 2016 Democratic presidential primaries. Examining primary elections is useful for my purposes because it allows me to test the influence of appearing racially progressive on vote choice when partisanship is held constant. I use the 1988, 2008, and 2016 Democratic presidential primaries as test cases because they are the only ones that had competitive primaries on the Democratic side during the period of interest. My dependent variable for this analysis is level of support for the candidate who ultimately won (i.e., support for Dukakis in 1988, support for Obama in 2008, and support for Clinton in 2016). This is measured by a question in the ANES that asks respondents who participated in the Democratic presidential primary who they supported. Those who supported a winning candidate were given a score of 1; all other participants were given a score of 0.

In addition to the primaries, I also assess electoral support for the Democratic candidate in the presidential election. To do so, I use the ANES question that asks, "For whom did [the respondent] vote for President?" I code those who supported the Democratic candidate as 1 and all others as 0. I should also note that I used the percentage of the two-party vote and excluded those who voted for a third party as an alternative dependent variable and this did not alter the results. My final dependent variable is whether respondents voted in the presidential election in November. Those who reported voting were given a score of 1, and all others were coded as 0.

It is important to note that this self-reported measure of voter turnout has some considerable drawbacks. Many respondents state that they voted when they did not. This phenomenon is known as social desirability response bias, and it occurs because voters are often too embarrassed to tell interviewers they did not vote because it appears as if they did not practice an important civic duty (Silver, Anderson, and Abramson 1986). While this problem raises some concerns about the following analysis, a real problem would only occur if individuals' perceptions of Democratic candidates' racial ideology were tied to their likelihood of misleading surveyors about their voting behavior. For example, there is no strong reason to believe that individuals who view a Democratic candidate as being liberal on racial issues would have a greater incentive to lie about their voting behavior than those who viewed a Democratic candidate as racially conservative.

My main independent variable of interest measures perceptions of racial progressivism. While an objective measure of racial appeals (e.g., content coding of a politician's statements or platform) has several advantages for measuring the influence of racial appeals on turnout and support, it also comes with the significant drawback that voters may not respond or even recognize such appeals as racial. As a result, I use a more subjective measure of individuals' perceptions of the candidates' racial progressivism that in all likelihood *is* tied to racial appeals. In fact, my own experimental analysis demonstrates that individuals who make racial appeals are perceived as being more racially progressive. See table 4.A1 in the appendix for this analysis.

The measure I use is derived from the ANES question that asks respondents, "Some people feel that the government in Washington should make every effort to improve the social and economic position of blacks. Suppose these people are at one end of a scale, at point 1. Others feel that the government should not make any special effort to help blacks because they should help themselves. Suppose these people are at the other end, at point 7. Where would you place the Democratic Presidential Nominee on this scale?" I reverse coded the answers to this question so that the highest score (7) indicates that individual perceived the Democratic candidate as believing that Washington should do everything in its power to improve the positions of blacks in society. This provides a subjective measure of how racially progressive a candidate is perceived to be.

Of course, there are hundreds of factors that may influence an individual's vote choice in any election. To try to minimize the influence of outside factors, I controlled for several variables. First, I controlled for whether the individual had been contacted by the campaign. This may matter little for vote choice, but mobilization plays a large role in predicting voter turnout. So much so that Gerber and Green (2000) suggest that the right mobilization efforts can increase turnout by almost 10 percent. I also control for individual-level factors such as age, income, education, and gender. Socioeconomic status has consistently been a strong predictor of voter turnout, while age and gender are strong predictors of vote choice (Leighley and Nagler 2013; Wolfinger and Rosenstone 1980). Finally, I control for the strength of the respondent's partisanship and whether the respondent resided in the South. Given the tumultuous racial history of the southern region of the United States, perceptions of racial progressivism may play a significant role in vote choice and turnout for individuals who live in this region (Key 1949).

Survey Results

Table 4.1 presents three separate logit regressions respectively predicting support for Dukakis in 1988, Obama in 2008, and Clinton in 2016 by those ANES respondents who participated in the Democratic primaries. Min-max probabilities were also estimated when perception of the candidate's racial ideology was a significant predictor of vote choice in the primaries. These min-max probabilities can be interpreted as how much respondents' likelihood of supporting the leading Democratic candidate in the primaries changed from when they perceived the candidate as having the lowest value on the "aid to blacks" scale to the highest value on this measure. Positive scores indicate that respondents' probability of supporting the Democratic candidate

TABLE 4.1. Logit regression predicting support for the leading Democratic presidential nominee candidate in the 1988, 2008, and 2016 Democratic presidential primaries

	Vote for Dukakis (1988)	Vote for Obama (2008)	Vote for H. Clinton (2016)
Candidate's "aid to blacks" score	−0.115 (0.105)	−0.350*** (0.0758)	0.0316 (0.0757)
Female	0.444 (0.301)	0.203 (0.255)	0.446** (0.186)
Age	0.0246*** (0.00893)	−0.00304 (0.00781)	0.0461*** (0.00566)
Income	0.00355 (0.00660)	−0.00443 (0.00293)	0.00853** (0.00376)
Education	0.0726 (0.0656)	0.148** (0.0644)	0.0222 (0.0434)
South	0.0469 (0.311)	−0.861*** (0.275)	0.430* (0.227)
Constant	−4.021*** (1.104)	−0.953 (1.069)	−3.781*** (0.797)
Observations	493	391	570

Source: ANES.

Note: Only individuals who participated in the Democratic primaries in these years are included in the models.

* $p<0.1$; ** $p<0.05$; *** $p<0.01$; standard errors in parentheses.

increases when the candidate is perceived as wanting to use government policies to aid blacks. Negative scores reveal the opposite.

The results in table 4.1 demonstrate that white Democratic primary voters who viewed Obama as believing the government should aid blacks were about 41 percent less likely to vote for him in the 2008 Democratic presidential primary than blacks who viewed him as believing blacks should help themselves. There is no significant relationship between perceptions of the candidate's racial liberalism and vote choice for either Dukakis or Clinton. The results suggest that only black candidates may be harmed in the primary for appearing as racially progressive. However, a separate analysis of Jesse Jackson's campaign in 1988 also revealed no relationship between perceptions of racial liberalism and vote choice. There may be something specific about Obama and the context of 2008 that made perceptions of racial liberalism damaging to whites who participated in the primary. In 2016, Clinton did not appear to pay a penalty in vote choice among white Democratic primary voters for appearing to be racially liberal.

Tables 4.2A–C estimate logit regression models predicting support for the Democratic candidate in presidential election years between 1980 and 2016 (with the exception of 1992, when the "aid to blacks" question was not asked). Table 4.2A includes only Democrats; table 4.2B includes only independents; and table 4.2C includes only Republicans. In addition to the regression models, I estimated min-max probabilities for the significant variables in the models. Overall, the results indicate that in 2016 attitudes about the Democratic presidential nominee's racial progressivism did not play a significant role in predicting their levels of support from white Democrats or white independents. Thus, most partisan groups were not largely moved to vote for or against the Democratic nominee based on their perceived stance on using government to assist the black population in 2016.

For Democrats, perceptions of the Democratic candidate as being too liberal on racial issues led to lower levels of support in 2008 and 2012, while holding constant other factors. Perceptions of racial liberalism had the largest influence on vote choice in 2012. In this year, white Democrats who viewed Obama as being the most racially liberal were 21 percent less likely to support him than white Democrats who viewed him as being racially conservative. Obama appears to pay a similar penalty in 2008. There may be something specific about Obama's race that made him particularly susceptible to being punished for being perceived as racially liberal. However, this may also have to do with the political context, in which many voters discounted racial discrimination as a problem. Nonetheless, the results indicate that perceptions of racial progressivism do not consistently hurt Democratic candidates among copartisan voters.

White independents appear to have punished Democratic candidates whom they perceived as being racially liberal in several cycles. For example, white independents who viewed Bill Clinton as the most racially liberal candidate in 1996 were 76 percent less likely to vote for him compared to similar individuals who perceived him as being racially conservative. Obama paid a similar penalty in 2008 and 2012 among white independents. However, by 2016 this relationship had dissipated, and Hillary Clinton was not punished by white independents for appearing as racially progressive.

White Republicans punished racially liberal Democrats in most of the elections examined in table 4.2C. In 2016, white Republicans were still about 16 percent less likely to support Hillary Clinton when she was perceived as being the most racially liberal. This suggests that if Democrats hope to attain the support of Republican whites, they may be able to do so by appearing

TABLE 4.2A. Logit regression predicting support for the Democratic presidential nominee for white Democrats only (1980–2016)

	Vote for Democratic presidential candidate							
Year	1980	1984	1988	1996	2004	2008	2012	2016
Candidate's "aid to blacks" score	−0.34	0.18	0.18	−0.53	0.56	−0.91***	−0.96***	−0.16
	(0.22)	(0.14)	(0.20)	(0.36)	(0.54)	(0.24)	(0.17)	(0.19)
Female	0.29	0.17	0.00	−0.66	−0.51	0.00	−0.79**	−0.39
	(0.42)	(0.34)	(0.49)	(0.68)	(1.11)	(0.69)	(0.40)	(0.47)
Age	−0.00	0.01	−0.00	−0.08***	0.02	−0.02	−0.02*	0.02
	(0.01)	(0.01)	(0.02)	(0.03)	(0.03)	(0.02)	(0.01)	(0.01)
Income	0.04	−0.27	0.15	−0.19	−0.15	−0.24	−0.18	0.20
	(0.26)	(0.19)	(0.27)	(0.43)	(0.55)	(0.44)	(0.18)	(0.21)
Education	−0.06	0.02	0.13	−0.42**	0.16	0.05	−0.12	0.36***
	(0.09)	(0.09)	(0.10)	(0.18)	(0.14)	(0.20)	(0.09)	(0.10)
7–point PID	−1.00**	−1.55***	−2.32***	−3.09***	−2.94***	−0.94	−1.95***	−1.87***
	(0.47)	(0.40)	(0.63)	(1.11)	(1.09)	(0.68)	(0.47)	(0.53)
South	−0.26	−0.51	−0.64	−1.26	−0.41	−2.23***	−0.25	−0.31
	(0.48)	(0.41)	(0.54)	(0.78)	(1.03)	(0.65)	(0.45)	(0.53)
Campaign contact	0.92	0.92	0.06	−0.30	0.91	2.12*	−0.73*	0.27
	(0.80)	(0.67)	(0.86)	(1.21)	(1.32)	(1.21)	(0.41)	(0.82)
Ideology	−0.31*	−0.53***	−0.80***	−1.58***	−1.32***	−0.63***	−1.02***	−0.98***
	(0.17)	(0.15)	(0.23)	(0.30)	(0.40)	(0.20)	(0.16)	(0.17)
Constant	6.33***	4.81**	5.58**	28.17***	7.16	11.90***	18.18***	3.41
	(2.40)	(2.02)	(2.33)	(6.33)	(4.68)	(4.05)	(2.54)	(2.24)
Observations	147	243	155	209	95	150	705	541

Source: ANES.

* $p<0.1$; ** $p<0.05$; *** $p<0.01$; standard errors in parentheses; PID=Party Identification.

TABLE 4.2B. Logit regression predicting support for the Democratic presidential nominee for white independents only (1980–2016)

	Vote for Democratic presidential candidate							
Year	1980	1984	1988	1996	2004	2008	2012	2016
Candidate's "aid to blacks" score	−0.35	0.21	−0.17	−0.59*	−0.07	−0.43**	−0.42***	−0.22
	(0.23)	(0.17)	(0.14)	(0.33)	(0.32)	(0.19)	(0.10)	(0.13)
Female	−0.09	−0.19	−0.36	−0.33	−0.89	−0.07	−0.21	−0.36
	(0.62)	(0.47)	(0.44)	(0.60)	(0.79)	(0.51)	(0.29)	(0.36)
Age	−0.04*	−0.02	−0.01	−0.02	−0.01	−0.00	−0.00	−0.01
	(0.02)	(0.01)	(0.02)	(0.02)	(0.03)	(0.01)	(0.01)	(0.01)
Income	−0.33	−0.25	−0.43	0.15	0.03	−0.02	−0.16	0.02
	(0.28)	(0.26)	(0.33)	(0.33)	(0.28)	(0.20)	(0.15)	(0.14)
Education	0.13	0.15	0.11	0.12	−0.15	0.03	0.25***	0.14*
	(0.13)	(0.11)	(0.09)	(0.12)	(0.17)	(0.11)	(0.07)	(0.07)
7-point PID	−1.09***	−2.02***	−1.99***	−1.79***	−1.91***	−1.35***	−2.09***	−1.75***
	(0.36)	(0.33)	(0.30)	(0.34)	(0.39)	(0.29)	(0.21)	(0.24)
South	−0.86	−1.79***	−0.80*	−1.75***	1.37	−0.14	−0.23	−0.51
	(0.54)	(0.53)	(0.42)	(0.60)	(0.84)	(0.45)	(0.31)	(0.39)
Campaign contact	1.33*	0.45	−0.80	0.04	−0.67	−0.24	0.24	0.20
	(0.76)	(0.65)	(0.69)	(0.84)	(0.76)	(0.74)	(0.30)	(0.55)
Ideology	−0.70**	−0.40*	−0.29	−0.76***	−0.68**	−0.61***	−0.68***	−0.63***
	(0.27)	(0.22)	(0.21)	(0.24)	(0.32)	(0.22)	(0.15)	(0.19)
Constant	9.63***	7.80***	10.65***	12.54***	13.41***	9.90***	10.46***	9.19***
	(2.81)	(2.16)	(2.62)	(3.36)	(3.52)	(2.19)	(1.66)	(1.57)
Observations	112	194	159	136	109	176	711	439

Source: ANES.

* $p<0.1$; ** $p<0.05$; *** $p<0.01$; standard errors in parentheses; PID=Party Identification.

TABLE 4.2C. Logit regression predicting support for the Democratic presidential nominee for white Republicans only (1980–2016)

	Vote for Democratic presidential candidate							
Year	1980	1984	1988	1996	2004	2008	2012	2016
Candidate's "aid to blacks" score	−0.44*	−0.03	−0.13	−0.66***	−0.08	−0.35**	−0.38**	−0.46***
	(0.23)	(0.20)	(0.29)	(0.21)	(0.41)	(0.14)	(0.15)	(0.12)
Female	0.86	0.95	0.59	0.45	−0.03	−0.71	0.52	0.11
	(0.93)	(0.87)	(0.70)	(0.55)	(1.00)	(0.63)	(0.48)	(0.44)
Age	0.02	−0.00	0.01	0.01	0.01	−0.00	−0.01	−0.03*
	(0.03)	(0.02)	(0.02)	(0.02)	(0.02)	(0.02)	(0.01)	(0.02)
Income	−0.35	−0.55**	−0.03	0.05	−0.09	−0.73**	0.04	0.55**
	(0.37)	(0.26)	(0.28)	(0.31)	(0.40)	(0.34)	(0.24)	(0.23)
Education	0.04	0.06	−0.14	0.11	0.13	0.00	0.23**	0.17
	(0.25)	(0.22)	(0.15)	(0.14)	(0.17)	(0.22)	(0.10)	(0.12)
7-point PID	−0.12	−1.10	^	−1.40**	−1.14	−0.63	−1.18**	−1.57***
	(0.96)	(0.80)	^	(0.63)	(1.44)	(0.89)	(0.55)	(0.53)
South	1.23	0.51	^	0.04	−0.37	1.33**	−0.65	−1.24*
	(1.00)	(0.90)	^	(0.65)	(0.98)	(0.61)	(0.47)	(0.66)
Campaign contact	−0.98**	−0.25	−0.32	−0.51*	−0.85***	−0.80***	−0.71***	−0.88***
	(0.44)	(0.27)	(0.32)	(0.28)	(0.31)	(0.25)	(0.17)	(0.19)
Ideology	^	^	^	0.06	0.69	−1.07	0.43	0.27
	^	^	^	(0.74)	(1.03)	(1.26)	(0.52)	(0.58)
Constant	3.63	5.42	1.92	9.70**	7.29	9.14	6.71*	11.74***
	(5.85)	(7.88)	(2.56)	(4.43)	(6.09)	(7.33)	(3.72)	(3.91)
Observations	133	238	69	244	159	223	846	677

Source: ANES.

* $p<0.1$; ** $p<0.05$; *** $p<0.01$; standard errors in parentheses; ^ no variation in this variable; PID = Party Identification.

as racially conservative. Overall, the analysis suggests that in the most recent election only white Republicans were persuaded by the perceived racially ideology of the candidate. As a result, Democrats who appear as racially liberal may be most hurt if they hope to win elections by putting together coalitions of Republicans along with their traditional base. However, given that Republicans are rarely a group that Democrats can rely on, the loss of these voters may not substantially alter elections. Particularly, if the use of racial appeals can provide advantages elsewhere.

Tables 4.3A–C respectively present logit regressions for white Democrats (A), white independents (B), and white Republicans (C). Each logit regression is estimated separately by year and by partisan group. Similar to the other analyses, I also estimate min-max predicted probabilities based on the estimates from the logit regressions. White Democrats who perceived Hillary Clinton as being racially progressive were significantly more likely to vote in the 2016 presidential election. Individuals who moved from perceiving Clinton as having the minimum racial progressive score to having the maximum score were about 14 percent more likely to turn out to vote. That year, however, was the only year in the analysis when the racial progressivism of the candidate motivated turnout among white Democrats. This suggests that in the current political context appeals to racial groups may mobilize white Democrats. In an era where base mobilization plays a large role in success, appearing as being racially progressive may actually help Democratic candidates. Moreover, a more mobilized Democratic base is likely to offset any losses from Republican whites who may oppose racially liberal candidates.

Moreover, this increase in participation from white Democrats does not appear to come with large levels of countermobilization among Republicans. While white Republicans were marginally more mobilized in 1984 and 1988 when they feared that the Democratic presidential nominee would favor the black community, there has mostly been no significant relationship between fears of the Democratic candidate providing assistance to blacks and heightened turnout rates among white Republicans.

Independents are much more likely to be mobilized by perceptions that the Democratic candidate is racially progressive. In about half of the elections in the thirty-six-year period, independents were mobilized by perceptions that the Democratic nominee favored using government to provide assistance to the black community. This occurred in 2016 as well. However, given that less is known about political independents' political preferences it is not known whether this increase in turnout benefits or hurts Democratic candidates. Given that Democrats are more mobilized, and Republicans are not affected by perceptions of the candidate's racial ideology, the results in this section

TABLE 4.3A. Logit regression predicting self-reported voter turnout for white Democrats only (1980–2016)

	Voted in presidential election							
Year	1980	1984	1988	1996	2004	2008	2012	2016
Candidate's "aid to blacks" score	0.00	0.05	0.11	0.17	−0.32	0.07	−0.01	0.37***
	(0.15)	(0.15)	(0.13)	(0.16)	(0.36)	(0.19)	(0.10)	(0.13)
Female	−0.05	0.76**	0.15	0.06	1.22	0.01	−0.14	−0.04
	(0.40)	(0.37)	(0.40)	(0.47)	(0.84)	(0.52)	(0.30)	(0.32)
Age	0.04***	0.05***	0.02	0.05***	0.04*	0.02	0.05***	0.04***
	(0.01)	(0.02)	(0.01)	(0.02)	(0.02)	(0.02)	(0.01)	(0.01)
Income	0.23	0.42**	0.31*	0.61***	−0.13	0.12	0.48***	0.29*
	(0.21)	(0.18)	(0.19)	(0.18)	(0.44)	(0.26)	(0.13)	(0.16)
Education	0.19**	0.30**	0.28***	0.41***	0.56**	0.39**	0.18**	0.24***
	(0.09)	(0.12)	(0.10)	(0.11)	(0.24)	(0.17)	(0.07)	(0.08)
7-point PID	−0.56	−1.56***	−0.94**	−1.29**	−1.52**	−0.65	−0.48	−0.26
	(0.44)	(0.42)	(0.46)	(0.51)	(0.69)	(0.76)	(0.33)	(0.36)
South	−0.28	−0.41	−0.53	−0.49	−0.31	−1.04*	−0.20	−0.89***
	(0.42)	(0.41)	(0.41)	(0.44)	(0.89)	(0.61)	(0.33)	(0.34)
Campaign contact	1.87*	0.36	^	0.52	2.13**	−0.17	0.63	−0.28
	(1.06)	(0.69)	^	(0.66)	(0.97)	(0.55)	(0.44)	(0.47)
Ideology	−0.00	−0.09	−0.02	0.11	−0.25	−0.14	−0.57***	−0.21
	(0.17)	(0.19)	(0.15)	(0.19)	(0.35)	(0.21)	(0.12)	(0.14)
Constant	−2.30	−2.81	−2.98	−6.77***	−3.55	−2.92	−1.54	−4.53***
	(2.31)	(2.57)	(2.04)	(2.25)	(3.61)	(2.69)	(1.36)	(1.49)
Observations	210	295	186	278	108	177	817	628

Source: ANES.

* $p<0.1$; ** $p<0.05$; *** $p<0.01$; standard errors in parentheses; ^ no variation in this variable; PID = Party Identification.

TABLE 4.3B. Logit regression predicting self-reported voter turnout for white independents only (1980–2016)

	Voted in presidential election							
Year	1980	1984	1988	1996	2004	2008	2012	2016
Candidate's "aid to blacks" score	0.08	0.18	0.31**	0.32*	−0.50**	0.05	0.02	0.19**
	(0.17)	(0.11)	(0.12)	(0.17)	(0.24)	(0.10)	(0.07)	(0.08)
Female	0.27	−0.11	0.52	0.29	−0.30	0.55	0.13	0.04
	(0.46)	(0.32)	(0.36)	(0.42)	(0.66)	(0.37)	(0.20)	(0.24)
Age	0.04***	0.04***	0.03**	0.05***	0.02	0.01	0.03***	0.03***
	(0.02)	(0.01)	(0.01)	(0.01)	(0.02)	(0.01)	(0.01)	(0.01)
Income	−0.06	0.26	0.65***	0.72***	−0.17	0.06	0.35***	0.18
	(0.24)	(0.18)	(0.20)	(0.20)	(0.29)	(0.19)	(0.09)	(0.12)
Education	0.28**	0.23**	0.22**	0.13	0.57***	0.43***	0.19***	0.23***
	(0.14)	(0.09)	(0.09)	(0.10)	(0.18)	(0.13)	(0.05)	(0.06)
7-point PID	−0.14	0.08	−0.34	−0.06	0.18	0.15	−0.06	0.13
	(0.32)	(0.21)	(0.22)	(0.24)	(0.35)	(0.24)	(0.16)	(0.18)
South	−0.42	0.33	−0.77*	0.19	−0.49	−0.51	−0.02	−0.44*
	(0.52)	(0.38)	(0.39)	(0.48)	(0.81)	(0.38)	(0.22)	(0.23)
Campaign contact	−0.34	−0.13	1.32	0.06	−0.41	0.07	1.02***	0.46
	(0.61)	(0.53)	(0.81)	(0.57)	(0.61)	(0.58)	(0.31)	(0.42)
Ideology	0.21	0.16	0.26*	0.02	0.29	0.04	0.07	−0.24**
	(0.21)	(0.14)	(0.14)	(0.18)	(0.31)	(0.17)	(0.10)	(0.11)
Constant	−4.12	−5.89***	−6.62***	−6.08***	−5.94*	−6.33***	−4.40***	−4.44***
	(2.56)	(1.66)	(1.72)	(1.96)	(3.18)	(1.93)	(0.95)	(1.10)
Observations	175	258	224	218	140	238	992	674

Source: ANES.

* $p<0.1$; ** $p<0.05$; *** $p<0.01$; standard errors in parentheses; PID = Party Identification.

TABLE 4.3C. Logit regression predicting self-reported voter turnout for white Republicans only (1980–2016)

	Voted in presidential election							
Year	1980	1984	1988	1996	2004	2008	2012	2016
Dem. candidate's "aid to blacks" score	0.11	0.22*	0.36*	0.09	−0.14	−0.03	0.12	0.03
	(0.15)	(0.11)	(0.20)	(0.18)	(0.31)	(0.18)	(0.08)	(0.08)
Female	−0.24	0.42	0.59	0.37	0.38	0.09	0.46*	0.36
	(0.45)	(0.34)	(0.46)	(0.48)	(0.74)	(0.57)	(0.26)	(0.28)
Age	0.03*	0.03**	0.03**	0.05***	−0.01	0.03**	0.04***	0.03***
	(0.02)	(0.01)	(0.01)	(0.02)	(0.02)	(0.01)	(0.01)	(0.01)
Income	0.18	0.35**	0.40*	0.29	0.41*	0.14	0.16	0.48***
	(0.25)	(0.16)	(0.24)	(0.21)	(0.24)	(0.28)	(0.12)	(0.12)
Education	0.35***	0.39***	0.15	0.44***	0.17	0.34*	0.23***	0.17**
	(0.11)	(0.10)	(0.12)	(0.16)	(0.13)	(0.17)	(0.07)	(0.07)
7-point PID	0.78	1.09***	0.36	2.01***	1.12	1.58**	0.82***	1.15***
	(0.51)	(0.35)	(0.47)	(0.56)	(0.80)	(0.74)	(0.31)	(0.36)
South	−0.89*	−0.42	−0.46	−0.78	−1.78**	0.47	−0.44*	0.17
	(0.53)	(0.42)	(0.53)	(0.50)	(0.77)	(0.68)	(0.27)	(0.33)
Campaign contact	0.39	0.82		1.82**	−0.33	−0.26	0.48	0.15
	(0.68)	(0.68)		(0.82)	(0.93)	(0.80)	(0.37)	(0.39)
Ideology	−0.17	0.06	0.24	0.37*	0.82***	−0.06	0.26*	0.20
	(0.24)	(0.15)	(0.20)	(0.22)	(0.28)	(0.22)	(0.13)	(0.14)
Constant	−9.20***	−14.36***	−7.83**	−22.26***	−10.78**	−13.75***	−11.17***	−12.35***
	(3.55)	(2.78)	(3.51)	(4.06)	(5.03)	(5.31)	(2.30)	(2.31)
Observations	191	319	236	296	174	247	980	783

Source: ANES.

* $p<0.1$; ** $p<0.05$; *** $p<0.01$; standard errors in parentheses; PID = Party Identification.

demonstrate that Hillary Clinton likely benefited from being perceived as a racial liberal through higher levels of Democratic turnout.

Latino Racial Appeals

Unfortunately, the ANES does not ask questions about perceptions of how government officials address aid to Latinos. Moreover, there does not appear to be a similar question about perceptions of how much candidates focus on Latino appeals. However, we can gain some insight into how whites respond to appeals to Latinos using Obama's immigration announcement on November 20, 2014. In this announcement, Obama stated that the new Deferred Action for Parents of Americans and Lawful Permanent Residents program would shield up to five million immigrants who were parents of U.S. citizens or legal residents, as well as expand protections for children who entered the country illegally with their parents. He also announced that these groups would be allowed to work in the United States legally after passing a background check and paying a fee. Many political pundits and scholars noted that these actions were meant to appeal to Latinos, who make up a disproportionate number of immigrants (Ayón 2017; Collingwood and O'Brien 2019). Additionally, a large number of individuals were aware of Obama's decision. In fact, 65 percent Americans, according to a 2014 Pew poll, said that they followed Obama's immigration actions either very closely or fairly closely (Dimock 2017).

As a result, this action serves as a good way to measure whether whites of different partisanships reward, punish, or ignore Latino racial appeals in the current political context. Moreover, Pew fortunately conducted two polls—on November 9 and December 7, 2014—following the announcement of Obama's new immigration program. Both surveys asked individuals whether they approved or disapproved of Obama. The proximity of the collection of the surveys better ensured that the main factor that could alter attitudes about Obama was his immigration announcement. The surveys therefore provide information about whether liberal-leaning politicians are punished for making high-profile racial appeals to Latinos.

Table 4.4 presents logit regressions predicting whether white Democrats, white Republicans, and white independents stated that they approved of Obama's performance as president. The main independent variable of interest is whether the respondents took the survey in December 2014, about two weeks after Obama's immigration announcement. The models control for age, gender, income, and education. Overall, the results demonstrate that approval for Obama remained unchanged among whites of all three partisanships after he made the immigration announcement. This result seems to indicate that

TABLE 4.4. Logit regression predicting whether respondents approved (1) or disapproved (0) of Obama before (Nov. 2014) and after (Nov. 2014) his DAPA announcement

	Obama approval rating		
	Democrat	Republican	Independent
After DAPA announcement	0.03	−0.42	−0.13
	(0.25)	(0.39)	(0.18)
Female	0.47*	−0.15	0.16
	(0.25)	(0.39)	(0.18)
Age	−0.01*	−0.03***	−0.01*
	(0.01)	(0.01)	(0.00)
Income	−0.03	−0.14*	−0.02
	(0.06)	(0.09)	(0.04)
Education	0.50***	0.04	0.28***
	(0.08)	(0.12)	(0.05)
Constant	−0.70	−0.41	−1.50***
	(0.58)	(0.77)	(0.38)
Observations	442	625	619

Source: Pew Research Center.
* $p<0.1$; ** $p<0.05$; *** $p<0.01$; standard errors in parentheses.

appeals to Latinos do not lead to a backlash among whites, regardless of their partisanship. As suggested above, increased polarization may make whites immune to altering their opinions based on racial appeals. Unfortunately, we cannot test whether actions like the one taken by Obama increase white political participation given the lack of available data. I do, however, attempt to address this shortcoming in the experiment discussed in the following section.

Experimental Results

While the public opinion surveys used in the previous sections have many advantages for testing the effect of racial appeals on political behavior, including allowing for a direct measure of perceptions of racial progressivism, they do have several disadvantages. For example, there may be other factors beyond perceptions of racial ideology that may influence the relationship between racial appeals, vote choice, and turnout. Moreover, lack of available data makes it difficult to determine whether racial appeals that include outreach to Latinos can mobilize whites of different partisanships. As a result, a complementary analysis that controls for all outside factors and better tests the relationship between Latino outreach and expressed turnout may provide more confidence in my findings.

I complemented the ANES and Pew analyses by implementing a separate survey experiment on Amazon Mechanical Turk. (See Notes on the Data for more information about the experiment. Also see table 4.A2 for demographic information on the sample.) Conducting a survey experiment helps to ensure that factors outside of racialization are not influencing my results. Moreover, it could better demonstrate whether racial appeals can directly influence vote choice and/or turnout. The combination of the survey experiment with the real-world data from the ANES and Pew would provide both external and internal validity to my study.

The survey experiment explored whether individuals respond to racial appeals and whether the race of the representative matters in their response. Respondents were told that they were being asked to review the webpage of a Democratic U.S. senator preparing to run for president in 2020. After this information was presented, respondents were randomly assigned to one of four conditions. The first pair of conditions separated the candidate by race. To do so, some respondents were provided a candidate with a white-sounding name (Wyatt McHarris) and others were assigned a candidate whose name sounded black (Malik Jackson). An analysis of respondents' perceptions of the race of the candidate demonstrated that a vast majority of individuals (76%) viewed the name Malik Jackson to be black and only 14 percent viewed the name Wyatt McHarris to be black. By separating the candidates by race, we can better understand if the negative impact of racially progressive views is particularly damaging to black candidates, as found in the previous section with Obama.

Additionally, respondents were also randomly assigned one of two issue-related webpages on the candidates' website. The first webpages for the candidate pair (one white, one black) were focused on racial justice (i.e., a racially liberal appeal) and argued for protecting voting rights, immigrant rights, and criminal justice reform. The second webpages for the candidate pair were centered on economic justice (i.e., a deracialized liberal appeal), such as fighting for workers' rights, a living wage, and union bargaining. The webpages were created to minimize differences between the language used in describing the candidate's platform and the design of the website. The main difference had to do with the subject of the information presented to the respondents. Manipulation checks demonstrated that voters viewed the racialized candidates as being the most racially progressive (see table 4.A1 in the appendix to this chapter). Using this 2 × 2 experiment, I first assessed whether black and/or white candidates who make racially liberal appeals as opposed to deracialized liberal appeals generate higher levels of turnout and electoral support. I then explored whether black and/or white candidates individually are rewarded or punished for advocating for racially progressive policies instead of deracialized progressive policies.

To measure differences in support for the racialized and deracialized candidates in the hypothetical primaries, I pitted the candidates who differed by issue type against Hillary Clinton and Bernie Sanders, the two leading candidates in the 2016 Democratic presidential primaries. In addition to being well known, both candidates also represent varying degrees of perceived liberal ideology. Respondents were asked whether they would support the hypothetical candidates or either Clinton/Sanders in a 2020 Democratic presidential primary matchup. Then they were asked whether they would support a hypothetical candidate over Donald Trump or Mitt Romney in a hypothetical 2020 presidential election matchup. Trump and Romney were the Republican nominees for each of the two previous presidential elections, with the former being ideologically extreme and the latter more moderate.

Finally, respondents were asked how likely they would be to vote if the hypothetical candidate (Wyatt McHarris/Malik Jackson) represented the Democratic Party in the 2020 presidential election, using a five-point scale from 1 (extremely unlikely) to 5 (extremely likely). Below, I present a test of means of the experimental data.

Table 4.5 presents the differences in levels of support for the hypothetical racially liberal candidate against support for the economically liberal deracialized candidate when they campaigned (1) for the Democratic nomination against either Hillary Clinton or Bernie Sanders and (2) for the presidential election against either Donald Trump or Mitt Romney. Positive scores indicate that the racialized candidate performed better than their deracialized counterpart and negative scores indicate the opposite. The table also presents a two-sample *t*-test comparing the significance of these differences.

Similar to the results for analysis of ANES data, the experiment results suggest that candidates do not pay a penalty for engaging in racial appeals among white Democrats. According to table 4.5, the racialized candidate performed equally as well statistically against high-profile politicians as the economically liberal candidate did among white Democrats. For example, the hypothetical candidates who focused on economic issues received 53 percent of the vote when pitted against Clinton in a 2020 Democratic presidential primary. The hypothetical candidates who focused on racial issues only received 1 percent more support (54%) against Clinton. With regard to Bernie Sanders, the difference in support for both sets of candidates was only

TABLE 4.5. Differences in stated support for hypothetical candidates Wyatt McHarris and Malik Jackson when they are presented as racialized or deracialized candidates and pitted against Hillary Clinton, Bernie Sanders, Donald Trump, and Mitt Romney in hypothetical 2020 matchups

	Clinton					
	Both	*N*	McHarris	*N*	Jackson	*N*
White Democrats	0.01 (0.07)	175	0.14 (0.10)	85	−0.11 (0.11)	90
White independents	−0.05 (0.07)	114	−0.06 (0.10)	53	−0.02 (0.11)	61
White Republicans	−0.26* (0.06)	115	−0.33* (0.09)	57	−0.20* (0.09)	58
	Sanders					
	Both	*N*	McHarris	*N*	Jackson	*N*
White Democrats	0.02 (0.07)	175	0.13 (0.10)	85	−0.07 (0.10)	90
White independents	−0.06 (0.09)	114	−0.04 (0.13)	53	−0.08 (0.12)	60
White Republicans	−0.21* (0.09)	115	−0.25+(0.13)	57	−0.18 (0.13)	58
	Trump					
	Both	*N*	McHarris	*N*	Jackson	*N*
White Democrats	−0.02 (0.03)	175	−0.01 (0.05)	85	−0.02 (0.04)	90
White independents	−0.11 (0.08)	114	−0.08 (0.12)	53	−0.12 (0.12)	61
White Republicans	−0.01 (0.08)	115	−0.10 (0.12)	57	−0.05 (0.09)	58
	Romney					
	Both	*N*	McHarris	*N*	Jackson	*N*
White Democrats	0.00 (0.04)	175	0.06 (0.06)	85	−0.05 (0.06)	90
White independents	−0.13 (0.09)	114	−0.10 (0.13)	53	−0.13 (0.13)	61
White Republicans	−0.11 (0.08)	115	−0.21+ (0.12)	57	−0.01 (0.10)	58

Source: Amazon Mechanical Turk survey.

Note: The "Both" column compares racialized and deracialized candidates of both races; the "McHarris" column compares only the racialized and deracialized McHarris candidate; and the "Jackson" column compares only the racialized and deracialized Jackson candidate. Positive scores indicate that the racialized candidate received more support than the deracialized candidate when pitted against an opponent.

* $p<0.05$; + $p<0.1$; significance based on a two-sample test of means; standard errors in parentheses.

2 percent. When disaggregating by race and message, it appears that white candidates who racialize tend to perform better than white economically liberal candidates among white Democrats. However, racialized black candidates tend to perform worse than their deracialized black counterparts. Nonetheless, there were no significant differences between candidates of the same race who differed by their use of racialized or deracialized appeals in the Democratic primaries.

In addition to white Democrats not displaying preferences for either racialized or deracialized candidates in the primaries, they also don't appear to be more supportive of either candidate type in hypothetical presidential election matchups against Donald Trump or Mitt Romney. White Democrats were overwhelmingly supportive of the hypothetical democratic candidate against both Republican nominees in 2020. For example, over 93 percent of white Democrats supported the hypothetical candidates, regardless of their message, over the Republican nominees in a potential 2020 matchup. Moreover, there was no significant difference between the levels of support for the deracialized and racialized candidates. In fact, in both potential matchups the hypothetical racially liberal candidate and the deracialized liberal candidate were only separated by 1 percent when analyzing candidates of both races at the same time. This finding mirrors the results in the previous section, which showed that racializing does not lead to lower levels of support among white Democrats.

Table 4.5 also presents the same differences among support for racialized and deracialized candidates of different races when pitted against high-profile politicians for white independents and white Republicans. The table suggests that white independents do not appear to significantly favor either racialized or deracialized candidates when pitted against any of the high-profile Democratic or Republican politicians. For example, just 5–6 percent of independent whites preferred the deracialized liberal candidate to the racially liberal candidate when pitted against Clinton or Sanders. This difference among white independents grows to double digits when this set of candidates is pitted against Republicans, but this difference remains statistically insignificant. Moreover, the race of the candidate appears to be inconsequential in determining the effectiveness of a racialized appeal among white independents in any of the hypothetical matchups. The combination of results suggests that neither black nor white candidates perform statistically worse when they focus on racially liberal policies among political independents than candidates who make economically liberal arguments.

While white Democrats and independents don't appear to respond differently to racially liberal appeals, the results in table 4.5 demonstrate that racialization does decrease support among Republicans in hypothetical matchups in the Democratic primaries against both Hillary Clinton and Bernie Sanders. Candidates who focused on economic justice received over 26 percent more white Republican support than the racial justice candidates against Hillary Clinton. Moreover, the deracialized candidates performed about 21 percent better against Bernie Sanders among white Republicans than their racialized counterparts. Both of these differences were significant based on a two-sample *t*-test. This indicates that if Republicans voted in Democratic primaries, they would support economic populist policies over racially progressive polices. However, given the low likelihood of white Republicans being the decisive vote in Democratic presidential primaries, there does not appear to be a high cost to losing Republican support in this context.

However, when the partisanship of the candidate varies, the effect of the message dissipates in most cases. White Republicans are marginally significantly more likely to support a white economic liberal than a white racial liberal when this individual is pitted against Romney, but not when pitted against Trump. However, outside of this case, white Republicans are not significantly more likely to support either the racialized or deracialized Democratic candidate to a greater degree when they are pitted against the two previous Republican presidential candidates. The results suggest that Democratic candidates who focus on racialized issues may lose Republican whites in some instances but perform equally as well as deracialized liberals among white Democrats and independents.

Unlike the analysis of observational data, the online experiment shows that racialized candidates did not increase white Democratic turnout to a greater degree than their economic-justice counterparts. Table 4.6 presents the average difference in levels of voting intentions in 2020 between candidates who focused on racial justice against those who focused on economic justice. This difference is disaggregated by the black candidate, white candidate, and both candidates together. For both candidate types, white Democrats expressed a high likelihood of intending to vote (~4.2 out of 5) when the hypothetical candidate is on the ballot. However, there does not appear to be any significant difference in white Democratic mobilization between candidates who racialize and those who do not. For example, just a tenth of a point on the five-point scale separates white Democrats' average voting intentions between black and white candidates who make racial appeals and those who focus on economically liberal policies. Even when disaggregating the candidates by race, there was no significant difference in turnout intentions among white Democrats between racially liberal and economically liberal candidates.

TABLE 4.6. Differences in voter enthusiasm (1 = low enthusiasm, 5 = high enthusiasm) if hypothetical candidates Wyatt McHarris and Malik Jackson are presented as racialized or deracialized candidates on the 2020 presidential ballot

	Both	*N*	McHarris	*N*	Jackson	*N*
White Democrats	−0.15 (0.15)	172	−0.08 (0.19)	84	−0.22 (0.21)	88
White independents	−0.72* (0.25)	112	−0.23 (0.31)	53	−1.125* (0.36)	60
White Republicans	−0.30 (0.28)	115	−0.40 (0.39)	57	−0.19 (0.41)	58

Source: Amazon Mechanical Turk survey.

Note: The "Both" column compares racialized and deracialized candidates of both races; the "McHarris" column compares only the racialized and deracialized McHarris candidate; and the "Jackson" column compares only the racialized and deracialized Jackson candidate. Positive scores indicate that the racialized candidate inspires more enthusiasm than the deracialized candidate.

* $p < 0.05$; + $p < 0.1$; significance based on a two-sample test of means; standard errors in parentheses.

The results may suggest that white Democrats are motivated to turn out and support any candidate whom they *perceive as progressive* regardless of whether this progressiveness is focused on racial issues or economic issues. There is some evidence for this in the fact that, in all cases, white Democrats expressed significantly more enthusiasm for voting in 2020 when the hypothetical candidates were on the ballot than white Republicans and white independents based a *t*-test comparing differences across party within issue type.

White independents tended to be less enthusiastic than white Democrats about voting in the 2020 election if either the deracialized or racialized hypothetical candidate was on the ballot. However, intention to turn out was significantly lower for white independents when the racialized candidate is on the ballot. On a one-to-five scale, white independents' levels of expressed desire to turn out declined by about three-quarters of a point when the Democratic candidate was racially liberal. This difference is in large part driven by white independents being less motivated to turn out to support a black racialized candidate. White independent turnout declines by 1.125 points on a five-point scale when a black candidate focused on racial issues rather than economic ones. This difference is not only large, but also statistically significant. However, given that independents do not have strong partisan attachments or voting preferences, one should not read too much into these results. For example, racially liberal candidates may limit turnout among independents who support either the Republican or Democratic Party. The former may actually help the Democratic candidate, while the latter would be problematic for the party.

Moreover, table 4.6 demonstrates that white Republicans do not countermobilize against candidates who racialized to a greater degree than the same candidates who focused on economic justice issues. Like Democrats, they are slightly less likely to vote when a racialized candidate is on the Democratic side, regardless of the race of the candidate, but these differences are statistically insignificant. In combination with the ANES analysis results, the results in this section suggest that racialized candidates don't appear to face an electoral backlash among white Republicans compared to economically liberal deracialized candidates.

Conclusion

At a 2016 campaign rally in Iowa, Donald Trump told an audience, "I could stand in the middle of 5th Avenue and shoot somebody and I wouldn't lose voters." While extreme, the comment was meant to signal the loyalty of Trump voters in the upcoming presidential election. Moreover, it also speaks to one of the major consequences of polarization in contemporary America. While committing a crime probably would test the limits of polarization, candidates can move further to the left or right without sacrificing large numbers of supporters. This change in the dynamic of American politics has fundamentally altered how candidates' campaign for elected office. As there are fewer persuadable voters in the electorate, campaigns must shift their tactics to increase their opportunities to win. The strategy that campaigns have adopted with some success in this changing political environment is to focus on mobilizing voters.

To mobilize voters, candidates take positions that are most salient to their base and work to appear as ideologically pure on the race issue as they can. In a period where race and perceptions of racial discrimination have become more salient, particularly among white Democrats, appearing as progressive on racial issues plays an important role in mobilizing Democratic white voters. The analysis in this chapter has demonstrated that in 2016, white Democrats who perceived Hillary Clinton as being most progressive on racial issues were much more likely to turn out to vote in the 2016 presidential election. As a result, Clinton's fault may not be that she focused on too many racial appeals, but that she was not perceived as being racially liberal enough. In part, any appeals she made to underrepresented groups may have been counteracted by attacks from opponents using statements she had made in the past (Stout and Baker 2019). Moreover, Clinton's unique position of being the first woman to run for the White House meant that her ex-president spouse played a larger role in discussions about her campaign than previous candidates (Elder, Frederick, and Burrell 2018). Perceptions of Bill Clinton as being racially conservative may have diminished trust in Hillary's ability to advance the interest of underrepresented groups, regardless of her racial rhetoric (Kim 2002).

In the experimental results, we found that a racially liberal position is statistically as likely to mobilize white Democratic voters as an economically liberal position. In both cases, Democratic voters on average noted that they were likely to vote if either a racialized candidate or economically liberal candidate was on the ballot. A liberal approach, regardless of whether it is racialized or not, appears to benefit Democratic candidates. This increase in enthusiasm from white Democrats does not appear to have been matched with higher levels of countermobilization among Republican voters. In sum, it appears that in the most recent election, and in the near future, appearing as racially progressive may help or at least not hurt Democratic candidates among white Democrats.

In the past the main drawback in appearing as a racial progressive was that it jeopardized the support of persuadable/swing voters. However, the analysis in this chapter suggests that this did not occur in the most recent presidential election. This implies that voters may be so set in their voting habits that the message of the candidate may not be enough to gain or lose a significant number of voters. This is important because white voters, and white independent voters in particular, were long believed to be the most turned off by candidates who appear as progressive on racial issues. If they are not, and such an appeal actually mobilizes supportive white voters, then there may need to be a change in how Democratic candidates address race in their campaigns.

However, the data also suggest that Republicans prefer deracialized Democrats to racialized Democrats. This may indicate that there are some benefits to deracializing. However, given that few Republican voters are likely to support a Democrat, the cost to racializing may be low. Moreover, if racialized liberals perform better among blacks and Latinos, a topic we will explore in future chapters, the loss of white Republicans would certainly be offset with gains from minorities who are becoming more consistently an important part of the Democratic coalition.

There are several important caveats that should be discussed here. The first relates to the 2016 election, which best exemplifies how the electorate has changed on racial issues is unique in numerous ways. The Republican nominee, Donald Trump held such regressive stances on racial issues that it may have drawn Democrats to become more interested in their candidates' positions on these issues. Additionally, neither of the major party candidates was well liked. This of course may have made persuasion, regardless of the position of the candidate, much more difficult. While there are numerous reasons for thinking 2016 to be unique, the overall changes in the political and racial context in the United States may be altering the way in which campaigns can address race and still perform well. Certainly, more research is necessary, but the fact that the results are consistent with the expectations outlined in this chapter and with the experimental analysis is promising.

Second, the most significant result is related to voter turnout. Self-reported voter turnout tends to overestimate turnout rates. However, given that we only have results for white Democrats in 2016 and that there is not strong reason to believe that attitudes toward racial progressivism may influence social desirability response bias, there is no strong reason to dismiss the analysis presented in this chapter.

Third, the analysis in this chapter has demonstrated that Obama faced a stiff penalty from all white voters for appearing as racially progressive. This may indicate that making racial appeals may be particularly damaging to black candidates. However, there is also reason to believe that the context in which Obama campaigned for the White House may have made racial appeals by a black candidate particularly off-putting for some white voters. As discussed in chapters 1 and 2, during 2008 and 2012 most whites had their highest levels of racial resentment and displayed their most skepticism that racism was a problem. As a result, if Obama was perceived in this context as favoring blacks, he may have been punished for rewarding what many whites perceived as an undeserving group.

Whether black candidates should still be concerned about making racial appeals in the current context requires more research in the future. However, there is some support for the idea that the context in which Obama campaigned made him particularly susceptible to being punished for appearing as racially liberal. As mentioned earlier, in the 1988 Democratic presidential primaries voters did not punish Jesse Jackson when they perceived him as being more racially liberal. Moreover, the black racialized candidate in the experiment discussed above did not face greater penalties in support from white Democrats, white independents, or white Republicans than a deracialized black candidate in hypothetical matchups with white Republican candidates. While more work in this area is necessary, there does appear to be some evidence that context interacts with the race of the candidate to make racial appeals more or less damaging.

The results in this first section of the book (chapters 1–4) demonstrate that candidates may be rewarded, or at least not punished, for appearing as racially progressive to white voters. This finding is surprising given that a deracialized approach has been hypothesized to be effective because it avoided alienating white voters who were worried about a progressive racial agenda. However, whether whites are unique in their turn toward being more approving of racially progressive candidates is unknown. Certainly, it is expected that blacks and Latinos should be the most supportive of candidates who advocate for improving racial inequality, but this needs to be empirically verified. Moreover, whether blacks and Latinos are becoming more concerned about racial progress and whether this translates into changes in political behavior needs further analysis. In chapter 5, I will explore whether changes in the political and social environment in the United States have made blacks more racially conscious.

TABLE APPENDIX 4.1. *t*-test assessing balance among white Democrats, white independents, white Republicans, blacks, and Latinos who received either the racialized or deracialized treatment

White Democrats	Female	Age	Education	Income	Ideology (conservative–liberal)
Deracialized	0.66 (0.07)	37.85 (2.05)	14.98 (0.28)	44.89 (5.88)	4.34 (0.11)
Racialized	0.43 (0.07)	36.7 (1.93)	15.33 (0.32)	60.18 (6.28)	4.39 (0.11)
Difference	0.22* (0.11)	1.15 (2.81)	−0.36 (0.43)	−15.29 (8.69)	−0.05 (0.15)
White independents	**Female**	**Age**	**Education**	**Income**	**Ideology (conservative–liberal)**
Deracialized	0.41 (0.09)	35.03 (1.93)	14.38 (0.26)	38.84 (3.36)	3.47 (0.16)
Racialized	0.21 (0.08)	36.5 (3.27)	14.75 (0.29)	48.04 (6.82)	3.57 (0.15)
Difference	−0.19 (0.11)	−1.47 (3.6)	−0.38 (0.39)	−9.2 (7)	−0.09 (0.23)
White Republicans	**Female**	**Age**	**Education**	**Income**	**Ideology (conservative–liberal)**
Deracialized	0.42 (0.09)	40.65 (2.44)	15.23 (0.34)	67.42 (7.38)	1.97 (0.1)
Racialized	0.54 (0.1)	38.19 (2.55)	15.15 (0.32)	60.88 (7.77)	2.08 (0.13)
Difference	−0.12 (0.13)	2.45 (3.54)	0.07 (0.47)	6.53 (10.76)	−0.11 (0.16)
Blacks	**Female**	**Age**	**Education**	**Income**	**Ideology (conservative–liberal)**
Deracialized	0.55 (0.04)	35.23 (1.05)	15.06 (0.14)	51.9 (2.87)	3.55 (0.08)
Racialized	0.65 (0.04)	33.95 (0.99)	15.21 (0.17)	56.12 (3.34)	3.68 (0.1)
Difference	0.095 (.062)	1.27 (1.45)	−0.16 (0.21)	−4.22 (4.38)	−0.13 (0.13)
Latinos	**Female**	**Age**	**Education**	**Income**	**Ideology (conservative–liberal)**
Deracialized	0.35 (0.06)	30.42 (1.13)	15.05 (0.21)	47.28 (3.96)	3.45 (0.14)
Racialized	0.41 (0.05)	31.1 (1.07)	15.1 (0.18)	52.55 (4.18)	3.67 (0.1)
Difference	0.055 (0.078)	−0.67 (1.57)	−0.05 (0.28)	−5.27 (5.88)	−0.22 (0.17)

Source: Amazon Mechanical Turk survey.

* $p < 0.05$; standard errors in parentheses.

TABLE APPENDIX 4.2. Manipulation check assessing whether respondents who received the racialized candidate rated them as higher on the "aid to blacks" scale

	White Democrats	White independents	White Republicans	Blacks	Latinos
Racialized candidate treatment	5.69 (0.15)	5.57 (0.22)	5.67 (0.24)	5.16 (0.14)	5.29 (0.17)
Nonracialized candidate treatment	5.11 (0.17)	4.87 (0.21)	4.54 (0.27)	4.4 (0.13)	4.61 (0.2)
Difference	0.58* (0.22)	0.7* (0.31)	1.14* (0.36)	0.76* (0.19)	0.69* (0.26)

Source: Amazon Mechanical Turk survey.

Note: Higher scores indicate candidate views government as a vehicle to aid blacks (i.e., racially liberal).

* $p < 0.05$; standard errors in parentheses.

5 The Return of Black Consciousness

Many African Americans viewed Obama's 2008 victory as a sign that the United States was moving toward a postracial society. Obama pollster Cornel Belcher noted, "I'm the new black politics. The people I work with are the new black politics. We don't carry around that history. We see the world through post-civil-rights eyes" (Bai 2008). Along the same lines, more blacks believed that with hard work and perseverance the significance of race would surely decline (see Stout and Le 2012). As the country moved away from the civil rights era and into the Obama era, many blacks were hopeful that racial barriers had disappeared.

In spite of this optimism, blacks were being confronted with images of police brutality and attacks on Obama that would raise questions about whether they were truly living in a postracial society. In fact, many of the high-profile shootings of black men and women raised questions about whether the United States had made any progress since the civil rights era. In a forum set up by the *New York Times* for students to react to the shooting of Trayvon Martin and the acquittal of George Zimmerman (see chapter 1), several students noted the connection between the current racial climate and the pre–civil rights era. One student wrote, "I am an African American and I feel extremely anxious that in 2012, African-American citizens have to rely upon the Federal Government to prosecute crimes against us that should be acted upon by local authorities. The Trayvon Martin tragedy is so reminiscent of the United States, 'Jim Crow' south of the 1950's and 1960's" (quoted in Ojalvo 2012). Barack Obama echoed these ideas by acknowledging that racism had never gone away; it was just something people preferred to believe did not exist (see Dyson 2016). In spite of hopes that Obama's election had moved blacks passed the barriers that had stifled progress for previous generations, Obama's presidency instead made racial discrimination more visible.

This increase in the visibility of racial bias may led to a resurgence in group consciousness among African Americans. When blacks viewed race as being less influential in their lives, they also experienced a decline in their sense of group consciousness and began to support more postracial policies (Tate 2010). However, with the greater visibility of racial discrimination, which was outlined in more detail in chapter 1, blacks may have returned to holding a strong sense of "linked fate," a measure of racial solidarity. The increasing salience of racial identify for African Americans in turn may have led them to be more liberal on race-based policies than they have been in the recent past.

In this chapter, I will explore changes in blacks' racial consciousness in recent years. I will begin by describing the move away from race as a salient identity for African Americans in the early twenty-first century. I will then discuss the role of perceptions of racial bias as influencing a sense of linked fate, a measure used to assess how important race is in one's political and social life. Following this discussion, I will use several data sets, including the National Black Election Study (NBES) for 1984, 1988, and 1996; the 2004 National Political Survey (NPS), and the 2008, 2012, and 2016 American National Election Studies (ANES), to explore whether blacks' levels of linked fate have changed over time. The results of this analysis demonstrate that while blacks had lower levels of linked fate in 2008 and 2012 than at any time during the period of this study, in 2016 this trend reverse and blacks displayed the highest levels of linked fate in the same period.

Following this analysis, I will also use the ANES, Pew Research Center polls and the General Social Survey (GSS) to explore whether this increase in linked fate translates into more support for progressive racial policies. I find that blacks were much more supportive of government providing aid to blacks, immigration, and affirmative action in 2016 than in the recent past. The results of this analysis indicate that blacks strongly prefer a racially progressive political agenda in the current political context.

Moving Away from Race

In the late twentieth and early twenty-first centuries, several scholars noted that more blacks were viewing race as becoming less central to their opportunities in life (Cose 2011; Mack 2011; Smith 2014; Wilson 1980). These studies focused on three main reasons for this decline in racial consciousness. First, internal divisions among blacks, such as the diversification of socioeconomic status, had become more predictive of blacks' life chances than race, and this had divided the black community. Second, the success of Obama made blacks more optimistic about their position in society and, as a result, they felt less defined by their race. Finally, some argued that as generations of blacks had been raised and socialized in a post–civil rights era, their different experiences with racism and black political leadership had been race less salient in their lives. In this section, I will explore each of these arguments in more detail.

Several scholars argue that blacks' racial consciousness declined after the civil rights era because of burgeoning opportunities for blacks in the middle and upper classes and declining opportunities for poorer blacks. The combination of these factors makes one's class more salient than one's race. The most prominent accounts of this changing dynamic are William Julius Wilson's *Declining Significance of Race* (1980) and *The Truly Disadvantaged* (1987). In short, Wilson argues that because of affirmative action programs, the increasing desire for diversity in both the private and public sector, and the dearth of blacks with the training to fill these jobs, blacks in the upper and middle classes would see an expansion in their opportunities. At the same time, because of the end of housing discrimination, wealthier blacks would move out of traditionally black neighborhoods and into the suburbs.

Blacks without these prospects would see declining opportunities for several reasons. First, the decline of manufacturing jobs would make it difficult for blacks with little education to make a decent wage. Second, blacks with elite backgrounds would leave majority-black neighborhoods, depriving younger blacks of role models. Finally, the declining tax base in cities would make it difficult for blacks who disproportionately resided in urban centers to have access to quality public resources. In combination, the divergent paths of poor and middle- and upper-class blacks would lead to intersections of class and race that would weaken the bond between these groups. These changes would make class more central to blacks' lives, and they would be less concerned about their race as a result.

In addition to greater class diversification in the late twentieth and early twenty-first centuries leading to a decline in racial consciousness, many point to the election of Obama to the presidency as being a factor in altering blacks' racial attitudes. To many, Obama optimizes the decline of discrimination and expanding opportunities for blacks that emerged from the successes of the civil rights movement. These improvements in race relations, they argued, would lead blacks to feel less connected to members of their racial group. By conducting a series of interviews, Cose (2011) found that blacks, and particularly blacks in the middle class, became much more optimistic after the 2008 presidential election. A black law professor told Cose, "If an African American can be elected president to the United States, I don't think there is anything in this country [we] can't do" (48). U.S. senator Cory Booker, meanwhile, noted that "Barack Obama could not have been elected president thirty years ago. It just would not have happened in the United States of America. So obviously I have, again thanks to my parents' generation's works, an expanded set of career options that they didn't have before" (49). These quotes suggest that many blacks, and in particular middle-class blacks, during the Obama administration saw expanding opportunities for their racial group as a result of the successes of the civil rights movement. This more optimistic outlook may be tied to blacks viewing their race as less central to their lives.

Additionally, some have argued that differences in experiences among blacks in different generations led younger blacks to reject the idea that their race defines them. Several scholars have argued that the post–civil rights generation (i.e., blacks born after 1964) tended to see the world through a more color-blind lens. Gillespie (2010) notes that younger blacks were less likely to perceive the struggles of their parents and grandparents as being *their* struggle. Instead, the focus of this new generation was on finding ways to incorporate themselves into the traditional power structure rather than change it by confronting racial inequalities (Bositis 2001). In another interview of Cose's (2011) interviews, a young black woman expressed her hopes that with hard work anything is possible: "For people of my generation, the biggest challenge is to adapt yourself to 'the norm'. . . . If you're willing to completely assimilate . . . people will overlook that you're from a minority" (46).

Along these lines, Mack (2011) found that young blacks were less likely to believe that their racial group faced greater levels of discrimination than had older African Americans. Watts-Smith (2014) demonstrated that blacks, and in particular young blacks, were much more likely to perceive lack of motivation as explaining lower levels of success for blacks in the 2000s than they had in the past. Overall, these studies suggest that as the post–civil rights generation becomes a larger part of the electorate, they will also bring with them a less racially conscious perspective.

Part of this optimism for the declining significance of race could be attributed to black politicians and elites whose rhetoric focused on problems of personal deficiencies rather than discrimination as the explanation for racial disparities in the United States. Gillespie (2010) outlines the goals and beliefs of what she defines as the third wave of black politicians. She argues that this third wave of black politicians is largely divorced from the civil rights context that influenced their parents' politics. Moreover, this group has taken a more traditional path to politics than their predecessors who had ties to the civil rights movement. This includes going to Ivy League colleges, working in the legal field, and taking centrist nonracialized positions. Gillespie (2010) and Tate (2010) both note that this new group of politicians has moved beyond race in their campaigns. This strategy may in part be driven by the different experiences of younger black politicians and their predecessors from the civil rights movement, but it also may be motivated by black politicians responding to perceptions that a deracialized campaign approach is the only path to higher-level elected offices.

Tate (2010) found that blacks, like other groups, often follow their political leaders in forming their political opinions. As black politicians deemphasized race in their campaigns to appeal to a broader electorate, black voters followed suit. Tate (2010) demonstrated that as black politicians became more conservative on issues like affirmative action, welfare, and crime policy, black voters too displayed more conservative values on these issues. In summary, the conditions of the post–civil rights generation made it so that blacks were less likely to have strong racial consciousness.

The Return to Consciousness

What factors may reinvigorate black racial consciousness? While there is a lot of debate on what influences group consciousness, most scholars agree that certain attributes must be present. At a basic level, there must be a group to which individuals feel connected to; there must be a polar effect (i.e., an in-group and an out-group); and, most importantly, there must be a feeling of expressed dissatisfaction about the power dynamics between the in-group and out-group (Miller et al. 1981). The final criterion appears to drive much of what influences perceptions of group consciousness. Although social and political disparities may exist between different groups, group consciousness is generally not activated until individuals perceive these differences as being driven by discrimination. As such, during the late 1990s and 2000s, where perceptions of racial discrimination were relatively low, it would not be surprising to find that blacks' level of racial consciousness was also low. However, if blacks have become more aware of racial inequality in recent years, they may be an accompanying increase in racial group consciousness.

The Obama years were marked with numerous high-profile racial events that increased blacks' perceptions that racial discrimination still occurs. From the treatment of Obama by the Tea Party movement to the acquittal of George Zimmerman, to the rise of the Black Lives Matter movement, few blacks would deny that race plays a role in determining their social and political outcomes in the twenty-first century. The Trayvon Martin shooting played a particularly significant role in sparking blacks' awareness of racial discrimination. While Obama symbolized progress, the acquittal of Martin's killer epitomized racial injustice. According to a poll conducted by Gallup shortly after the shooting, 72 percent of blacks felt that race was a major factor in Zimmerman following and shooting the black teenager. Only 8 percent said that race played no role in the shooting (Newport 2012). In addition to viewing

Zimmerman's motives as being based on race, many blacks viewed his treatment in the courts as being too lenient given that he had killed an unarmed teenager. In the same Gallup Poll, 72 percent of blacks felt that Zimmerman would have been arrested more quickly had he killed a white teenager. Following the acquittal of Zimmerman, blacks largely believed that the system was discriminatory against blacks. No less than 86 percent of blacks in a poll conducted by the *Washington Post* and ABC News felt that blacks and other minorities don't receive equal treatment under the law (Thompson and Cohen 2012).

The acquittal of Zimmerman reminded some blacks that they were not too far removed from the pre–civil rights era. In particular, many blacks equated the shooting of Trayvon Martin to the murder of Emmett Till, a black teenager killed by white men in Mississippi in the summer of 1955. Like Till, Martin's murder was unprovoked and driven by racial biases. Moreover, like Till's murderers, Martin's murderer was acquitted of all charges.

Many in the black community felt that the Martin case awoke a sense of group consciousness and activism that had been missing since the civil rights movement. Activist and filmmaker Bree Newsome described the Martin shooting and Zimmerman acquittal as being a defining moment in her engagement in social activism. In an interview with CNN, Newsome noted that Martin was "kind of like the Emmett Till of my time" (Rickford 2016). Moreover, the acquittal of Zimmerman is cited as a motivating factor for the beginning of the Black Lives Matter movement. In the "herstory" section of the movement's website, Alicia Garza, one of the founders of Black Lives Matter, tied the origins of the movement to the shooting of Martin. "I created #BlackLivesMatter with Patrisse Cullors and Opal Tometi, two of my sisters, as a call to action for Black people after seventeen-year-old Trayvon Martin was posthumously placed on trial for his own murder and the killer, George Zimmerman, was not held accountable for the crime he committed."

The Martin shooting came as an eye-opener to many who felt that race no longer defined them. In an interview with CNN, Kim Coleman, a black attendee of the 2008 Democratic Convention, expressed hope following the election of Obama. She noted, "I had hope running through my veins" (Blake 2016). However, after the Martin shooting and a string of other police killings, she returned to a realization that racism had not disappeared. In the same interview, she commented, "I didn't realize how many people were racist until all of this—police killings, racism online" (Blake 2016).

Moreover, the perception that with hard work, high socioeconomic status, or power the significance of race recedes was largely shattered by how Obama was treated during his presidency. Many saw him as working hard to make race a less salient issue and perceived much of the Republicans' effort to block his agenda in Congress as being racially motivated (Dowe et al. 2010; Tesler 2016). Blacks in particular felt that Obama was treated unfairly because of his race. Even shortly after Obama's election in 2009, a period where blacks tended to be more optimistic about race relations, almost 70 percent of blacks in a Pew poll felt that opposition to Obama's presidency was in part driven by racial biases (Tesler 2016). Obama himself argued that racism in part played a role in how he was assessed by the public. When asked by CNN correspondent Fareed Zakaria whether racism played a role in how voters evaluated him, Obama stated, "Absolutely. . . . There's a reason why attitudes about my presidency among whites in Northern states are very different from whites in Southern states" (quoted in Desmond-Harris 2016).

Such developments led to the realization among many blacks that if even Obama, who held the highest office in the United States and worked to make race a less salient feature in his politics, faced discrimination, then there was little hope for the average African American. In an interview with CNN, Linnyette Richarson-Hall, a black event planner, argued that the negative things that her associates would say about Obama led her to the realization that they may have held the same biases about her: "These are people I've known for years, I was like, 'If you think this about him, what do you think of me?'" (Blake 2016).

Given that perceptions of discrimination play a large role in influencing attitudes about group consciousness, it follows that blacks may have experienced a return to group consciousness following the events of the Obama era. If even Obama could not receive fair treatment from whites, then blacks may now view race as a more salient part of their own lives. Moreover, the high-profile shootings of African Americans and the lack of accountability has raised questions about whether blacks truly are treated equal in contemporary society. Many blacks feel that more work needs to be done to address racial discrimination in the United States, and they may display both higher levels of linked fate and support for progressive racial policies as a result.

Data

Linked Fate

Dawson (1994) and Tate (1994) both outline the significance of a common consciousness or linked fate in determining black political opinion and behavior. Linked fate refers to the sense that an individual's life chances are inextricably tied to those who share some similar characteristic. A sense of linked fate relies on a group orientation when evaluating social and political contexts, with a collective "we" in mind rather than a view that one's outcomes in life are removed from the well-being of the group. Higher levels of linked fate play an important role in influencing blacks' opinions about racial issues. If their own well-being in life is tied to their race, then they will have a stronger preference for racial policies and politicians who address racial inequities.

To measure linked fate, I use a variety of sources to best measure this concept over a long period of time. The concept was first popularized in the NBES and featured in 1984, 1988, and 1996 editions. The 1984 and 1988 NBES were actually panel studies featuring many of the same respondents. A large number of African Americans were asked about their political opinions and their assessment of linked fate. The 2004 NPS was a multiracial survey that included a large sample of black, Latino, and Asian American respondents. While the survey included many questions about race relations across different groups, it also included a question that asked the respondents about their levels of linked fate. Finally, because the ANES contained an oversample of black and Latino respondents in 2008 and 2012, the authors began expanding the questions that they used around racial issues. One such addition was asking white, black, and Latino respondents about their levels of linked fate. As a result, the 2008, 2012, and 2016 ANES all include questions about this measure. I therefore use the 1984, 1988, and 1996 NBES; the 2004 NPS; and the 2008, 2012, and 2016 ANES to measure changes in black linked fate over time.

While there is some inconsistency in how questions on linked fate have been asked over time, the basic structure remains unchanged across surveys. In the 1984, 1988, and 1996 NBES; the 2004 NPS; and the 2008 and 2012 ANES, linked fate was measured using two questions. The first asked, "Do you think that what happens generally to black people in this country will have something to do with what happens in your life?" Those who answered affirmatively to this question then answered a follow-up question: "How much does what happens to blacks affect you?" Responses to this second question were on a three-point scale: (1) "a little", (2) "some", and (3) "a lot." The 2016 ANES combined these two questions into one and asked, "How much do you think that what happens generally to black people in this country will affect what happens in your life." The responses were on a four-point scale and ranged from (1) not at all, (2) not very much, (3) some, and (4) a lot. For all but the 2016 ANES, I used the two-question format to create a four-point scale. Those who answered "no" to the first question were given score of 1; those who answered "a little" to the second question were given a score of 2; those who answered "some" to the second question were given a score of 3; and those who answered "a lot" to the second question were given a score of 4. This coding scheme is shared by those who have explored linked fate for blacks and other groups (see Dawson 1994; Junn and Masuoka 2008; Sanchez and Masuoka 2010; Stokes 2003).

Figure 5.1A presents blacks' average levels of linked fate over a more than thirty-year period. In most years, the average black respondent was between having a little (2 on the four-point scale) and some (3 on the four-point scale) linked fate. For example, in 1984 blacks on average had a linked fate score of 2.67. This increased slightly in 1988 and 1996 and then dipped downward, leading to a low of 2.49 in 2012. Consistent with expectations, blacks as a group tended to have the lowest levels of linked fate in the early Obama years. As Obama's election demonstrated to some the declining significance of race, blacks' levels of linked fate decreased. However, in 2016 blacks displayed their highest levels of linked fate. Blacks on average had a linked fate score of 3.14 that year, which is almost a quarter of a point greater than the previous high in 1996 (2.91) and almost three-quarters of a point higher than the figure for 2012. A test of means comparing blacks' linked fate in 2016 to their previous high in 1996 demonstrated that the difference was statistically significant. As expected, blacks reported a significant increase in linked fate in the latter part of the Obama years.

Of course, it could be argued that differences in the question wording in 2016 might have in part driven these differences. In particular, the fact that the question was asked over two separate parts in the pre-2016 years with slightly different responses ("a little" vs. "not much") may be skewing these results. To address this possibility, I compared the percentage of blacks who said that they had a lot of linked fate with other blacks across my period of interest. Given that this option remained the same across the time periods, if I were to find similar results across time I can be more confident in these results. Figure 5.1B presents the percentage of blacks who stated that they had "a lot" of linked fate from 1984 to 2016. The results confirm that blacks did indeed report a greater level of linked fate at a greater rate in 2016 than in previous years.

About a third of blacks in any given year stated that they had a lot of linked fate. However, in 2012 this number decreased substantially. In fact, in that year less than a quarter of blacks felt that they had high levels of linked fate. This was significantly lower than in 2008 based on a two-sample *t*-test. However, in 2016 this figure has risen to about 46 percent, indicating that almost half of blacks felt strongly connected to those who share their race. This 10 percent difference from the previous high point in 1996 is also statistically significant based on a two-sample *t*-test. The results in figure 5.1 provide evidence that blacks have experienced a recent resurgence in linked fate. However, whether

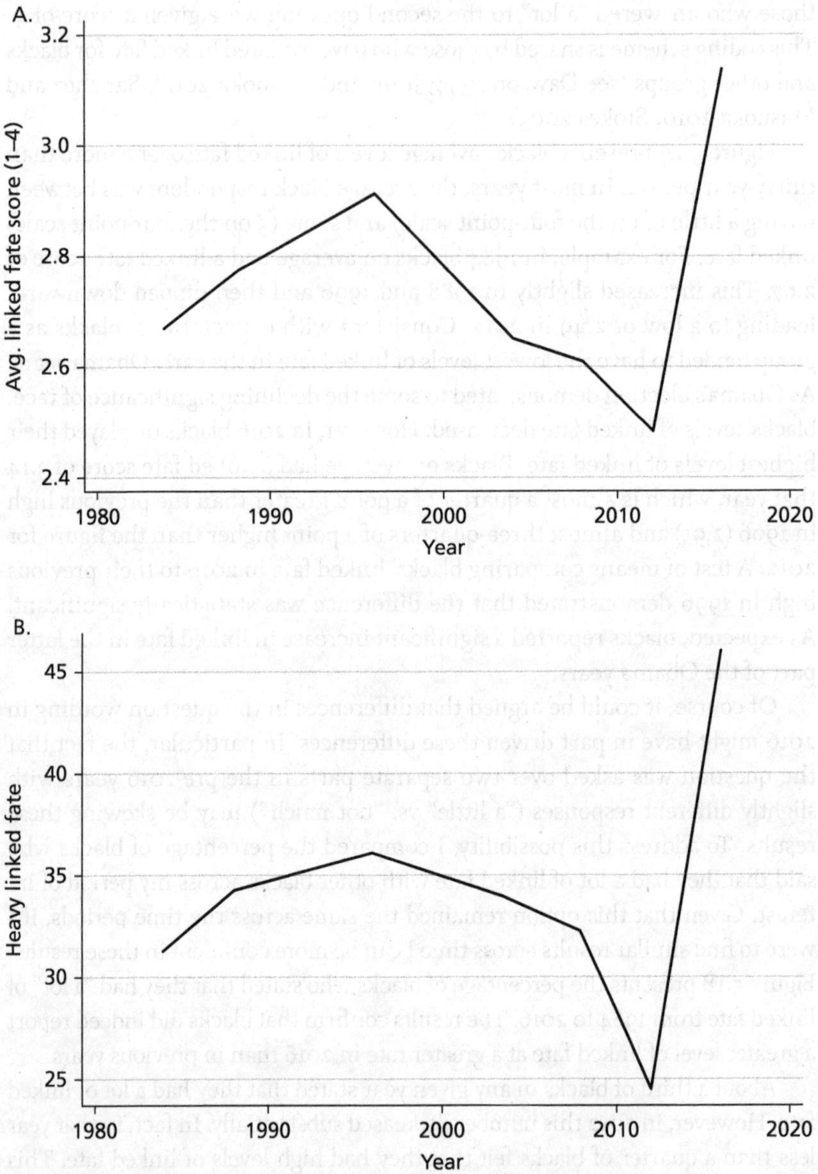

FIGURE 5.1. Blacks' levels of linked fate (1984–2016): A: average levels; B: heavy levels

Sources: 1984, 1988, and 1996 NBES; 2004 NPS; 2008, 2012, and 2016 ANES.

this resurgence in consciousness translates into more progressive liberal attitudes, as suggested by Dawson (1994) and Tate (1994), is yet to be seen.

Does a Resurgence of Group Consciousness Influence Blacks' Policy Preferences?

If blacks display higher levels of linked fate, but do not alter their support for progressive racial policies, then there may be little reason to expect that this reinvigorated connection of blacks to their racial group will yield much policy change. To assess this possibility, I returned to the ANES and the GSS to explore whether blacks' levels of support for explicitly race-based policies have changed over time. In particular, I explored whether blacks were more likely to support affirmative action, to view immigrants more positively, and oppose allowing owners to discriminate when selling homes, as well as their attitudes about whether government should provide aid to blacks to address racial inequality.

Figure 5.2 presents black respondents from the period 1984–2016 and assesses their support for affirmative action using the question, "Some people say that because of past discrimination blacks should be given preference in hiring and promotion. Others say that such preference in hiring and promotion of blacks is wrong because it gives blacks advantages they haven't earned. What about your opinion—are you for or against preferential hiring and promotion of blacks?" Those who answered "yes" to this question were given a score of 1 and those who answered "no" to this question were given a score of 0. Figure 5.2 presents the average number of "yes" responses over time.

The results in figure 5.2 present evidence that blacks' position on affirmative action has improved in recent years. Unsurprisingly, a majority of blacks are supportive of affirmative action in most years. In fact, in 1990, 73 percent of blacks said that they supported the program. However, this number declined throughout the 1990s and early 2000s. In 1996, fewer than 50 percent of blacks said that they supported affirmative action. However, the percentage who supported affirmative action began to increase again in 2012. In 2016, about 69 percent of blacks supported the program, this represents about a 7 percent increase from four years earlier. This growth in support is statistically significant based on a two-sample *t*-test. Outside of 1990, when the highest percentage of blacks supported affirmative action, 2016 represents the highest level of support for the program. Moreover, there difference in the percentage of blacks who supported affirmative action in 1990 and 2016 was not statistically significant based on a two-sample *t*-test. Overall, this result seems to suggest that blacks' higher levels of linked fate do translate into more support for racial policies.

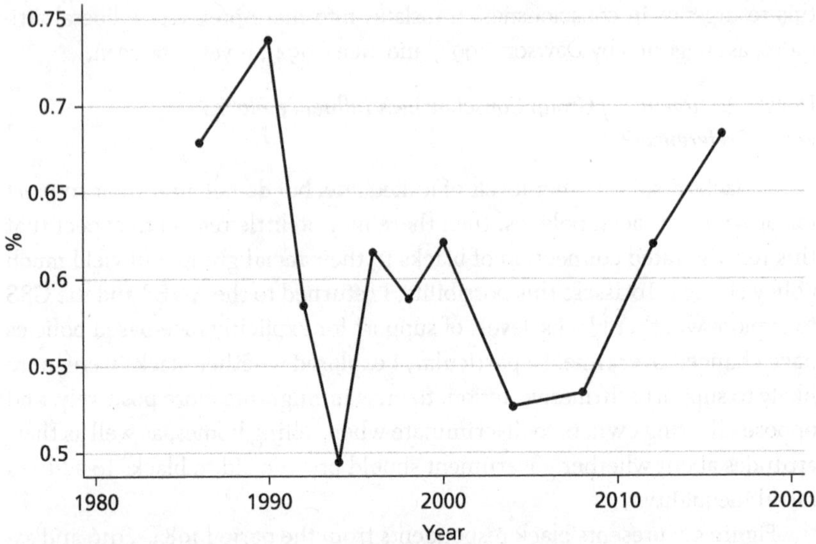

FIGURE 5.2. Blacks' support for affirmative action (1984–2016)
Source: ANES.

Figure 5.3 explores whether blacks were more supportive of government providing aid to blacks again using the ANES. The figure presents blacks' yearly average score on a seven-point scale based on the question, "Some people feel that the government in Washington should make every possible effort to improve the social and economic position of blacks (7). Others feel that the government should not make any special effort to help blacks because they should help themselves (1). Where would you place yourself on this scale?" Higher scores on this scale indicate that blacks were more supportive of public policy changes being made to improve the position of blacks in the United States. The results in figure 5.3 present somewhat of a U-shaped pattern. Blacks in the 1982 and 1984 were largely supportive of more government aid. On a seven-point scale, blacks in these years had a score of around 5.1, indicating that they were much more likely to believe that government should aid blacks given continuing racial disparities rather than that these disparities could be alleviated through hard work alone.

This average score dips to below 4 in the year 2000, indicating that blacks were more likely to believe that blacks should help themselves to achieve racial equality than they were to believe that government should aid blacks. The average score increased to about 4.7 in 2004, but then declined to about 4.5 in 2012 before shooting up to 5.1 in 2016. The difference in perceptions of aid to blacks between 2012 and 2016 is statistically significant based on a

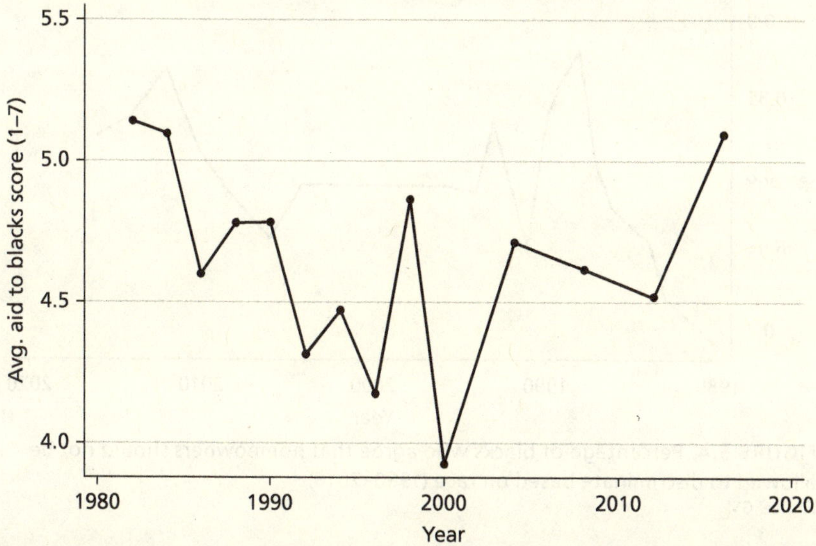

FIGURE 5.3. Blacks' average score on the "aid to blacks" scale (1–7) (1980–2016)
Source: ANES.

two-sample *t*-test. Moreover, blacks' perceptions of the government's role in addressing racial inequality in 2016 matched what they were during the 1980s, at the height of blacks' advocacy for more government intervention to address racial inequality.

Figure 5.4 explores blacks' attitudes about whether owners should be able to discriminate based on race when they sell their homes. This question is measured using the GSS, which asks, "Suppose there is a community-wide vote on the general housing issue. There are two possible laws to vote on 1: 'The Owner Decides' or 2: 'The Owner Can't Discriminate Based on Race.' Which law would you vote for?" The question was asked for all years between 1980 and 2016. I recoded this variable so that "The Owner Can't Discriminate Based on Race" was given a score of 1 and "The Owner Decides" was given a score of 0.

Figure 5.4 presents some evidence that attitudes about housing discrimination did not become more racially progressive in 2016 for blacks. While blacks became more supportive of affirmative action and government aid to blacks in the latter stages of the Obama presidency, they were not more likely to believe that homeowners should be prohibited in discriminating in 2016 than they were in years past. However, it is important to note that there may be a ceiling effect on this variable, whereby there is not much room to improve. For example, in 2012, 86.8 percent of black respondents

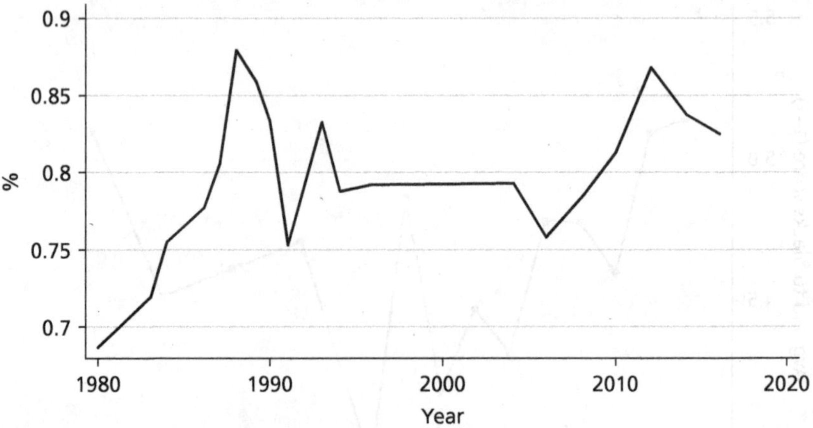

FIGURE 5.4. Percentage of blacks who agree that homeowners should not be allowed to discriminate based on race (1980–2016)
Source: GSS.

felt that owners should not be able discriminate based on race. This number decreased by about 4 percent to 82.5 percent in 2016. However, this decline is not statistically significant based on a two-sample *t*-test. Thus, blacks still overwhelmingly disapprove of discrimination in home selling. However, there was not a large amount of growth in this area, unlike attitudes about the role of government found in the previous set of questions presented in figures 5.2 and 5.3.

Blacks are not only becoming more racially liberal on issues concerning their racial group, they also appear to be becoming more supportive of immigration. While some have argued that immigration drives a wedge between blacks, Latinos, and the Democratic Party (see McClain et al. 2006), the results in figure 5.5 demonstrate that blacks are much more likely to view immigrants as strengthening the nation in recent years. Figure 5.5 is derived from a series of six Pew polls from 2006, 2010, 2013, 2014, 2015, and 2016. In these surveys, Pew said to respondents, "As I read each pair, tell me whether the first statement or the second statement comes closer to your own views—even if neither is exactly right. . . . Immigrants today strengthen our country because of their hard work and talents, immigrants today are a burden on our country because they take our jobs, housing and health care." For each year, those who stated that immigrants strengthened our country were given a score of 1 and those who viewed immigrants as being a burden on our country were given a score of 0. Respondents who stated they were unsure were excluded from the analysis.

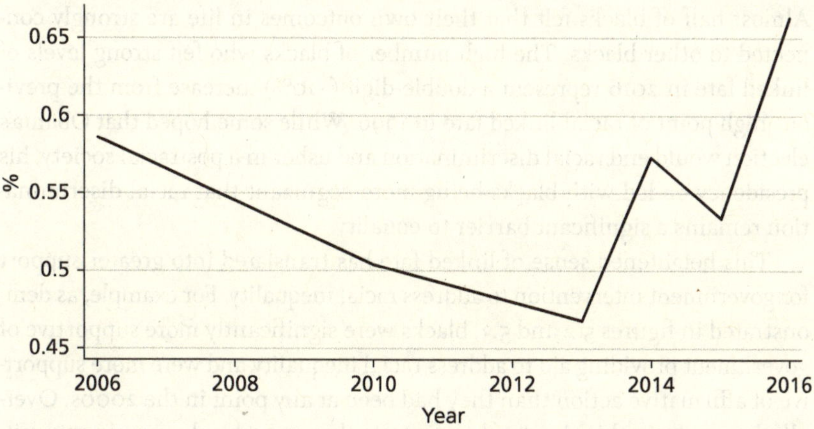

FIGURE 5.5. Percentage of blacks who agree that immigrants improve society (2006–16)
Source: Pew Research Center.

Figure 5.5 presents the percentage of blacks who agreed with the statement "Immigrants strengthen the United States" at multiple points in time between 2006 and 2016 based on Pew Research Center polling. The figure shows that a majority of blacks have always felt that immigrants strengthen the nation. However, in 2016 more blacks agreed with this statement than before. Moreover, in just a four-year period between 2012 and 2016 blacks' perceptions of immigrants improving the nation increased by over 10 percent. In 2016, a supermajority (67%) of blacks agreed that immigrants strengthen the United States. The results suggest that the current political climate may make it easier for the Democratic Party to appeal to Latinos without sacrificing black voters. In fact, such appeals may improve the party's standing with the black community.

Conclusion

The results of this chapter demonstrate that blacks returned to a state of high linked fate in the latter part of the Obama administration. Moreover, in many cases this return to consciousness correlates with more support for a racially progressive agenda. While there was a lot of research published in the 2000s demonstrating the decline of black group consciousness, the teens of the new millennium have led to a reawakening of racial linked fate. Through a series of dramatic events, blacks have become more cognizant of the role that race plays in shaping their social and political outcomes. This has led blacks to have a heightened sense of connection to others who share their race.

Almost half of blacks felt that their own outcomes in life are strongly connected to other blacks. The high number of blacks who felt strong levels of linked fate in 2016 represent a double-digit (~10%) increase from the previous high point of racial linked fate in 1996. While some hoped that Obama's election would end racial discrimination and usher in a postracial society, his presidency ended with blacks being more cognizant that racial discrimination remains a significant barrier to equality.

This heightened sense of linked fate has translated into greater support for government intervention to address racial inequality. For example, as demonstrated in figures 5.2 and 5.3, blacks were significantly more supportive of government providing aid to address racial inequality and were more supportive of affirmative action than they had been at any point in the 2000s. Overall, the results in this chapter demonstrate that many blacks remain committed to addressing racial inequality. These results suggest that candidates who want to maximize their support among the black electorate may be able to do so by demonstrating their willingness to address racial disparities rather than ignore it, as suggested by the deracialization strategy. In the following chapter, I will explore this possibility by assessing whether black voters are more supportive of candidates whom they perceive as addressing racial inequality.

6
The Increasing Importance of Racial Appeals for Black Voters

In 2002, two African Americans, Harvard-educated assistant U.S. attorney Artur Davis and Democratic congressman and former civil rights activist Earl F. Hilliard faced off for Alabama's seventh district congressional seat. The campaign exemplified the changes in black politics that were occurring in the early 2000s. On one hand, Davis represented what political scientist Andra Gillespie (2010) has described as the "Ivy League Upstarts," whose path into politics was comparable to the average white politician. These candidates graduated from prestigious colleges and law schools, took centrist positions on salient political issues, and deemphasized race in their campaigns. On the other hand, Hilliard represented the traditional black politician. Hilliard's roots were in the civil rights movement; he was for the most part ideologically liberal and focused on race in his campaigns for elected office. In essence, the campaign pitted the old school black politician against the new school black politician. In the end, Davis succeeded because he was able to put together a large enough coalition of younger blacks and liberal whites.

Given Davis's deracialized campaign strategy, it was surprising that he did so well with the black electorate. Many scholars argue that a deracialized campaign approach should help candidates attract white voters, but the trade-off is that it often leads to lower levels of support in the black community. The campaign of Davis and those of others like him demonstrated that during the late 1990s and 2000s the thinking that black voters may have a strong preference for racialized candidates may no longer apply. In particular, as blacks had become more racially conservative and declined in their sense of racial consciousness, their preference for deracialized politicians increased (see Gillespie 2012; McIlwain and Caliendo 2011; Tate 2010). This made running a deracialized campaign less of risky strategy. The approach allowed deracialized candidates to appeal to white voters without sacrificing black support. In essence, the deracialized approach allowed candidates to have their cake and eat it too.

However, if blacks' levels of group consciousness have rebounded in recent years and they have become more cognizant of racial discrimination as a severe problem (see chapters 1 and 5), then a deracialized approach may no longer be as attractive to black voters as it was during the pre-Obama/early Obama years. As blacks become more aware of racial discrimination and more supportive of a racially progressive agenda, they may become more likely to reject deracialized politicians who they perceive as not caring enough about these topics.

This speaks to the significance of accountability to black voters. As blacks have increasingly felt alienated by political parties and growing levels of racial inequality (Frymer 1999; Harris 2012), many black leaders have pushed government officials to be more accountable to black interests if they want to receive black votes. Walters (2007) describes black political accountability as politicians demonstrating that they will champion issues that are most directly relevant to the black community. When politicians appear unconcerned about racial issues, blacks with higher levels of racial consciousness question the benefits they will derive from individuals from their preferred party being elected and are less enthusiastic to support their campaign. As black voters grow in racial consciousness and become more important players in the Democratic Party, finding ways to motivate and attract their support may be essential for the party to succeed. As such, knowing whether racially progressive Democratic candidates engage black voters significantly more than deracialized candidates is crucial.

In this chapter, I explore whether black voters prefer candidates who appear as racially progressive. I begin by reviewing literature on how black voters respond to candidates who make deracialized and racialized campaign appeals. From this review, I will argue that as blacks became more racially conservative in the mid-1990s and early 2000s their preference for deracialized candidates increased. However, given changes in the current political context, blacks are again displaying strong preferences for candidates whom they perceive as aiding the black community.

To test this hypothesis, I will explore the connection between perceived racially liberal ideology and vote choice in presidential elections between 1980 and 2016 and recent competitive Democratic presidential primaries using the American National Election Studies (ANES). Moreover, I will use a survey experiment with an oversample of black respondents to test whether blacks prefer coracial or white politicians who take either a racially liberal or an economically liberal approach. Across these analyses, I find evidence that blacks in recent years are much more motivated to turn out and be supportive of Democratic candidates whom they believe are racially liberal. The results of this chapter demonstrate that candidates who engage in racial appeals do improve their standing with black voters and do a much better job mobilizing this electorate.

The Rise of Deracialization

In his seminal article on deracialization, Charles V. Hamilton (1977) notes that the deracialization strategy may not be successful in a majority-black setting because it may upset black voters. Moreover, in their work on deracialization, McCormick and Jones (1993) warn that candidates who run an overtly deracialized campaign may face a backlash from black voters who feel ignored. The warnings that a deracialized campaign may hamper a candidate's ability to attract black support played out in several elections in the 1980s and early 1990s. For example, Atlanta mayor Andrew Young failed in his 1990 bid for the Georgia governorship in large part due to his lackluster support from black voters. In spite of his background in the civil rights movement, Young's inability to excite the black community was attributed by many to his deracialized campaign approach and focus on the white electorate (Pierannunzi and Hutcheson 1991). Similarly, in 1982 Los Angeles Democratic mayor Tom Bradley was defeated by about 1 percent of votes in an extremely competitive campaign. Again, analysis performed after the election attributed Bradley's defeat to his strategy of distancing himself from the black community, which led to lackluster minority turnout (Pettigrew and Alston 1988). These studies suggest that black voters preferred racialized over deracialized candidates in the 1980s and early 1990s.

However, by the late 1990s and 2000s it appeared that deracialized candidates were no longer being punished by black voters. In fact, during this period there were several high-profile examples of deracialized candidates performing well with African Americans. Bill Clinton in the 1990s took a number of steps to distance himself from racial issues by chastising hip-hop artist and activist Sister Souljah and supporting welfare reform. Despite these deracialized tactics, Clinton was extremely popular in the black community (Wickham 2004). Moreover, others argue that Obama's deracialized campaign did little to disengage black voters, who remained supportive of him in spite of his lack of racial appeals (Harris 2012).

McIlwain and Caliendo (2011) conducted a nationally representative experiment of black voters, exploring how they respond to racialized and deracialized appeals. The authors found that contrary to expectations, black voters in the late 2000s preferred deracialized candidates to their racialized counterparts. McIlwain and Caliendo's (2011) research demonstrated that deracialized candidates may actually perform better among blacks than their racialized counterparts, with all else being equal.

Why would a deracialized approach turn off black voters in the 1980s and early 1990s but not in later years? Research that argued that deracialized candidates could perform well among blacks focused on the growing racial moderation in the black community and the increasing interest among blacks to increase black representation in government. As the previous chapters have demonstrated, during the George W. Bush and Obama years, blacks' attitudes about the salience of race in their lives decreased. Thus, politicians who focused on race may have been perceived as disingenuous and as only using racial divisions to propel themselves into elected office. Hajnal (2006) and McIlwain and Caliendo (2011) argue that racial appeals generally operate to remind blacks that they are a distinct group who faces unique challenges. McIlwain and Caliendo (2011) argue that these appeals are most effective when black voters have a strong sense of group consciousness and are concerned about their racial group's position in society. However, in cases where racial group consciousness is low among blacks, as it was in the 2000s and early 2010s, then a racialized approach may be less effective. The combination of these factors may have led to lower levels of black support for racialized candidates in the early twenty-first century.

Moreover, some argue that blacks are willing to compromise policy representation to ensure that someone who shares their values is in elected office (Harris 2012). Several political scientists have argued that a large proportion of blacks understand that for coracial and copartisan individuals to succeed outside of majority-minority districts they would have to minimize their connection to the black community (Harris 2012; McCormick and Jones 1993; R. Smith 1990). Many blacks were willing to make this compromise, given their lower levels of group consciousness during the early Obama years. Harris (2012) argues that many black voters supported Obama even though he did not expressly campaign on racial issues because they hoped that his presence in the White House would ultimately lead to positive changes. Along the same lines, candidates who engage in racial appeals may not be perceived as competitive (Stout 2015). If competitiveness is a necessary condition for liberal candidates to inspire higher levels of black turnout (see Keele et al. 2017), then it is possible that candidates—and especially black candidates—who engage in racial appeals may not generate much excitement around their candidacy and not mobilize blacks.

The Fall of Deracialization

Several changes to the political context in recent years may have made racial appeals more important to black voters. The growth in black representation following Hamilton's (1977) article in combination with disappointment in the pace of change in race relations provides a context where black voters may hold liberal and coracial politicians more accountable. This may be particularly true as blacks have now held all major positions of power in government, from mayoral offices to governors' offices and from Congress to the White House; the barriers have been broken across government. However, in spite of the success of black politicians, blacks as a group have faced significant setbacks. For example, Obama's early years in the White House overlapped with some of the highest levels of black unemployment since the 1980s. At the same time, blacks as a group were more likely to have their homes foreclosed than their white counterparts, as the racial divide in poverty and wealth grew significantly.

Outside of national politics, blacks faced significant challenges in many cities. At the same time that blacks and Democrats were reliably winning mayoral offices in most large cities, many businesses moved out of the cities and into the suburbs. The resulting changes in population patterns brought with them declining tax revenue in cities. Friesema (1969) labeled the newfound success of blacks and white Democrats in cities as a hollow prize. While liberals were gaining political power, they no longer had the resources to help improve the situation of black voters.

Structural limitations aside, black and liberal elected officials were perceived as being unable or unwilling to advance black political interest (Gillion 2016; Owens and Brown 2014; Spence and McClerking 2010). This change led several scholars to identify a disempowerment effect among black voters in cities. As Hamilton (1977) had suggested, a deracialized campaign must be met with pressure among blacks to ensure that government officials are responsive: "The real burden of a de-racialized strategy, in fact, is not to lay one's self open to having been coopted, but require continued diligent political mobilization to be able to reward and punish" (4). Hamilton's (1977) arguments may be most applicable to the current period where blacks have seen numerous black and Democratic politicians in elected office since the 1980s but have seen their position in society worsen. The growing realization among many blacks that the racial dynamic in the United States has worsened may make them less supportive of candidates who they feel take their vote for granted.

Racialization and Mobilization

To ensure that liberal politicians are serious about addressing racial inequality, many blacks may withdraw from participating in elections when these candidates ignore race in their campaigns. Conversely, there are good reasons to believe that black voters may feel more energized when candidates are perceived as being more racially liberal. Individuals often make decisions about their levels of political activity based on the perceived benefits they would receive should their preferred candidate be elected (Blais 2000; Downs 1957). When voters perceive neither candidate as representing their political interest or working hard for individuals like themselves, they are much more likely to not only avoid voting, but also to drop out of the political system entirely (Piven and Cloward 1980). Wattenberg (2002), for example, shows that young Americans largely abstain from electoral politics because they perceive neither of the two major parties as caring about individuals like themselves. When individuals perceive neither party/candidate as being empathetic nor concerned with their position, it is not surprising that they would distance themselves from governmental affairs.

Conversely, there is evidence that suggests that voters are particularly mobilized when a candidate devotes significant outreach efforts to individuals with deeply held identities. Former president George W. Bush's public appeals to religious voters through his personal narrative as a born-again Christian is argued to have inspired a significant growth in turnout among Christian voters in 2004 (Hillygus and Shields 2005). Christian voters were more enthusiastic about Bush's candidacy because they believed he had a better understanding of the religious community. Additionally, Marcus and MacKuen (1993) demonstrated that voters are much more participatory in campaign activities when they are more enthusiastic about their party's nominee for elected office. This level of enthusiasm is partially driven by perceptions that the candidate is sympathetic to voters like themselves (Marcus and MacKuen 1993).

Similar to these studies, there is evidence that suggests blacks make decisions about whether to participate based on the level of concern candidates/parties show for individuals like themselves (Dawson 1994; Hajnal and Lee 2011; Kaufmann 2004; Tate 1991). Tate (1991), for example, argues that black voter turnout decreased significantly in the 1988 general election because blacks felt that the Democratic Party did not show enough concern for black voters through their poor treatment of Jesse Jackson. Similarly, Kaufmann (2004) hypothesized that black turnout decreased in the 2001 New York mayoral election because the Democratic nominee, Mark Green, was not perceived as a sympathetic figure in the black community.

Why would candidates working to advance blacks' interests increase their levels of political participation? Moreover, why would a racialized approach matter more now than before? Blacks' long sociohistorical legacy of discrimination in the United States and greater recognition of racial inequality in recent years has led many to see their political advancement as individuals as tied to the advancement of their racial group (Dawson 1994; Tate 1994). As demonstrated in chapter 5, this sense of linked fate was significantly higher in 2016 than it was at any point in the past thirty years.

As a result, blacks may be much more likely to vote and be enthusiastic about candidates whom they perceive as caring about individuals like themselves. An empathetic candidate may be expected to be more interested in improving conditions for African Americans and, by extension, such work should advance the position of blacks. This may be especially crucial in a period where blacks are increasingly concerned about their position in society. As a result, the potential benefits derived from the election of a candidate who is vocal about addressing racial inequality should motivate blacks to become more involved in politics.

Racialization and Vote Choice

Unlike whites, who have always included significant, if varying, numbers of swing voters, blacks as a group have been extremely loyal to the Democratic Party since the 1964 Civil Rights Act. So much so that some have argued that black voters are loyal to the Democratic Party to a fault (Frymer 1999). As a result, whether a candidate is perceived to be racially liberal or not should not alters black voter support in presidential elections. Regardless of their levels of racialization, every Democratic presidential nominee over the past thirty years has received over 85 percent of the two-major-party black vote. Most blacks feel that regardless of how much or little the Democratic Party addresses racial inequality, the Republican Party is not a viable alternative (Frymer 1999; Philpot 2009). As a result, racial appeals may be effective in mobilizing blacks but are unlikely to alter vote choice in elections between Democratic and Republican candidates.

However, in cases where partisanship is held constant, such as in nonpartisan elections or primaries, it is likely that black voters will prefer the candidate who actively appeals to the black community over a deracialized candidate. In the 2010 Alabama Democratic gubernatorial primary, for example, black voters supported white candidate Ron Sparks over the coracial candidate Artur Davis in large part because Sparks was more vocal about addressing racial inequality in the state. This result indicates blacks' growing preference for substantive representation even outweighs the opportunity to expand black representation. Given growing concerns in the black community that the deck is stacked against them, many may feel that the best way to alleviate this problem is to support politicians who actively address inequality. Thus, if blacks have a choice between a racially liberal and racially conservative

Democrat, they should display a strong preference for the racially progressive candidate.

Data and Analysis from the American National Election Study

To explore the impact that perceptions of racial progressivism have on vote choice and turnout for African Americans, I will return to the ANES. The ANES include a measure of perceptions of how racially progressive a Democratic candidate is using a question that asks respondents, "Some people feel that the government in Washington should make every effort to improve the social and economic position of blacks. Suppose these people are at one end of a scale, at point 1. Others feel that the government should not make any special effort to help blacks because they should help themselves. Suppose these people are at the other end, at point 7. And, of course, some other people have opinions somewhere in between, at points 2, 3, 4, 5, or 6. Where would you place [Democratic presidential nominee] on this scale?" I recoded this scale so that a score of 7 indicates that the voter perceives the candidate to believe that government should provide aid to blacks and a score of 1 indicates the voter believes that blacks should help themselves.

While it is unlikely that perceptions of candidates' racial progressivity will matter in blacks' presidential election vote choice, it is possible that the use of racial appeals may improve a candidate's ability to attract black voter support in the Democratic presidential primaries, where the party of the candidates is held constant. To test the relationship between perceived candidate racial liberalism and vote choice, I begin by analyzing the ANES for the Democratic presidential primaries of 1988, 2008, and 2016. As mentioned in chapter 4, I use these years because vote intention for the Democratic primaries was not asked of respondents outside of this time frame. In addition to the primaries, I also explore vote choice in the presidential election for all years between 1980 and 2016.

For the primaries, my dependent variable measures support for the winning candidate on a dichotomous scale (1 = voted for the winning Democratic candidate in the primary, 0 = voted for a candidate other than the winning Democratic candidate in the primary). For the presidential election, I coded those who voted for the Democratic candidate as being a 1 and those who voted for someone else as having a score of 0. My final dependent variable for this section is whether the respondent reported voting in the presidential election in any given year. This is a binary variable; respondents who reported voting were given a score of 1, and those who did not were given a score of 0.

It is important to note that the aforementioned dependent variables are self-reported measures of various forms of political participation. The self-reported nature of the ANES combined with incentives for respondents to overstate their political activity has often led to large gulfs between reported and actual behavior (see Ansolabehere and Hersh 2012; Silver, Anderson, and Abramson 1986). Nonetheless, there are reasons to believe that the examination of differences in political participation in this analysis will not be diminished too much because of problems with social desirability response bias. My dependent variables measure change in political behavior over time using the *same* survey (i.e., the ANES). While blacks may be more likely to overstate their levels of political participation, a problem would only arise if they were systematically more likely to do so in years where they perceived the Democratic candidate as being more racially progressive. While multiple factors may influence when voters overstate participation, perceptions of racial progressivity alone are unlikely to exert additional pressure to lead respondents to lie about voting.

Given that many factors influence turnout and vote choice, I control for several variables. First, I control for the socioeconomic status of the respondent. Previous research demonstrates that voters with higher levels of income and education are much more likely to report voting than their lower-socioeconomic-status counterparts (Harris, Sinclair-Chapman, and McKenzie 2005). I also control for gender as black women tend to be much more politically active and liberal than black men (Brown 2014). Beyond demographic characteristics, I control for the partisanship of the respondent on a seven-point scale that ranges from 1 (Strong Democrat) to 7 (Strong Republican). Additionally, I control for whether the respondent was contacted by a political campaign during the presidential election. Previous research has identified campaign contact as one of the most important predictors of turnout in elections and vote choice (Goldstein and Ridout 2002). Finally, I control for whether the respondent resided in the South. Given the tumultuous racial history of the southern region of the United States, this control is necessary.

ANES Results

Table 6.1 presents the results from three separate logit regression models predicting the effect of perceptions of Democratic candidates' racial liberalism on vote choice for the leading candidate in the Democratic presidential primaries in 1988 (Michael Dukakis), 2008 (Barack Obama), and 2016 (Hillary Clinton). The results of this analysis demonstrate that in 2016, blacks' perceptions of Clinton as being racially liberal significantly increased their likelihood of voting for her. In fact, holding all else equal, blacks who viewed Clinton as being the most racially liberal were about 30 percent more likely

TABLE 6.1. Logit regression predicting support for the leading Democratic presidential nominee candidate in the 1988, 2008, and 2016 Democratic presidential primaries

	Vote for Dukakis (1988)	Vote for Obama (2008)	Vote for H. Clinton (2016)
Candidate's "aid to blacks" score	0.20 (0.27)	0.05 (0.09)	0.37** (0.14)
Female	0.28 (0.98)	−0.27 (0.36)	0.30 (0.47)
Age	0.06** (0.03)	−0.00 (0.01)	0.08*** (0.02)
Income	0.00 (0.02)	0.00 (0.01)	−0.01 (0.01)
Education	0.22 (0.17)	0.05 (0.10)	−0.10 (0.11)
South	0.88 (0.94)	0.26 (0.34)	0.64 (0.44)
Constant	−9.59*** (3.47)	0.41 (1.49)	−2.26 (1.65)
Observations	94	211	177

Source: ANES.

Note: Only individuals who participated in the Democratic primaries in these years are included in the models.

* $p<0.1$; ** $p<0.05$; *** $p<0.01$; standard errors in parentheses.

to vote for her over her competitors in the 2016 Democratic presidential primaries. In contrast, perceptions of the racial liberalism of neither Obama in 2008 nor Dukakis in 1988 were significant predictors of black vote choice in these years. This result suggests that in the most recent primary elections the racially liberal candidate had an advantage over others who shared their partisanship.

Table 6.2 presents the results from several logit regressions predicting support for the Democratic presidential candidate in the general elections for black respondents only. Unfortunately, for many years in the ANES there was neither enough variation in vote choice nor an adequate number of black voters to estimate black support for the Democratic candidate in the presidential election. Thus, I estimate support for the Democratic presidential candidate only in 1984, 2004, 2012, and 2016. The results of the analysis demonstrate that blacks are mostly not significantly more likely to support the Demo-

TABLE 6.2. Logit regression predicting black support for the Democratic presidential nominee (1980–2016)

	Vote for Democratic presidential candidate			
Year	1984	2004	2012	2016
Candidate's "aid to blacks" score	0.36	−0.15	−1.04**	2.22
	(0.28)	(0.26)	(0.42)	(1.57)
Female	0.27	−0.72	2.21**	0.78
	(0.77)	(1.58)	(0.94)	(1.62)
Age	−0.05	−0.09*	−0.04	−0.31
	(0.03)	(0.05)	(0.03)	(0.19)
Income	−0.11	−0.87	0.37	0.56
	(0.65)	(2.27)	(0.44)	(1.46)
Education	−0.22	−0.46	−0.34*	−1.96*
	(0.15)	(0.39)	(0.18)	(1.17)
7-point PID	−0.24	−1.31***	−1.86***	−4.54*
	(0.31)	(0.34)	(0.36)	(2.58)
South	0.33	−2.04	−1.86	2.81***
	(0.81)	(4.66)	(1.58)	(0.99)
Campaign contact	−0.84		−2.69***	
	(1.18)		(1.01)	
Ideology	−0.11	0.02	−2.10***	−4.70**
	(0.17)	(0.67)	(0.49)	(2.33)
Constant	6.38**	23.16**	32.42***	69.24*
	(3.18)	(10.26)	(6.20)	(38.13)
Observations	67	54	612	129

Source: ANES.

* $p<0.1$; ** $p<0.05$; *** $p<0.01$; standard errors in parentheses; PID = Party Identification.

cratic presidential nominee when he or she is perceived as being more racially liberal in the presidential election. The one exception to this is in 2012. In this year, blacks who perceived Obama as being the most racially liberal were 10 percent less likely to support him. This suggests that during a period when blacks had the lowest levels of linked fate and most optimism about a postracial society, black candidates like Obama could be punished for appearing as racially liberal. However, in most years and including 2016, perceptions of racial liberalism did not alter blacks' vote choice. Given blacks' high levels of support for the Democratic Party in the presidential election, racialization may not matter too much for Democratic candidates in persuading blacks who turn out at the polls.

Table 6.3 presents eight logit regression models predicting whether a respondent reported voting in the presidential election in that year. The models only include black respondents. The results provide support for my argument that black voters respond to perceptions of the candidate's racial progressiveness and that this has been most likely to occur in recent years. Perceptions of the Democratic candidate's support for government to provide aid to blacks was a significant predictor of black turnout in 2012 and 2016 only. All else being equal, moving from the minimum to the maximum perception of Hillary Clinton being racially liberal increased the likelihood that a black respondent would report voting by 14 percent in 2016. In 2012, the impact of the perceived racial liberalism of Obama increased a black respondent's likelihood of voting by 9 percent. Overall, the results of my analysis provide support for the claim that in recent elections candidates who were perceived as being more racially liberal increased turnout among black voters. As a result, it appears that candidates may be able to maximize black turnout by working to appeal to the black community. Moreover, this appears to be true for both black candidates like Obama and white candidates like Clinton.

Latino Racial Appeals

The results in the preceding section demonstrate that Democratic candidates who appear as being racially liberal are better able to mobilize black voters and gain their support in presidential primaries. The analyses focused on appeals that are directly related to blacks; the measure of racial liberalism in the previous section explicitly mentions how the candidate is perceived on providing aid to blacks. The Democratic Party often makes appeals that are directed at Latinos or Asian Americans as well. How blacks respond to these appeals is unknown but plays a large role in the Democratic Party's strategy to build multiracial coalitions.

To test blacks' reactions to racial appeals that are not centered on their interests, table 6.4 presents a logit regression predicting approval for Obama (1 = approve, 0 = oppose) before and after he made the high-profile announcement to shield parents of undocumented children known as Dreamers from deportation in 2014 (see chapter 4 for more information about this action). Similar to the analysis in chapter 4, the logit regression model in table 6.4 combines two Pew Research Center surveys from about two weeks before and after Obama made the announcement. These surveys allow me to test whether Obama's level of support in the black community changed after he made this announcement. Given that blacks are much less likely to be immigrants than are Latinos and Asian Americans, an assessment of how they respond to

TABLE 6.3. Logit regression predicting self-reported black voter turnout (1980–2016)

	Voted in presidential election							
Year	1980	1984	1988	1996	2004	2008	2012	2016
Candidate's "aid to blacks" score	–0.69**	–0.09	–0.09	–0.18	0.01	0.10	0.26**	0.33***
	(0.33)	(0.18)	(0.15)	(0.20)	(0.19)	(0.12)	(0.10)	(0.12)
Female	0.06	0.97	–0.06	0.83	0.80	0.27	–0.00	1.22**
	(1.02)	(0.61)	(0.57)	(0.64)	(0.78)	(0.45)	(0.36)	(0.52)
Age	0.03	0.03	0.02	0.07**	0.02	0.02	0.03***	0.02
	(0.03)	(0.02)	(0.02)	(0.03)	(0.02)	(0.01)	(0.01)	(0.01)
Income	0.14	0.39	–0.03	0.05	1.00***	0.61**	0.41***	1.04***
	(0.34)	(0.29)	(0.24)	(0.39)	(0.32)	(0.26)	(0.16)	(0.29)
Education	0.23	0.22*	0.23*	0.66***	–0.07	0.07	0.28***	0.12
	(0.28)	(0.13)	(0.13)	(0.22)	(0.14)	(0.11)	(0.10)	(0.12)
7-point PID	–0.40	–0.35	–0.46**	–0.16	0.09	–0.38**	–0.58***	–0.36**
	(0.31)	(0.24)	(0.20)	(0.31)	(0.30)	(0.16)	(0.12)	(0.16)
South	0.35	–0.01	–1.16**	–0.14	0.53	–0.32	–0.42	–0.47
	(0.91)	(0.58)	(0.56)	(0.66)	(0.68)	(0.47)	(0.39)	(0.48)
Ideology	0.26	–0.10	–0.18	0.30	0.04	–0.17	–0.06	0.69***
	(0.31)	(0.19)	(0.18)	(0.23)	(0.24)	(0.14)	(0.12)	(0.19)
Campaign contact		0.06		–0.13	–0.04	0.41	0.31	0.72
		(0.86)		(0.99)	(0.92)	(0.61)	(0.56)	(0.68)
Constant	0.06	–2.54	0.08	–10.81***	–2.40	–0.25	–3.55**	–6.88***
	(5.36)	(2.28)	(2.57)	(4.19)	(2.58)	(1.69)	(1.38)	(1.95)
Observations	48	93	96	82	79	233	714	214

Source: ANES.

* $p<0.1$; ** $p<0.05$; *** $p<0.01$; standard errors in parentheses; PID = Party Identification.

TABLE 6.4. Logit regression predicting whether black respondents approved (1) or disapproved (0) of Obama before (Nov. 2014) and after (Dec. 2014) his DAPA announcement

	Obama approval rating
After DAPA announcement	−0.02
	(0.40)
Female	−0.15
	(0.41)
Age	0.02
	(0.01)
Income	−0.20*
	(0.11)
Education	0.10
	(0.13)
Democrat	1.52***
	(0.46)
Republican	−0.80
	(0.82)
Constant	0.94
	(0.78)
Observations	238

Source: Pew Research Center.
* $p<0.1$; ** $p<0.05$; *** $p<0.01$; standard errors in parentheses.

Obama's outreach to these groups will provide information about whether racial appeals toward Latinos or Asian Americans can improve left-leaning candidates' standing with the black community.

The results of the logit regression presented in table 6.4 suggest that a direct appeal to Latinos and Asian Americans did not statistically significantly shift blacks' approval of Obama. This result may in part be driven by blacks' high levels of approval for the first black president, which provides little room to grow. However, it also demonstrates that direct appeals to Latinos and Asian Americans from the Democratic Party do not dampen support among blacks. This indicates that the party will not face a significant backlash from blacks for appealing to other racial/ethnic groups that some have argued are perceived as rivals by the black community (see McClain et al. 2006).

Experimental Analysis

In addition to using observational data gathered by the ANES and Pew Research Center, I also examined whether black respondents would be more motivated to turn out in an election for a candidate whose website focuses on racial justice as opposed to a candidate who focuses on economic justice using an online experiment. I also use this experiment to assess whether individuals are more likely to support a racialized or deracialized candidate against candidates of the same party and those of a different party. As a reminder (see the introduction and chapter 4 for more detail), I implemented an online survey on Amazon Mechanical Turk and presented respondents with one of four treatments. The first half of respondents were presented with either a candidate with a white-sounding name (Wyatt McHarris) or a candidate with a black-sounding name (Malik Jackson), both of whose webpages focused on racial justice. In particular, these candidates advocated for strengthening the Voting Rights Act, addressing the criminal justice system, protecting immigrant rights, and advocating for comprehensive immigration reform. The other half of respondents were presented with either Wyatt McHarris or Malik Jackson, but this time the candidates' webpages advocated for economic justice in the form of strengthening the national labor relations act, fixing the financial system, protecting workers' rights, and advocating for a living wage. The former condition represents a racialized appeal and the latter represents a deracialized appeal.

To measure intention to vote, the respondents were asked, "If Malik Jackson/Wyatt McHarris runs for President in 2020, how likely are you to engage in the following activities around his campaign: Vote?" The response scale ranged from 1 (extremely unlikely) to 5 (extremely likely). The main independent variable for this model was whether the respondent received the racial justice treatment or the economic treatment. I also varied the race of the candidate to test whether black voters respond differently to racial appeals made by black versus white candidates. As a result, in addition to testing whether voters respond differently to the same set of candidates who make racial appeals, I also disaggregated candidates by their race to assess whether blacks respond uniquely to racial appeals made by coracial individuals.

In addition to turnout, I also analyzed the efficacy of racial appeals on vote choice using the aforementioned experiment comparing the hypothetical candidates Wyatt McHarris or Malik Jackson when they focused on either racial issues or economic issues (i.e., deracialized issues). To explore whether racial appeals improve a candidate's likelihood of succeeding in the primaries,

I asked respondents whether they would prefer my hypothetical candidates to Hillary Clinton or Bernie Sanders in a 2020 Democratic primary matchup. To assess the effect of racialization in the general election, I asked respondents to select between my hypothetical candidate and either Donald Trump or Mitt Romney in a hypothetical 2020 matchup.

The selection of opponents explored the effect of racial appeals relative to deracialized appeals on vote choice in matchups between well-known moderate candidates (Hillary Clinton and Mitt Romney) and well-known ideologically extreme candidates (Bernie Sanders and Donald Trump). Because there were no imbalances in key independent variables due to the random assignment of the treatments, I simply present the results of the *t*-tests comparing how well the racialized candidates performed relative to the deracialized candidates.

Experimental Results

Table 6.5 presents the average level of support black respondents gave to candidates who did racialize (i.e., focused on racial justice on their webpage) and candidates who didn't racialize (i.e., focused on economic justice on their webpage) against potential primary challengers and opponents in hypothetical 2020 presidential election matchups. The table disaggregates responses for the white candidate (Wyatt McHarris), the black candidate (Malik Jackson), and both candidates combined. In particular, table 6.5 compares the average level of black support for the hypothetical candidates by issue type against Hillary Clinton. The table also compares these same candidates in a hypothetical 2020 Democratic presidential primary matchup against Bernie Sanders, as well as in potential 2020 presidential election matchups against Donald Trump and Mitt Romney.

The results in table 6.5 provide support for the hypothesis that racialized candidates tend to perform better among blacks during primaries, but do not have an advantage in the presidential election. According to the results, both the racial justice and economic justice candidates were preferred to Hillary Clinton, regardless of the race of the candidate. In a hypothetical matchup against Clinton in 2020, 78 percent of blacks selected the candidates who focused on racial issues. In contrast, 63 percent of blacks supported the same candidates when they focused on economic justice. This 15 percent difference was statistically significant based on a two-sample *t*-test.

The largest effect appears to be for black candidates who racialize against those who do not. Malik Jackson performed 23 percent better when he focused on racial issues against Hillary Clinton than the same-race candidate who focused on nonracial issues. This difference is statistically significant at

TABLE 6.5. Differences in stated support for hypothetical candidates Wyatt McHarris and Malik Jackson when they are presented as racialized or deracialized candidates and pitted against Hillary Clinton, Bernie Sanders, Donald Trump, and Mitt Romney in hypothetical 2020 matchups

	Clinton					
	Both	*N*	Jackson	*N*	McHarris	*N*
Deracialized candidate	0.63 (0.04)	134	0.57 (0.06)	63	0.69 (0.06)	71
Racialized candidate	0.78 (0.04)	113	0.8 (0.06)	50	0.76 (0.05)	63
Difference	**−0.14* (0.06)**	**247**	**−0.23* (0.09)**	**113**	**−0.07 (0.08)**	**134**
	Sanders					
	Both	*N*	Jackson	*N*	McHarris	*N*
Deracialized candidate	0.32 (0.04)	134	0.25 (0.06)	63	0.38 (0.06)	71
Racialized candidate	0.42 (0.05)	113	0.32 (0.07)	50	0.51 (0.06)	63
Difference	**−0.1+ (0.06)**	**247**	**−0.07 (0.09)**	**113**	**−0.13 (0.09)**	**134**
	Trump					
	Both	*N*	Jackson	*N*	McHarris	*N*
Deracialized candidate	0.84 (0.03)	134	0.9 (0.04)	63	0.79 (0.05)	71
Racialized candidate	0.87 (0.03)	113	0.84 (0.05)	50	0.89 (0.04)	63
Difference	**−0.02 (0.05)**	**247**	**0.06 (0.06)**	**113**	**−0.1 (0.06)**	**134**
	Romney					
	Both	*N*	Jackson	*N*	McHarris	*N*
Deracialized candidate	0.88 (0.03)	134	0.87 (0.04)	63	0.89 (0.04)	71
Racialized candidate	0.82 (0.04)	113	0.78 (0.06)	50	0.86 (0.04)	63
Difference	**0.06 (0.05)**	**247**	**0.09 (0.07)**	**113**	**0.03 (0.06)**	**134**

Source: Amazon Mechanical Turk survey.

Note: The "Both" column compares racialized and deracialized candidates of both races; the "McHarris" column compares only the racialized and deracialized McHarris candidate; and the "Jackson" column compares only the racialized and deracialized Jackson candidate. Positive scores indicate that the racialized candidate inspires more enthusiasm than the deracialized candidate.

* $p<0.05$; $+p<0.1$; standard errors in parentheses; significance is based on a two-sample test of means.

0.05. Wyatt McHarris performed only about 6 percent better when he focused on racialized issues rather than deracialized issues against Clinton. This difference is statistically insignificant. It appears that black candidates who racialize in primaries may enjoy a unique advantage over deracialized black candidates among black voters.

However, the relationship between racialization and vote choice weakens when the comparison primary candidate changes. According to table 6.5, the hypothetical candidates who focused on racial justice instead of economic justice performed 10 percent better in a hypothetical matchup against Bernie Sanders. This difference was significant at 0.10 based on a two-sample *t*-test. When disaggregating by the race of the candidate, neither the black nor white candidate appears to be uniquely driving these effects. Nonetheless, the results demonstrate that blacks tend to be much more supportive of candidates who make racial appeals than those who make economic appeals in Democratic primaries. When partisanship is held constant, black voters display a strong preference for racialized candidates.

Partisanship, however, overwhelms message when black voters make decisions between the hypothetical candidates and politicians of another party. The results in table 6.5 show that black voters were statistically equally likely to support the deracialized and racialized candidates over their Republican foes, regardless of the race of the candidate. As was found with the observational data, blacks tended to support Democrats at high levels (over 80% in all cases), leaving very little room for significant variation. As a result, the significance of partisan loyalties drowns out the influence of racial messaging for black voters.

Not only is there strong support for my hypothesis that racialized candidates increase black turnout more than their deracialized counterparts using real-world data, I also find support for my claim that blacks are more motivated to turn out with hypothetical candidates who engage in racialized appeals in my experimental analysis. Table 6.6 presents black voters' stated intention to vote in the 2020 presidential election when hypothetical candidates Malik Jackson or Wyatt McHarris appear on the ballot as a racialized liberal or an economic liberal. The table explores the difference in support for these candidates by issue type and separately for the white candidate (Wyatt McHarris), the black candidate (Malik Jackson), and both candidates combined.

The results demonstrate that blacks generally responded positively to liberal candidates. However, blacks were more likely to vote for the same candidate when they focused on racial issues on their campaign webpage. Blacks who read the racialized message for both candidates scored on average 4.10

TABLE 6.6. Differences in voter enthusiasm (1 = low enthusiasm, 5 = high enthusiasm) if hypothetical candidates Wyatt McHarris and Malik Jackson are presented as racialized or deracialized candidates on the 2020 presidential ballot

Candidate type	Both	*N*	Jackson		McHarris	*N*
Deracialized candidate	3.73 (0.11)	134	3.73 (0.16)	63	3.73 (0.14)	71
Racialized candidate	4.1 (0.1)	112	3.92 (0.16)	50	4.24 (0.13)	62
Difference	**−0.37* (0.15)**	**246**	**−0.19 (0.23)**	**113**	**−0.51* (0.19)**	**133**

Source: Amazon Mechanical Turk survey.

Note: The "Both" column compares racialized and deracialized candidates of both races; the "McHarris" column compares only the racialized and deracialized McHarris candidate; and the "Jackson" column compares only the racialized and deracialized Jackson candidate. Positive scores indicate that the racialized candidate inspires more enthusiasm than the deracialized candidate.

* $p<0.05$; + $p<0.1$; standard errors in parentheses; significance based on a two-sample test of means.

on the five-point voter enthusiasm scale. Blacks who read the deracialized website from the same set of candidates had an average score of 3.73 on this scale. The difference of over a third of a point in the average scores is significant at 0.05 according to a two-sample *t*-test.

When I disaggregated by the race of the candidate, blacks responded to both the white and coracial candidate more than their deracialized counterparts, but this difference is only statistically significant when a white candidate racializes. Blacks were about half a point more likely on a five-point scale to state their intention to vote when they were presented with a racialized white candidate over a deracialized white candidate. This difference was statistically significant based on a two-sample *t*-test. Furthermore, blacks were about 0.2 points on a five-point scale more likely to vote for a racialized black candidate over a deracialized black candidate, which is statistically insignificant at 0.05. In combination with the observational data, the results from this experiment demonstrate that blacks are much more likely to vote when a candidate is racially liberal. This appears to be particularly true for white candidates.

Conclusion

The results of this chapter demonstrate that Democratic candidates who can appear as racially liberal improve turnout among African Americans. Moreover, such candidates perform better in Democratic primaries with black voters. Given the changing political landscape in the United States, the Democratic Party may be increasingly reliant on increasing black turnout to ensure success at the national level. While Hillary Clinton won the popular vote by almost three million votes, she was defeated because she lost key swing states. In particular, black turnout was lower in states like Wisconsin, Michigan, Pennsylvania, and Florida than it was four years earlier when Barack Obama carried these areas. Many political pundits saw Clinton's inability to mobilize blacks, in spite of spending comparable amounts of money to Obama on mobilization, as key to her defeat. For example, in Michigan Clinton lost to Trump by just ten thousand votes. The decline in turnout in Detroit alone was 75,000. In Wisconsin, where Trump only won by about 23,000 votes, black turnout in the state declined by over 20 percent. Had Clinton been able to maintain the levels of black turnout Obama enjoyed in 2012, she would have won the 2016 presidential election.

Of course, many political observers have noted that Clinton did make appeals to the black community in the 2016 presidential election. From having a section on her website focused on racial justice and equality to inviting the Mothers of the Movement (a group affiliated closely to Black Lives Matter) to speak at the Democratic National Convention to saying she keeps hot sauce in her bag (a cultural reference meant to appeal to black voters), Clinton went out of her way to mobilize blacks. For the most part this was successful in leading blacks to feel that she would use government to aid blacks. Blacks rated Clinton higher on the seven-point racially liberal scale (4.60) than any white Democratic presidential candidate in the past thirty years.

Nonetheless, during Clinton's campaign video surfaced of her making a speech in New Hampshire in 1996 saying that gang members were not kids, they were "super-predators." While Clinton never explicitly mentions African Americans, her critics, and in particular, Republican National Committee chair Reince Preibus said that she was using this terminology "super-predator" to paint African Americans as animals (Stout and Baker 2019). While the quote was twenty years old and she apologized for it, her critics used this as evidence that Clinton did not truly care about the black community.

Moreover, some have speculated that targeted messages focused on demobilizing African American voters worked hard to amplify the belief that Clinton did not care about blacks. These messages, communicated by both the Trump campaign and Russian troll farms posing as black activists, may have counteracted any appeals that the Clinton campaign hoped to make. Analysis of Russian troll farms has revealed rumors being spread that the Democratic Party accepted money from the Ku Klux Klan, encouraging blacks not to accept the lesser of two evils between Clinton and Trump (Stout and Baker 2019). These explicit demobilization strategies may have been effective in getting blacks to question Clinton.

This may in part explain why in spite of her greater substantive outreach to the black community, Clinton was seen as much less racially liberal than

Obama among blacks. Of course, it is also probable that many blacks inferred Obama to be more caring given their shared racial background (see Stout 2018). Regardless, given the substantial and significant influence that perceptions of racial liberalism had on black turnout, it is likely that had Clinton been perceived as racially liberal as Obama, she may have inspired more blacks to vote and won the presidency. While counterfactuals are unprovable, maximizing black turnout may be essential for Democrats in the near future.

In addition to turnout, it may benefit Democratic candidates in the primaries to make racial appeals. The growing levels of Democratic partisanship among blacks during the Obama years, and the declining numbers of white Democrats, make the black vote crucial for Democratic presidential hopefuls (Stout and Garcia 2015). Some have argued that Sanders's poor performance with the black community may have been his downfall in 2016. As the analysis of both observational and experimental data of this chapter demonstrates, when partisanship is held constant, candidates who can appear as racially liberal tend to perform much better than those who focus on deracialized topics. As a result, Democratic candidates who hope to draw support in the primaries can't afford to run on a message that does not aggressively address racial inequality.

As the nation becomes more diverse, there will be significant changes to the campaign strategies employed by politicians. In particular, the growth of the Latino community will make this electorate a key part of any winning coalition. While there is a lot of literature exploring black-Latino coalitions, less is known about whether Latinos will be supportive of candidates who make racial appeals. In the following chapters, I will explore whether Latinos have experienced a resurgence in linked fate in recent years, leading them to be more supportive of racial policies.

7
Making the Connection
HOW THE CURRENT POLITICAL CLIMATE HAS INCREASED LATINO PANETHNIC LINKED FATE

In 2004, George W. Bush's chief campaign strategist Karl Rove argued that Latinos could easily become part of the Republican Party's coalition under the right conditions. In several preelection polls, Latinos stated that their number-one concerns were jobs and the economy (Barreto and Nuño 2011). Latinos are disproportionately Catholic, and this religious identity better aligned with the Republican Party than the Democratic Party. Finally, Latinos largely differed from blacks in that they tended to have low levels of both ethnic and panethnic group consciousness.

While blacks are also more religious than whites on average, their high levels of group consciousness made it difficult for a party that did not focus on race to appeal to them. Latinos did not pose the same problem for the Republican Party. Instead, as long as Republicans were not hostile to Latinos, they could garner a substantial amount of support from this underrepresented community with the right message. Moreover, their low levels of panethnic group consciousness mean that Republicans could focus on nonracial issues and still enjoy substantial support from the Latino community.

Whether or not there has been a change in Latino linked fate in recent years will largely determine whether a deracialized approach can still be effective in attracting this growing electorate. In previous chapters, I presented evidence that African Americans have grown in their racial linked fate and that this corresponds with higher levels of support for racially progressive policies and politicians. Moreover, I argue that much of the growth in linked fate among blacks is driven by growing perceptions of discrimination against their racial/ethnic group.

The same process may be occurring for Latinos. Latinos as a group have not been immune from policies that disproportionately disenfranchise them from the political process. Moreover, Latinos were one of Donald Trump's primary targets in the 2016 presidential election. From getting his crowds to chant "build a wall" along the Mexican-American border to arguing that many Mexicans in the United States were rapist and drug dealers, Trump's campaign took numerous hostile actions toward Latinos. At the same time, hate crimes against Latinos grew 15 percent between 2015 and 2016 (Iwama 2018). For these reasons, it is not surprising to find that 80 percent of Latinos in a 2017 Pew Research Poll (see chapter 1) believed that Latinos face a lot of discrimination in the United States. While Latinos have long been the target of restrictive legislation, the high visibility of the discrimination that Latinos have faced in recent years may have led them to have a higher sense of panethnic group linked fate. This in turn may have led them to display more progressive attitudes on racial issues that both directly and indirectly influence their opportunities in the United States.

In this chapter, I will explore whether the current political and racial context in the United States has heightened Latinos' sense of panethnic linked fate, leading them to display stronger preferences for racially progressive issues. I first review the literature explaining why Latinos have traditionally displayed lower levels of panethnic linked fate. I will then describe how policies such as voter identification laws, Trump's presidential campaign, and growing levels of racial inequality may have increased Latinos' sense of a common consciousness. Using the 2004 National Political Survey (NPS) and the 2008, 2012, and 2016 American National Election Studies (ANES), I find that Latinos have displayed higher levels of panethnic linked fate in recent years.

Furthermore, I argue that this change in Latinos' racial identity has made them more likely to support racial policies that are both explicitly connected to both issues that disproportionately affect them and issues that are only tangentially related to them. I test this hypothesis using data from the ANES, the General Social Survey (GSS), and Pew Research Center polls. Overall, I show that Latinos have become more racially progressive on a number of issues following Trump's rise to the presidency. In combination, the results of this chapter provide evidence that Latinos are increasingly perceiving the political advancement of minorities as important in influencing their own opportunities.

Why Latinos Tend to Have Lower Levels of Linked Fate

While a shared history and culture for most African Americans makes it easier for them to find a bond with each other, Latinos don't have the same shared experiences in the United States. "Latino" is an umbrella term for individuals from different national origin groups who originate in Latin America. It is a panethnic identification that ties individuals together based on the shared experience of Spanish colonization. However, in terms of ethnicity—often described as one's country of origin—Latinos are much more diverse.

This diversity in national origin creates significant challenges for Latinos around developing a unified identity.

For example, beyond language and a shared experience of Spanish colonization little ties individuals from Cuba, Mexico, Puerto Rico, and other Latin American countries. Moreover, many of these countries have preexisting rivalries that may make it difficult for those who immigrate into the United States to feel connected to each other. Mexico and Guatemala, for example, have had many conflicts about their shared border. These preexisting rivalries often lead to divisions for Latinos of different national origins when they arrive in the United States.

Additionally, Latinos' experiences in the United States both historically and in the present have largely differed by their nationality and generation in the country. Historically, many Mexican Americans in the southwestern states resided in these territories before they were annexed into the United States and thus have been here for numerous generations. As a result, a sizable number of Mexican Americans can trace their ancestry in the United States back to the Treaty of Guadalupe Hidalgo (1848). In comparison, most Cuban Americans came to the United States following the overthrow of the Batista regime in 1959. Differences in the number of generations Latinos have been in the United States play a large role in whether they perceive commonalities between each other. Latinos who have been in the United States for a shorter period of time tend to display higher levels of linked fate, in part because of their greater use of the Spanish language and their proximity to other Latino immigrants (Sanchez and Masuoka 2010).

In contemporary America, Latinos largely differ by their citizenship status. For example, Puerto Ricans are American citizens who don't share the same immigrant experience as Mexican Americans, who are disproportionately undocumented. Moreover, Cubans had an easier time entering the United States between 1965 and 1978 than Latinos from other Central American countries due to their refugee status. Along these lines, many of these national-origin groups live in areas that are disproportionately of their own nationality and thus have few panethnic connections. For example, Cuban Americans disproportionately live in Florida, where they would have less contact with Mexican Americans, who mostly reside in southwestern states such as Arizona, California, and New Mexico.

To make collective action even more difficult for these groups, ethnicity often intersects with race. Similar to the United States, colorism leads to different opportunities for and connections between lighter-skin and darker-skin Latinos (Hunter 2007; Lavariega Monforti and Sanchez 2010). Darker-skin Latinos often encounter more discrimination than their lighter counterparts.

This may in part explain why Afro-Latinos are more likely to perceive a common identity with others who share than panethnicity (Masuoka and Sanchez 2010).

For these reasons, Latinos have historically had lower levels of linked fate compared to their black counterparts. According to the 2004 NPS less than 1 in 5 Latinos expressed having a lot of Latino linked fate. Moreover, differences in perceptions of panethnic linked fate are often tied to some of the aforementioned factors. For example, Latinos who can trace their origins to Central America or Mexico are much more likely to see the Latino panethnic identity as more meaningful to them than Latinos who can trace their ties to Cuba (Masuoka 2006). Latinos who are darker skinned, meanwhile, are more likely to identify as Latino than those with lighter skin (Masuoka 2006). These differences between different Latino groups have been tied to perceptions of discrimination. Overall, it is important to note that while it may appear that Latinos are a homogenous group with similar behaviors, there is a significant amount of social diversity among them that has important consequences for their political attitudes and behaviors.

The Rise of Latino Linked Fate

The rise of the Tea Party movement's influence on state legislatures around the country came with a slew of legislation that was perceived as being anti-immigrant and as targeting Latinos more than other groups. Reich (2017) and Gulasekaram and Ramakrishnan (2015) found that since Obama's election to the White House there has been a significant increase in punitive immigration legislation at the state level. Moreover, many of these pieces of legislation garnered a lot of media attention. Arizona Senate Bill 1070 (SB 1070), which allowed police officers to detain a person and check their immigration status, was national news for several weeks and motivated several large-scale protests (Toomey et al. 2014). This bill was viewed by some as a way for police officers to racially profile Latinos or others with brown skin without much cause (Toomey et al. 2014).

A similar bill in Alabama, House Bill 56 (HB 56), also received national news coverage because there were several boycotts of the state as a result of its passage (Zhang, Palma, and Xu 2016). Like SB 1070, HB 56 was perceived by many as providing police officers with an excuse to harass Latinos (Mohl 2016). While these bills do not explicitly mention Latinos and may also impact other communities of color, they were perceived as being a racially motivated attack on Latinos. Moreover, Almeida et al. (2016) found evidence that Latinos in states where these types of legislation are passed are much more likely to encounter discrimination based on their race/ethnicity. Given this research, it would not be surprising to find that the rise of punitive immigration laws has increased Latinos' levels of linked fate. Vargas, Sanchez, and Valdez (2017) found that Latinos who live in states that pass more punitive immigration legislation have significantly higher levels of panethnic linked fate. They argue that this change in feelings of closeness to other Latinos is driven by perceived hostility from government officials and increases in perceptions of discrimination.

In addition to punitive immigration legislation, many state legislatures have also enacted numerous laws that disenfranchised Latino voters, such as voter identification laws. Hajnal, Lajevardi, and Nielson (2017) found that Latinos are the most disadvantaged by voter identification laws. Assaults on voting also came in the form of ending early voting and decreasing the number of precincts in minority communities (King 2017). Despite increased interest in the 2016 presidential election among Latinos, many precincts in heavily Latino-populated areas like Maricopa County, Arizona, decreased the number of polling stations, increasing wait times for Latino voters. Arizona was not alone; heavily Latino areas in states like Texas, Alabama, and North Carolina also had decreased numbers of polling places. As a result of these and other changes, on average both Latinos and blacks wait significantly longer to vote than their white counterparts in most elections (Stewart 2012). Again, the growth in legislation that disproportionately affects Latinos may have led to higher levels of panethnic linked fate.

Additionally, Latinos were the frequent target of racially charged attacks from Donald Trump during the 2016 presidential campaign. This was best exemplified by Trump's campaign launch, in which he suggested that immigrants from Latin countries where largely undesirable. "When Mexico sends its people, they're not sending their best. . . . They're sending people that have lots of problems, and they're bringing those problems with us. They're bringing drugs. They're bringing crime. They're rapists." Similarly, Trump was a strong advocate for building a wall along the Mexican-American border and defunding sanctuary cities. He also made numerous mentions of the shooting of Kate Stienle, a white woman who was killed by an undocumented immigrant from Mexico.

On the campaign trail, Trump suggested that evangelicals should question Texas U.S. senator Ted Cruz's ties to his religion because his father was from Cuba (Newman, Shah, and Collingwood 2018). In the first year of his presidency, Trump was accused of being slow to respond to the disaster in Puerto Rico caused by Hurricane Maria. Moreover, in a tweet he blamed Puerto Ricans rather than the federal government for their inability to rebuild the island after the hurricane. Many viewed his unwillingness to help the island recover and his response as being racially motivated (Newman, Shah, and Collingwood 2018). In all, many accused Trump of playing on fears of Latinos to appeal to his base (Newman, Shah, and Collingwood 2018; Sanchez and Gomez-Aguinaga 2017).

As political elites such as Trump increase negative rhetoric around Latinos of different ethnicities, Latinos may feel more connected to their panethnicity. Scholars who explore factors that give rise to Latino panethnic group consciousness argue that the different ethnic groups need to perceive some shared objectives/concerns. For example, Padilla (1985) demonstrated that Puerto Ricans and Mexican Americans in Chicago coalesced around the issue of education and fears that Spanish speakers were being singled out by school boards. Common goals could also come in the form of a common enemy. Meier and Stewart (1991) demonstrated that Latinos as a group may form bonds when they perceive a common threat. Trump's attacks on Latinos from different national-origin groups may have led many Latinos to unite in their concern about discrimination from elected officials. This may have led many Latinos to feel linked to those who share their panethnicity. Moreover, Trump serving as a political adversary may have played a significant role in uniting the Latino community.

In addition to the actions of elected officials, Latinos, like blacks, have experienced a decline in socioeconomic status relative to whites in recent years. The Pew Research Center has demonstrated that levels of wealth and income inequality between Latinos and whites have grown after the great recession. While whites' wealth was on average 8.2 times greater than Latinos' average wealth in 2007, by 2013 this ratio had grown to whites having 10.3 times the wealth of Latinos on average (Ovink and Kalogrides 2015). Much of this decline was driven by lower incomes and fewer job opportunities for Latinos, who as a group tend to have lower levels of education. Moreover, the decline of public sector jobs has led to a disproportionate decline in the Latino middle class (Tran and Valdez 2017). Given these factors, Latino households experienced on average a 9 percent decrease in income between 2010 and 2013, while whites experienced only a 1 percent average decrease in income over the same time period (Ovink and Kalogrides 2015).

Finally, demographic changes in the Latino community may have led to stronger perceptions of a common consciousness among this group. Mexican Americans and non-foreign-born individuals are making up a larger portion of Latinos in the United States. According to Pew, Mexican Americans made up about 60 percent of the Latino population in 2000, and this number had grown to 65 percent in 2015 (Gómez 2018). Mexican Americans on average have higher levels of panethnic linked fate than other Latino national-origin groups (Masuoka 2006).

Moreover, as Latino immigration has slowed in recent years, the Latino population is increasingly made up of individuals who are not foreign-born. In 2000, about 55 percent of the adult Latino population was born outside of the United States according to Pew. However, by 2014 foreign-born Latinos made up less than 50 percent of the population. Moreover, by some estimates the size of the foreign-born Latino population will decline to about 36 percent by 2030 (Gómez 2018). Latinos who have resided in the United States for more than one generation tend to have higher levels of panethnic linked fate (G. Sanchez and Masuoka 2010). Based on these estimates, groups that generally have higher levels of linked fate have grown in recent years.

Have Latinos Experienced a Growth in Their Common Consciousness?

To explore whether Latinos have grown in their levels of common consciousness over time, I will explore changes in panethnic linked fate in the 2004 NPS and the 2008, 2012, and 2016 ANES. While the span of time I examine Latino panethnic linked fate is shorter than my examination of black linked fate, the period covered in this analysis still spans twelve years. Moreover, the 2016 ANES corresponds with Trump's presidential campaign and election, which as I argued above may have played a significant role in increasing Latino panethnic linked fate.

Linked fate is measured using two questions in the 2004 NPS and in the 2008 and 2012 ANES. The first question asks respondents, "Do you think that what happens generally to Hispanic people in this country will have something to do with what happens in your life?" Those who answer affirmatively to this question are then asked the follow-up question: "How much does what happens to Hispanics affect you?" Responses to this second question are on a three-point scale: (1) "a little"; (2) "some"; and (3) "a lot." As mentioned in chapter 5, the 2016 ANES used a slightly different format and combined these two questions into one, asking, "How much do you think that what happens generally to black people in this country will affect what happens in your life." Regardless of how the question was asked, the same four-point scale is used, with the options being "not at all," "not very much," "some," and "a lot."

Table 7.1 demonstrates that Latinos have experienced a substantial growth in their levels of linked fate over time. The table gives the percentages of Latino respondents who reported having no linked fate, a little linked fate, some linked fate, and a lot of linked fate between 2008 and 2016. The results are stark. In 2004 and 2012, about half of Latinos reported having no linked

TABLE 7.1. Latino perceptions of panethnic linked fate (2004–16)

	2004	2008	2012	2016
None	53%	42%	49%	14%
A little	5%	5%	7%	22%
Some	23%	29%	30%	38%
A lot	19%	25%	14%	26%
Average	2.08	2.37	2.09	2.76

Sources: 2004 NPS and the 2008, 2012, and 2016 ANES.

fate. However, by 2016 only 14 percent of Latinos reported no linked fate. Moreover, the number of Latinos who reported having some or a lot of Latino linked fate in 2016 was 10 percent greater compared to 2008 and 20 percent greater than in 2012 and 2004. On a four-point scale, Latinos' average level of linked fate in 2016 was 2.76, which is statistically significantly higher than Latinos' average linked fate in 2012 (2.09), 2008 (2.37), and 2004 (2.08). The results suggest that Latinos, like African Americans, have experienced a significant amount of growth in their levels of linked fate in recent years.

Latino Attitudes on Racial Policies in Recent Years

There is good reason to believe that the increase in linked fate among Latinos in recent years may correspond with growing racial liberalism among this underrepresented group. Like African Americans, there is a significant amount of research that demonstrates that Latinos with higher levels of linked fate tend to be more racially progressive. This is driven by the fact that Latinos who are connected to their panethnic group are more willing to support policies that they view as expanding opportunities for Latinos. For example, Hurwitz, Peffley, and Mondak (2015) found that Latinos with high levels of linked fate are more likely to support protections for minorities in the justice system. Along the same lines, G. Sanchez (2006) showed that high-linked-fate Latinos were more supportive of protections for immigrants and were stronger advocates for bilingual education.

In addition to high-linked-fate Latinos being more approving of policies that disproportionately affect their panethnic group, there is also evidence that such Latinos are more likely to join in coalitions with other racial/ethnic minorities. McClain et al. (2006) showed that Latinos with high levels of linked fate were more likely to view blacks as a group favorably. More recently, Hurwitz, Peffley, and Mondak (2015) found that Latinos with high levels of linked fate were more likely to recognize that they had much in common with African Americans. Given these findings, it follows that Latinos may have displayed more support for racially progressive policies in recent years even if they do not directly affect their panethnic group, given their substantial growth in linked fate.

Unfortunately, most time series surveys do not ask questions explicitly about Latinos or Latino-related issues for a long period of time, the same way that they do for African American issues. As a result, this section will use Latinos' attitudes about racial issues connected to African Americans as a proxy to test whether Latinos have become more racially liberal in recent years. The two exceptions to this will be the examination of Latinos' attitudes toward immigrants, who tend to be disproportionately Latino, and their attitudes about limiting homeowners' abilities to discriminate based on race.

Nonetheless, there are good reasons to use Latinos' attitudes toward black racial issues as a measure for changes in the former's racial attitudes in recent years. Moreover, these measures would be better than questions that asked about whites' position in society, given the overlapping opportunities and challenges that blacks and Latinos face in the United States. Many policies that affect African Americans also impact the well-being of Latinos, given their similar socioeconomic status in society. For example, an expansion of affirmative action policies generally leads to more blacks *and* Latinos in the workplace and on college campuses because both groups are targets of implicit racism (Hinrichs 2012). Similarly, voter identification laws, which disproportionately disenfranchise blacks, also make it harder for Latinos to vote (Hajnal, Lajevardi, and Nielson 2017).

In addition to policy tying these groups together, Latinos and blacks are often the subject of attacks from the same politicians and political organizations. Donald Trump's 2016 campaign, it is argued, used racial hostility against minorities to increase support among racially resentful voters (Sides, Tesler, and Vavreck 2017). By championing the end of political correctness, a concept meant to protect underrepresented groups from hostile speech, Trump and politicians like him may create a greater sense of commonality between blacks and Latinos.

At the same time, the Democratic Party, which has increased its focus on attracting Latinos and blacks, has tied these group's interests together. For example, on Hillary Clinton's presidential campaign website she had a segment in her issues section titled "Racial Justice." The section combined both appeals to black and Latino voters under the same umbrella. Clinton is not alone in this tactic. Bernie Sanders, the runner-up in the 2016 Democratic presidential primaries, used the term "people of color" ten times and mentioned

African Americans and Latinos in the same sentence six times in the "Racial Justice" section of his own presidential campaign website. The grouping of the interests of blacks and Latinos by both Democratic and Republican elites may have led Latinos to see more of a connection between policies that address racial inequality for blacks as applying to themselves as well. While not perfect, the use of questions around African Americans may be a good proxy for racial liberalism given the placing of blacks and Latinos into the same category by politicians and the disproportionate impact of public policy influencing these groups' opportunities jointly.

Before I begin this analysis, it is important to note that there are several cleavages in the Latino community that may influence their racial ideology. For example, Latinos who are not first-generation are generally more racially progressive (see Cisneros 2017). Similarly, Mexican Americans and Puerto Ricans tend to be more racially liberal and supportive of cross-racial coalitions (Cisneros 2017). More obviously, we would expect that Latinos who identify as liberals or Democrats should also be more racially progressive than their conservative and Republican counterparts. Given this, I would prefer to disaggregate Latinos into different categories as I did for whites in chapters 1–4. However, given the small number of Latinos in time series surveys such as the ANES, GSS, and Pew Research Center surveys, I am unable to provide a more nuanced analysis. Nonetheless, given that some subsections of Latinos may not change in their attitudes over time, a test of change for all Latinos is probably a more conservative test. For example, a drastic movement in support for affirmative action among liberal Latinos would only appear as a small movement for the group if others within the Latino community hadn't changed their opinion on the topic or moved in the opposite direction.

To test whether Latinos have become more racially liberal in recent years, I again use multiple measures from either the ANES, GSS, or Pew Research Center surveys. The first measure comes from a series of six Pew polls from 2006, 2010, 2013, 2014, 2015, and 2016. In these surveys, Pew asked respondents, "As I read each pair, tell me whether the first statement or the second statement comes closer to your own views—even if neither is exactly right.) . . . Immigrants today strengthen our country because of their hard work and talents, immigrants today are a burden on our country because they take our jobs, housing and health care." For each year, I coded respondents as 1 if they stated that immigrants strengthened our country and as 0 if they viewed immigrants as being a burden on our country. Respondents who stated they were unsure were excluded from the analysis.

In addition, I also analyze the ANES measure that asks Latino respondents to place themselves on a seven-point scale based on the question "Some people feel that the government in Washington should make every possible effort to improve the social and economic position of blacks. Others feel that the government should not make any special effort to help blacks because they should help themselves." A score of 1 on the scale indicates that the individual believes that blacks should help themselves without any favors, while a score of 7 indicates that the individual believes government should make a special effort to help blacks. I also assessed Latinos' attitudes about affirmative action using a question from the ANES that asks respondents, "Some people say that because of past discrimination blacks should be given preference in hiring and promotion. Others say that such preference in hiring and promotion of blacks is wrong because it gives blacks advantages they haven't earned. What about your opinion; are you for or against preferential hiring and promotion of blacks?" This was coded simply as a dichotomous variable, with a 1 indicating support and a 0 indicating opposition to affirmative action.

Finally, I assess Latinos' attitudes about prohibitions to housing discrimination using a question on the GSS that asks respondents, "Suppose there is a community-wide vote on the general housing issue. There are two possible laws to vote on: 1: "The Owner Decides" or 2: "Can't Discriminate Based on Race" Which law would you vote for?" I recoded this variable so that the response "can't discriminate" was given a score of 1 and the response the "owner decides" was given a score of 0.

Figure 7.1 presents the percentage of Latinos who believed that immigrants strengthen this country rather than burden it. The results demonstrate that in all the years surveyed a vast majority of Latinos believed immigrants strengthen rather than burden the country. This result is not surprising given that Latinos are disproportionately either first- or second-generation immigrants and have strong ties to immigrant communities. However, the current political context has led to a significant growth among Latinos who view immigrants as strengthening the nation. In 2010, about 70 percent of Latinos held that opinion, but this figure had grown to 81 percent in the 2016 survey. This difference is statistically significant based on a two-sample *t*-test. The results of this analysis suggest that Latinos are more likely to have displayed higher levels of linked fate in recent years and that this is correlated with more positive attitudes about immigrants in the United States.

Figure 7.2 explores whether Latinos are more likely to support government providing more aid to blacks using the seven-point scale from the ANES. Higher scores on this measure indicate that Latinos believe that government should provide more aid to blacks, whereas lower scores indicate that Latinos

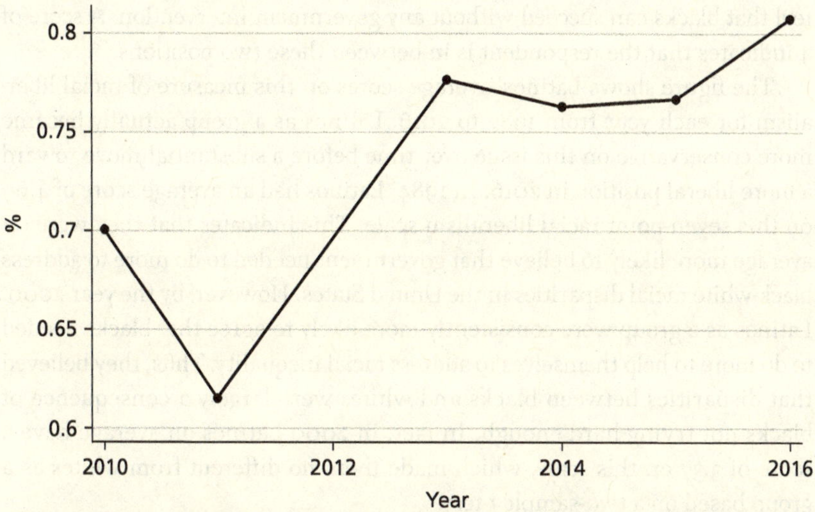

FIGURE 7.1. Percentage of Latinos who agree that immigrants strengthen the United States (2010–16)
Source: Pew Research Center.

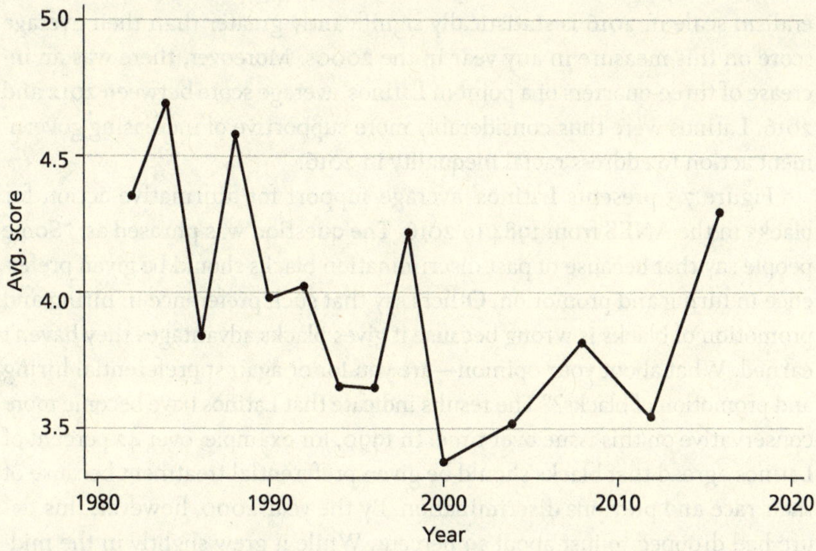

FIGURE 7.2. Latinos' average score on "aid to blacks" scale (1–7) (1980–2016)
Source: ANES.

feel that blacks can succeed without any government intervention. A score of 4 indicates that the respondent is in between these two positions.

The figure shows Latinos' average scores on this measure of racial liberalism for each year from 1982 to 2016. Latinos as a group actually became more conservative on this issue over time before a substantial move toward a more liberal position in 2016. In 1984, Latinos had an average score of 4.69 on this seven-point racial liberalism scale. This indicates that they were on average more likely to believe that government needed to do more to address black-white racial disparities in the United States. However, by the year 2000, Latinos as a group were consistently more likely to agree that blacks needed to do more to help themselves to address racial inequality. Thus, they believed that disparities between blacks and whites were largely a consequence of blacks not trying hard enough. In fact, in 2000 Latinos on average have a score of 3.37 on this scale, which made them no different from whites as a group based on a two-sample *t*-test.

In 2016, however Latinos' levels of racial liberalism had increased substantially. Latinos were more ready to believe that government aiding blacks was a better solution to address racial inequality that year than they had been in almost twenty years. Their average score of 4.29 on the seven-point racial liberalism scale in 2016 is statistically significantly greater than their average score on this measure in any year in the 2000s. Moreover, there was an increase of three-quarters of a point in Latinos' average score between 2012 and 2016. Latinos were thus considerably more supportive of increasing government action to address racial inequality in 2016.

Figure 7.3 presents Latinos' average support for affirmative action for blacks in the ANES from 1984 to 2016. The question was phrased as: "Some people say that because of past discrimination blacks should be given preference in hiring and promotion. Others say that such preference in hiring and promotion of blacks is wrong because it gives blacks advantages they haven't earned. What about your opinion—are you for or against preferential hiring and promotion of blacks?" The results indicate that Latinos have become more conservative on this issue over time. In 1990, for example, over 42 percent of Latinos agreed that blacks should be given preferential treatment because of their race and previous discrimination. By the year 2000, however, this figure had dropped to just about 19 percent. While it grew slightly in the mid-2000s, by the time Obama was running for reelection in 2012 only a quarter of Latinos supported affirmative action when phrased as providing blacks preferential treatment.

As was true with other measures of racial liberalism, Latinos became significantly more supportive of affirmative action for blacks in 2016. About a

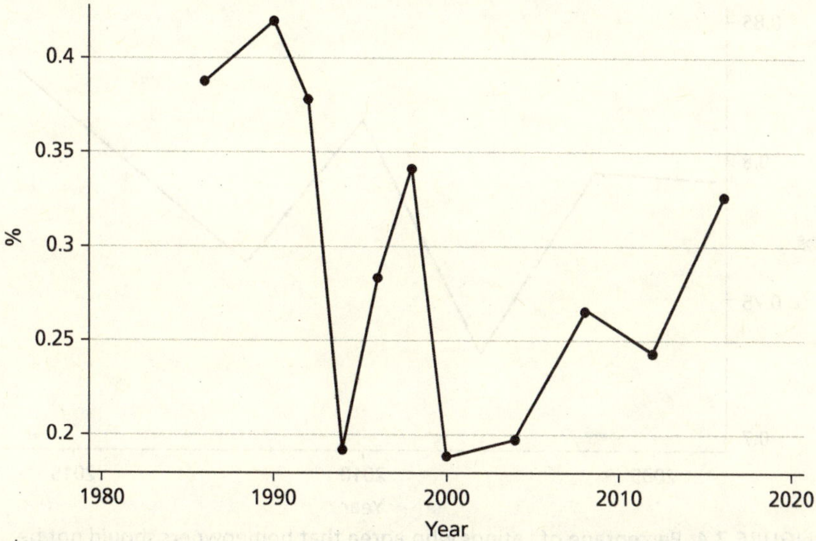

FIGURE 7.3. Latinos' support for affirmative action on a four-point scale (1984–2016)
Source: ANES.

third of Latinos in 2016 believed that blacks should be given preferential treatment because of previous forms of discrimination. This represents an 8 percent increase from 2012 and a 14 percent increase from 2000. Moreover, this growth in support for affirmative action among Latinos between 2012 and 2016 is significant at 0.05 based on a two-sample *t*-test. However, the lower levels of support (around 33%) for affirmative action as phrased as preferential treatment in 2016 may indicate the limit of what Latinos will support. While they may believe that more progress is necessary to address racial inequality, they may also feel that providing one group preferential hiring is not the best way to address this problem.

Finally, figure 7.4 presents the percentage of Latinos who believe that owners should not be able to discriminate when they sell their homes. The results are derived from the GSS for the years 2004–16. Latinos have become much more racially cognizant in their attitudes about housing discrimination over the past ten years. In 2008, for example, 73 percent said that an owner should not be able to discriminate when selling their home. In 2016, this figure grew by 10 percent, which is statistically significant based on a two-sample *t*-test. Moreover, between 2012 and 2016, Latinos became about 4.5 percent more likely to agree that homeowners should not discriminate by race. This difference is marginally significant based on a two-sample *t*-test ($p < 0.10$). Consistent with the results in this section, the growing levels of

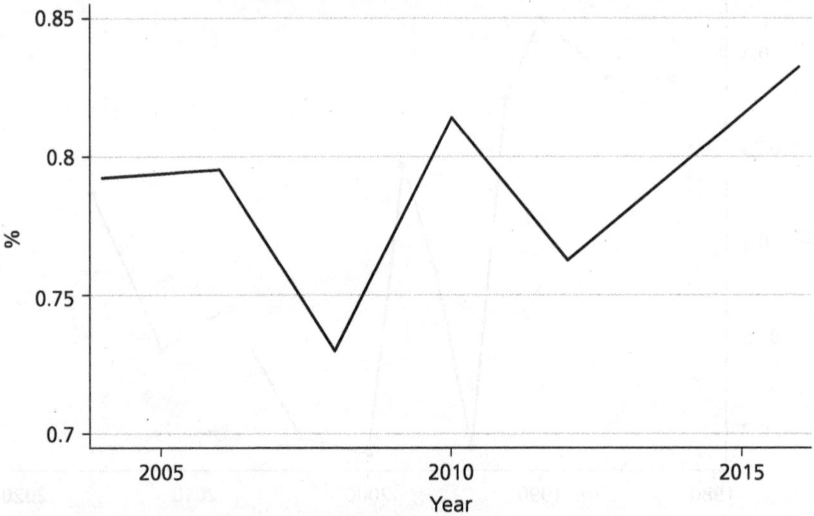

FIGURE 7.4. Percentage of Latinos who agree that homeowners should not be allowed to discriminate based on race (2004–16)
Source: GSS.

Latino group consciousness appear to correspond to greater support for racially liberal policies and ideas.

Conclusion

By the year 2050, Latinos will make up about 30 percent of the nation's population (Gómez 2018). They already make up the plurality of residents in California, the nation's largest state, and by 2030 will account for the majority of residents in other states such as Texas. The growing number of Latinos certainly makes them a central player in American politics. However, there are significant debates about whether Latinos as a group will shed their ethnicity to the same degree as the previous waves of immigrants from Ireland, Italy, Germany, and Eastern Europe (DeSipio 1996). If Latinos do abandon their panethnic interests, the growth in their population may not have so large an impact on politics because these groups will incorporate into the polity and be less of a cohesive voting bloc.

Others argue though that Latinos are a unique immigrant group and over time may behave more like African Americans in terms of being cognizant of their ethnic group's interests when making political decisions (see, e.g., Huntington 2004). The analysis in this chapter provides some support for the second expectation, at least in the current political context. Latinos as a group displayed their highest levels of panethnic linked fate in 2016, and this corresponds with the rise of anti-immigrant legislation and the Trump presidency. The results in table 7.1 above demonstrate than almost two-thirds of Latinos expressed either having a lot or some linked fate in 2016. This suggests that Latinos are becoming more conscious of the role their panethnic identity plays in explaining their own individual outcomes.

This change in thinking lends itself well to increasing support for racial issues. The results in the chapter demonstrate that in many areas Latinos now hold more progressive racial attitudes. In 2016, Latinos were the most likely to believe that immigrants strengthened the United States. Moreover, in the same year Latinos were more likely to believe that government should aid blacks than they were at any point in the new millennium; were more supportive of providing preferential hiring to blacks in 2016 than they were in almost twenty years; and were more likely to support bans on racial/ethnic discrimination in home selling that at any other time the GSS has asked respondents their attitudes on this issue. In sum, Latinos appear to be more ethnically aware and more racially progressive now than in the past.

As mentioned earlier, the results are averages across all groups of Latinos and do not account for differences based on nationality, generation, or even partisanship. As discussed in the literature review, Latinos are divided in their views on racial/ethnic issues like immigration by how many generations they or their descendants have lived in the United States and by their country of origin. As a result, it is possible that some groups like Mexican Americans have become more racially liberal while other groups like Cuban Americans have not changed in their attitudes. Given the dearth of data on Latinos over time, I am unable to address this possibility. As better data become available, future researchers should explore which groups of Latinos have been most affected by the racial context in altering their public opinion. One thing is certain, however: Latinos on average have become more racially liberal.

These changes in Latinos' attitudes may lead this growing panethnic group to reward rather than punish politicians whom they perceive as addressing the needs of racial/ethnic minorities. Latinos may feel that politicians who address racial inequality for underrepresented groups may be more caring for individuals like themselves. Moreover, Latino voters may want politicians to address growing disparities in opportunities for blacks and Latinos rather than focus exclusively on nonracial issues. In the chapter 8, I will assess whether Latinos' greater levels of racial liberalism in recent years has translated into more support for racially progressive politicians.

8
The Leaning Giant
LATINOS AND RACIAL APPEALS

In the 2001 Los Angeles mayoral election, Antonio Villaraigoisa was vying to become the first Latino mayor of Los Angeles since 1872. He hoped to put together a coalition of liberal white, Latino, and African American voters to defeat Los Angeles city attorney James Hahn. Gaining the support of whites and blacks, however, would be difficult. First, the strong preference that individuals have for coracial politicians provided Hahn a natural advantage with white voters. Hahn also had a strong legacy with the black community in Los Angeles that was in part connected to his father Kenneth Hahn. Kenneth Hahn had been a Los Angeles City Council member and a civil rights activist. Citing this legacy, James Hahn worked hard to appeal specifically to black voters, even arguing that he would retain black police chief Bernard Parks (something he ultimately would not do) if elected. James Hahn also received the endorsements of key black political figures, including former NBA star Magic Johnson. Given Hahn's campaign strategy, mobilizing and winning a vast majority of the Latino vote would be crucial for Villaraigoisa.

Unlike Hahn, Villaraigoisa shied away from explicit appeals to black and Latino voters. Instead, Villaraigoisa focused on deracialized issues such as the economy and education to appeal to Latinos in hopes of not alienating other racial/ethnic groups. He made it clear that in spite of the historic nature of his campaign, he would focus on economic divisions instead of race or ethnicity should he be elected. In a speech to Angelinos, Villaraigoisa noted, "It's about class, not race. . . . What divides us most is not language or skin color. It is class" (quoted in Wright Austin and Middleton 2004). In the end, Hahn received the vast majority of the black vote and a significant amount of support from white voters. Moreover, some argued that Villaraigoisa's deracialized campaign failed to mobilize Latinos, whose turnout was much lower than expected (see Wright Austin and Middleton 2004). In combination, it may have been Villaraigoisa's deracialized campaign that led to his downfall.

While most previous studies of deracialization have focused on white and black voters, the growing number of Latinos in the United States has sharply altered the strategies of political campaigns. As whites, and in particular working-class whites with high racial resentment, have become more Republican in recent years, the Democratic Party has become more reliant on Latino voters. As a result, more research needs to be done to determine whether Latinos will be supportive of racially liberal candidates.

In this chapter, I will explore whether Latinos are more likely to support or punish candidates whom they perceive as being racially progressive. Moreover, I will assess whether racially liberal politicians have received greater levels of support from Latinos in recent years. I begin by discussing previous research that explores whether Latinos respond positively to campaigns that make racial appeals. Following this, I assess whether perceptions of the racial progressivity of Democratic presidential candidates between 1998 and 2016 have influenced vote choice or turnout among Latino voters. Additionally, I examine whether Barack Obama's intention to expand the Deferred Action for Childhood Arrivals (DACA) program via the Deferred Action for Parents of Americans and Lawful Permanent Residents (DAPA) program in 2014 led Latinos to be more approving of his presidency. Finally, I use an online experiment to assess how Latinos respond to racially liberal versus economically liberal candidates.

Similar to the findings for blacks and white Democrats in previous chapters, I find that Latinos who perceived Hillary Clinton as being racially liberal were much more likely to vote for her in the primaries. The link between perceptions of the Democratic presidential candidate's racial progressivism and turnout/vote choice for Latinos was for the most part not present before this period. Moreover, Latinos' approval for Obama grew significantly after he expanded DACA to cover more individuals. Finally, the experimental analysis demonstrates that Latinos are currently expressing more enthusiasm for turning out to support racially progressive candidates in presidential elections. Overall, the results suggest that Latinos, a crucial part of the Democratic coalition, respond positively to racially progressive candidates.

Latinos and Racialization

Despite the rapid growth of Latinos in the United States, it was not until relatively recently that political scientists focused on the political behavior of this underrepresented group. As a result, most previous research exploring the links between racialization and voter behavior focuses almost exclusively on blacks and whites. The lack of research in this area is problematic as candidates who make racial appeals often pin their hopes on winning the support of left-leaning whites and racial/ethnic minority groups such as blacks and Latinos. While one of the major disadvantages of a deracialized campaign is that blacks will often be less enthusiastic about the candidate, earlier research on this topic found that Latinos remained supportive of and engaged in campaigns with candidates who shied away from racial issues (Gonzalez Juenke and Sampaio 2010). As a result, deracialized candidates may be able to win by putting together coalitions of white and Latino voters. Juenke and Sampaio (2010) found that Latinos, and particularly conservative Latinos, were supportive of both John (U.S. House) and Ken Salazar (U.S. Senate), who ran deracialized campaigns for two federal offices in the state of Colorado in 2004. The authors argue that Latino voters were not turned off by the brothers' appeals to white voters and that Latino voters do not punish candidates when they don't make explicit appeals to the Latino community.

This does not mean that Latinos won't reward candidates who make race-based appeals, however. Alamillo and Collingwood (2017), for example, demonstrated that Latinos were more supportive of white candidates who spoke Spanish and had Latino relatives. Along the same lines, Collingwood, Barreto, and Garcia-Rios (2014) showed that candidates who appear as being progressive on immigration issues generally enjoy greater levels of support from Latino voters. My own analysis of black U.S. Senate and gubernatorial candidates between 1982 and 2010 also found that Latinos were more likely to vote in elections in which black candidates engaged in racial appeals (Stout 2015).

Why would Latinos be more sympathetic to candidates who make racial appeals? A significant amount of research shows that Latinos are much more supportive of individuals like themselves. Barreto (2010) and McConnaughy et al. (2010), for example, demonstrated that Latinos were much more likely to turn out and support individuals who share their ethnicity. Similarly, Nuño (2007) and Bedolla and Michelson (2012) found that coethnic mobilizers were much more effective in getting Latinos to vote. All of these studies argue that coethnics are effective at mobilizing Latinos because they are more trusting that individuals who share their ethnicity will look out for their best interests.

The same logic may explain why candidates who make racial appeals should be able to mobilize Latinos. While voters may assume that coethnic politicians will protect their interests based on their shared ethnicity, politicians of a different ethnicity may be able to incite the same levels of enthusiasm by openly advocating for issues that disproportionately influence Latinos. Along these lines, Alamillo and Collingwood (2017) argue that white politicians who make racial appeals limit the perceived political distance between themselves and Latino voters. As a result, Latinos are more trusting that such politicians will work to advance Latino political interests. This in turn inspires higher levels of support and enthusiasm among Latinos for racialized candidates.

Furthermore, previous research demonstrates that Latinos are more responsive to politicians whom they perceive as caring about individuals like themselves. Collingwood, Barreto, and Garcia-Rios (2014) showed that one of the reasons Latinos were supportive of Obama in 2012 was because they believed he cared about the Latino community. The authors argue that this was driven by Obama's support for immigration policies. Similarly, I found that Latinos viewed black candidates who racialized as being more concerned about their panethnic group and this inspired a higher level of turnout (Stout 2015).

In addition to believing that racially progressive candidates care more about them, Latinos may also be more supportive of politicians whose policies align with their own interests. As Latinos have increasingly perceived themselves as being treated poorly because of their ethnicity (see chapter 1) and become increasingly conscious of their panethnic linked fate (see chapter 7), they have also become more supportive of racially progressive policies (see chapter 7). In recent years, Latinos have become more likely to view government as being necessary to address disparities between blacks and whites, to view immigrants as strengthening the nation, and to be more supportive of laws that would limit housing discrimination. This change in their attitudes may have made them more supportive of racialized candidates in recent years as these candidates are most likely to advocate for these racial issues. As a result, during periods where Latinos perceive government as being necessary to address racial inequality, they may be more supportive of politicians whom they view as being racially progressive.

Additionally, Latinos with the highest levels of panethnic consciousness appear to be the most responsive to racial appeals. For example, Soto and Merolla (2006) found evidence that Latinos who had the highest levels of ethnic group consciousness were the most responsive to Spanish-language ads put out by federal office candidates in 2000. Along the same lines, Michelson (2003) showed that Latinos with high levels of ethnic group consciousness were more responsive to mobilization efforts from Latino political groups (see also Valenzuela and Michelson 2016). In combination, the results suggest that Latinos are the most responsive to racial appeals when they have high levels of ethnic group consciousness. Based on this research and the results presented in chapter 7, the growth in Latino linked fate in recent years may have made Latinos more responsive to candidates whom they perceive as appealing to their panethnic community. These racially progressive candidates may be perceived as expanding opportunities for Latinos by addressing racial inequities in society.

What about Black Racial Appeals?

It is important to note that some of the measures used below to measure racial progressivity are tied explicitly to black voters. For example, I examine how Latinos' placement of Democratic presidential candidates on a scale that ranges from believing government should help blacks to believing blacks should help themselves influences their likelihood of turning out to vote and vote choice. While this measure of racial progressivism may be focused on African Americans, there are good reasons to expect that Latinos may view candidates who are progressive on black issues as also being supportive of Latino concerns.

When candidates engage in racialized campaigns, it is rarely targeted at only one racial group (Stout 2015). In general, a candidate who makes racial appeals to blacks generally needs the support of Latinos as well. Thus, most racialized candidates make panminority racial appeals rather than appeals directed exclusively at one racial group. This is particularly true at the national level, where a racialized candidate can only succeed by combining the support of blacks with the support of a mobilized group of Latinos and liberal whites.

This can be examined empirically by analyzing recent presidential campaigns. As mentioned in chapter 7, the 2016 presidential campaign websites of both Bernie Sanders and Hillary Clinton had "Racial Justice" sections focusing on issues that are important to both the black and Latino community. In his 1984 speech to the Democratic National Convention, Jesse Jackson made mobilizing Latinos and blacks a priority: "Reagan won Illinois by 300,000 votes—800,000 unregistered blacks, 500,000 Hispanics, rocks just laying around . . . pick up your slingshot, pick up your rock, and declare [that] our time has come, a new day has begun!" (quoted in Stout 2015). As a result, it is likely than when candidates are perceived as caring for the black community, they may also be perceived as caring for Latinos as well.

Moreover, Latinos and blacks are increasingly overlapping in their political interests. While Latinos have generally been less Democratic than African Americans, they have become much more likely to identify with the Democratic Party in recent years. This makes them more like African Americans in their partisanship. According to the Pew Research Center, 64 percent of Latinos either identified as Democrat or leaned toward the Democratic Party in 2016. In comparison, only 49 percent of Latinos had the same levels of Democratic partisanship ten years earlier in 2006. As Democratic leaders increasingly discuss the importance of addressing racial discrimination, Latinos as a group may be more willing to heed this call (Levendusky 2010).

Moreover, because Latinos and blacks largely occupy the same political space, Latinos may view advances for blacks as being good for their coalition and by extension good for themselves.

Along the same lines, while divisions may exist between black and Latino citizens, there is work to suggest that black and Latino representatives are consistent allies in government (Casellas 2009). Hero and Preuhs (2009) found that black and Latino legislators often vote similarly on bills. Moreover, black and Latino advocacy groups most often prioritize the same issues and advocate on behalf of each other's causes (Hero and Preuhs 2009). Illinois U.S. House representative Luis V. Gutierrez, for example, made a speech on the House Floor in 2016 advocating for a national strategy to address the shooting of black men by police. Gutierrez told the House, "I think black lives matter and I think this Congress should be the place where America comes together to decide what we are going to do about young black men getting shot by police" (Hero and Preuhs 2009). As Latinos' group consciousness increases, they may become more trusting of and persuaded by the actions and words of coethnics in government. This may increase Latinos' likelihood of being supportive of policies that advance black political interests. Moreover, it may increase perceptions of black interests as overlapping with Latinos' own preferences.

Do Perceptions of Racialization Matter in Vote Choice for Latinos?

To test whether Latinos are more supportive of and mobilized by politicians who are perceived as being racially progressive, I return to Pew Research Center polls, the American National Election Study (ANES), and my online experiment discussed in previous chapters. As noted in chapter 4, on November 20, 2014, Obama made an announcement that he was going to expand the DACA program, which shielded undocumented individuals who came into the United States as children, to also include the parents of those children, by establishing the DAPA program. Many have noted that this executive action was meant to appeal to Latinos, who are disproportionately undocumented (Bell 2016; Cisneros 2017). Fortunately, Pew Research conducted two polls around the date of this announcement that included a large number of Latinos respondents. The first was taken on November 9, 2014, and the second was taken roughly a month later on December 7. Both polls included about 170 Latino respondents. If Obama's appeal to Latinos influenced their attitudes toward him, we should expect that his approval rating would be higher among this group in the December poll than in the November one.

To test this possibility, I estimated a logit regression predicting Obama's approval rating (1 = Approve, 0 = Don't Approve) using whether the Latino

TABLE 8.1. Logit regression predicting whether Latino respondents approved (1) or disapproved (0) of Obama before (Nov. 2014) and after (Dec. 2014) his DAPA announcement

	Obama approval rating
After DAPA announcement	0.70**
	(0.27)
Female	0.17
	(0.28)
Age	0.00
	(0.01)
Income	−0.05
	(0.07)
Education	0.05
	(0.08)
Democrat	1.47***
	(0.31)
Republican	−1.26***
	(0.41)
Constant	−0.38
	(0.51)
Observations	287

Source: Pew Research Center.
* $p<0.1$; ** $p<0.05$; *** $p<0.01$; standard errors in parentheses.

respondent was asked about support for Obama before (November 2014) or after (December 2014) he made his DAPA announcement. To ensure that other factors were not biasing the results, the models controlled for the gender, age, income, education, and partisanship of the respondents.

Table 8.1 presents a logit regression predicting approval rating for Obama before and after he made his DAPA announcement. The table also presents corresponding predicted probabilities. While the DAPA announcement did not alter Obama's approval ratings among whites (see chapter 4) or blacks (see chapter 6), Latinos were much more likely to approve of Obama after he made this racial/ethnic appeal. Holding all else equal, Latinos were 16 percent more likely to approve of Obama after his announcement. Consistent with the results of Collingwood, Barreto, and Garcia-Rios (2014), I find strong evidence that Latinos respond to racial appeals made my prominent politicians. Thus, to maximize support among Latino voters, candidates should not shy away from issues that disproportionately affect this underrepresented group. However, whether or not general perceptions of racial progressivism matter in Latino vote choice and participation is not yet known. In the following section, I will assess whether Latinos were more supportive of candidates whom they perceived as being racially progressive.

Racial Progressivism, Vote Choice, and Turnout

To assess whether Latinos have become more supportive and enthusiastic for racially progressive candidates, I turn to the ANES. Using this data set, I first examine whether Latinos were more supportive of the ultimate winner of the Democratic presidential nomination in 2008 and 2016 based on perceptions of these candidates' racial liberalism. In previous chapters, I also examined the 1988 Democratic presidential primary for whites and blacks. However, there were too few Latinos who participated in the 1988 Democratic presidential primary in the ANES data set to draw any meaningful conclusions.

I also examined whether Latinos were more supportive of the Democratic nominee in all presidential elections between 2008 and 2016. While the previous chapters explored black and white vote choice for a longer period of time, the ANES did not collect a large enough sample of Latino voters until recently. Moreover, in several years there was not enough variation in vote choice among Latinos for the models to make adequate predictions. Nonetheless, I measured support for the Democratic candidate using the question that asks respondents who they voted for in the general election in these years. I coded those who supported the Democratic nominee as 1 and all others as 0. Finally, I explore whether perceptions of the racial liberalism of the Democratic candidate in 1998, 2008, 2012, and 2016 inspired higher levels of Latino turnout. Respondents for this measure were given the score of 1 if they reported voting in the presidential election year and a 0 if they did not.

Similar to previous chapters, my main independent variable of interest is perceptions of the Democratic candidate's racial progressivism, which is scored on a seven-point scale based on the ANES question that asks respondents: "Some people feel that the government in Washington should make every effort to improve the social and economic position of blacks. Suppose these people are at one end of a scale, at point 1. Others feel that the government should not make any special effort to help blacks because they should help themselves. Suppose these people are at the other end, at point 7. Where would you place the Democratic presidential nominee on this scale?" Responses were coded so that a score of 1 indicates that the individual perceives the Democratic presidential candidate as believing that blacks should help themselves to address racial disparities and a score of 7 indicates that

TABLE 8.2. Logit regressions predicting Latinos' support for the leading Democratic presidential nominee candidate in the 1988, 2008, and 2016 Democratic presidential primaries

	Vote for Obama (2008)	Vote for H. Clinton (2016)
Candidate's "aid to blacks" score	−0.16	0.27*
	(0.11)	(0.14)
Female	0.16	0.57
	(0.45)	(0.46)
Age	−0.04***	0.05***
	(0.02)	(0.01)
Income	−0.01	0.01
	(0.01)	(0.01)
Education	−0.07	−0.09
	(0.09)	(0.10)
South	−0.98**	−0.11
	(0.43)	(0.60)
Constant	3.43**	−2.68*
	(1.71)	(1.41)
Observations	132	104

Source: ANES.

Note: Only individuals who participated in the Democratic primaries in these years are included in the models.

* $p<0.1$; ** $p<0.05$; *** $p<0.01$; standard errors in parentheses.

the respondent perceives the Democratic candidate as believing the government should aid blacks to alleviate racial inequality.

To better isolate the relationship between the perceived racial progressivism, vote choice, and turnout, I controlled for several demographic variables such as the respondents' age, income, education, and gender. In addition, I controlled for whether the respondent resided in the South and whether the respondent was second-generation or more. Finally, I controlled for whether the respondent was a Democrat or a Republican.

Table 8.2 includes two logit regressions predicting Latino respondents' support for the winning candidate in the 2008 Democratic presidential primaries (Barack Obama) and the 2016 Democratic presidential primaries (Hillary Clinton). Along with these estimations, I also calculated min-max predicted probabilities. The results demonstrate that Latinos who viewed Obama as favoring the black community in 2008 were not significantly more or less supportive of his candidacy in that year. However, as Latinos have grown in their levels of panethnic linked fate (see chapter 7) and have displayed more racially liberal attitudes, they have also displayed a stronger preference for racially liberal candidates. In 2016, Latinos who perceived Clinton as being racially liberal were substantially more supportive of her compared to her Democratic rivals. In fact, all else being equal, Latinos who voted in the Democratic primaries and viewed Clinton as believing government should aid blacks were 38 percent more likely to support her over her democratic rivals. The results provide some evidence that racialized appeals may improve Latino voters' support for Democratic candidates when partisanship is held constant.

While perceptions of racial liberalism mattered when there were few differences between Democratic candidates, the effect of polarization on vote choice appears to have muted differences in perceptions of racialization in recent years. Table 8.3 presents three logit regressions predicting support for Democratic candidates based on Latinos' perceptions of their racial liberalism for 2008, 2012, and 2016. I calculated min-max probabilities for significant variables in these regression models. Overall, the results suggest that perceptions of the racial liberalism of the Democratic presidential candidate rarely influence Latinos' vote choice in presidential elections. In fact, in only one of the previous three presidential elections were perceptions of racial liberalism a significant predictor of their vote choice. When Latinos perceived Obama as being racially liberal in 2012, they became much less likely to support him. In fact, holding other variables at their mean, Latinos who viewed Obama as being the most racially liberal were 15 percent less likely to vote for him than those who perceived him as being opposed to using government to aid blacks.

By 2016, there appears to have been no relationship between racialization and vote choice. Similar to the same analysis for whites (see chapter 4) and blacks (see chapter 6), Latinos did not appear to punish or reward Hillary Clinton for her perceived racial ideology. This may suggest that using racialization to persuade voters in a presidential election is unlikely to be successful. However, it also demonstrates that candidates who appear as working to address inequality for blacks do not lose support among Latinos in the presidential election. Some may argue that this is likely a Trump phenomenon, where few Latinos would support Trump regardless of Clinton's stances on race. However, according to the ANES, Trump performed statistically as well among Latinos as Romney did four years earlier.

Table 8.4 presents four separate logit regressions predicting self-reported voter turnout for Latinos in the 1996, 2008, 2012, and 2016 presidential elections. I also calculated min-max predicted probabilities for significant variables. As noted above, there were too few Latinos in the ANES before this year to draw any meaningful inferences about their political behavior. In the

TABLE 8.3. Logit regressions predicting Latinos' support for the Democratic presidential nominee (1980–2016)

	Vote for Democratic presidential candidate			
Year	1996	2008	2012	2016
Candidate's "aid to blacks" score	0.43 (0.58)	−0.13 (0.16)	−0.35** (0.15)	−0.15 (0.30)
Female	−7.72 (5.41)	0.33 (0.54)	0.04 (0.46)	1.05 (0.98)
Age	−0.01 (0.10)	−0.02 (0.02)	−0.01 (0.02)	0.05 (0.04)
Income	0.75 (2.28)	−0.93*** (0.25)	−0.10 (0.22)	−0.27 (0.30)
Education	−1.95 (1.41)	0.08 (0.11)	0.01 (0.08)	0.42*** (0.14)
7-point PID	−1.76 (1.29)	−0.65*** (0.15)	−1.07*** (0.18)	−1.24*** (0.31)
South	0.34 (2.46)	−0.24 (0.53)	0.14 (0.47)	−0.72 (0.99)
Ideology	−3.22* (1.95)	−0.54*** (0.19)	−0.44** (0.19)	−1.55*** (0.54)
Campaign contact	−8.93 (5.87)	0.33 (0.54)	−0.30 (0.55)	0.35 (0.91)
Constant	52.66* (31.10)	9.21*** (2.16)	9.39*** (1.89)	6.40** (3.03)
Observations	54	181	503	155

Source: ANES.
* $p<0.1$; ** $p<0.05$; *** $p<0.01$; standard errors in parentheses; PID = Party Identification.

years where data are available, it appears that unlike blacks and white Democrats analyzed in previous chapters, Latinos do not appear to be mobilized by the use of racial appeals. This null finding may be in part driven by the fact that my measure for racial liberalism is specific to blacks. To explore whether a more multiracial appeal may motivate Latino turnout, I now turn to the experimental analysis.

Experimental Data

In addition to the ANES and Pew Research, I also included a large number ($N = 160$) of Latino respondents in my survey experiment comparing voters'

TABLE 8.4. Logit regressions predicting Latinos' self-reported voter turnout (1980–2016)

	Voted in presidential election			
Year	1996	2008	2012	2016
Dem. candidate's "aid to blacks" score	0.54**	0.04	0.08	0.12
	(0.22)	(0.09)	(0.08)	(0.11)
Female	−0.15	0.25	0.23	0.27
	(0.70)	(0.36)	(0.28)	(0.35)
Age	0.06**	0.03*	0.02***	0.03**
	(0.02)	(0.02)	(0.01)	(0.01)
Income	−0.09	0.28	0.33**	0.42**
	(0.33)	(0.18)	(0.14)	(0.17)
Education	0.23	0.36***	0.22***	0.19***
	(0.18)	(0.07)	(0.07)	(0.07)
7-point PID	−0.27	−0.16*	−0.08	−0.29***
	(0.23)	(0.09)	(0.08)	(0.10)
South	0.05	0.13	−0.24	−0.62*
	(0.76)	(0.37)	(0.28)	(0.36)
Ideology	0.59**	−0.02	0.05	0.43***
	(0.26)	(0.12)	(0.11)	(0.15)
Campaign contact	1.20	1.09**	0.33	0.73
	(1.36)	(0.56)	(0.42)	(0.52)
Constant	−8.12***	−5.63***	−4.05***	−5.21***
	(3.12)	(1.24)	(0.99)	(1.19)
Observations	78	269	712	254

Source: ANES.

* $p<0.1$; ** $p<0.05$; *** $p<0.01$; standard errors in parentheses; PID = Party Identification.

reactions to two candidates—one white and one black—who focus on either economic or racial justice. An experimental analysis that holds everything equal but the race and agenda of the candidate provides internal validity to my study. As mentioned earlier, the collection of this experimental data took place using Amazon Mechanical Turk over four days from July 6 to July 10, 2017. Respondents were paid 50 cents to complete a survey that took about nine minutes to complete on average.

Respondents in the experiment were shown one of four webpages; two were for a candidate with a black-sounding name (Malik Jackson) and two were for one with a white-sounding name (Wyatt McHarris). Each candidate's webpages discussed either racial justice by focusing on issues like voting rights, police brutality, and immigrant rights, or economic justice, which focused on issues like workers' rights, collective bargaining rights, and raising the minimum wage. Respondents were told that the candidate was a U.S. senator who many considered to be a credible presidential candidate for the Democratic Party in 2020. Respondents were assigned to one of four treatments: a black racialized candidate, a white racialized candidate, a black deracialized candidate, or a white deracialized candidate.

Following the presentation of the treatment, I asked respondents who they would support in a potential matchup between Hillary Clinton in 2020 for the Democratic nomination. I then asked whether they would support the hypothetical candidate against Bernie Sanders in the same year for the Democratic nomination. Following questions about the Democratic primaries, I also asked respondents whether they would support the hypothetical candidates against Donald Trump in a potential 2020 presidential election matchup or Mitt Romney in a potential 2020 matchup. My dependent variable for this part of the analysis was simply whether the respondent selected the hypothetical candidate or the well-known Democrat in the Democratic primaries or the hypothetical candidate over the well-known Republican in the 2020 presidential election. Given that random assignment ensures balance between the treatment groups on variables like age, income, education, and partisanship, I simply estimated a two-sample *t*-test comparing how well the racial justice candidate performed against the economic justice candidate of the same race.

Table 8.5 compares Latino respondents on their levels of support for a hypothetical pair of candidates who advocated for racial justice against the same candidates who advocated for economic justice when pitted against a) Hillary Clinton only, b) Bernie Sanders only, c) Donald Trump only, and d) Mitt Romney only. The results demonstrate that Latinos were equally supportive of the racial justice candidates as they were the economic justice candidates, regardless of the opponent in the Democratic presidential primaries. The difference in the margin of victory for either the black racialized or deracialized candidate against Clinton or Sanders is less than 5 percent. Moreover, in the case of the hypothetical black candidates being matched up against Sanders, Latinos preferred both the deracialized and racialized candidates equally. The same relationship appears to hold for the hypothetical white candidates when they are pitted against Clinton or Sanders. In both cases, about 4 percent separates the white deracialized and racialized candidates in their reported support from Latino respondents. None of these differences were statistically significant.

TABLE 8.5. Differences in Latinos' stated support for hypothetical candidates Wyatt McHarris and Malik Jackson when they are presented as racialized or deracialized candidates and pitted against Hillary Clinton, Bernie Sanders, Donald Trump, and Mitt Romney in hypothetical 2020 matchups

	Clinton					
	Both	*N*	McHarris	*N*	Jackson	*N*
Deracialized candidate	0.7 (0.06)	67	0.74 (0.08)	34	0.67 (0.08)	33
Racialized candidate	0.71 (0.05)	92	0.7 (0.07)	50	0.71 (0.07)	42
Difference	**–0.01 (0.07)**	**159**	**0.04 (0.1)**	**84**	**–0.05 (0.11)**	**75**
	Sanders					
	Both	*N*	McHarris	*N*	Jackson	*N*
Deracialized candidate	0.36 (0.06)	67	0.38 (0.08)	34	0.33 (0.08)	33
Racialized candidate	0.34 (0.05)	92	0.34 (0.07)	50	0.33 (0.07)	42
Difference	**0.02 (0.08)**	**159**	**0.04 (0.11)**	**84**	**0 (0.11)**	**75**
	Trump					
	Both	*N*	McHarris	*N*	Jackson	*N*
Deracialized candidate	0.78 (0.05)	67	0.71 (0.08)	34	0.85 (0.06)	33
Racialized candidate	0.87 (0.04)	92	0.9 (0.04)	50	0.83 (0.06)	42
Difference	**–0.09 (0.06)**	**159**	**–0.19 (0.08)**	**84**	**0.02 (0.09)**	**75**
	Romney					
	Both	*N*	McHarris	*N*	Jackson	*N*
Deracialized candidate	0.77 (0.05)	66	0.79 (0.07)	33	0.76 (0.08)	33
Racialized candidate	0.79 (0.04)	92	0.81 (0.06)	42	0.78 (0.06)	50
Difference	**–0.02 (0.07)**	**158**	**–0.02 (0.09)**	**75**	**–0.02 (0.1)**	**83**

Source: Amazon Mechanical Turk survey.

Note: The "Both" column compares racialized and deracialized candidates of both races; the "McHarris" column compares only the racialized and deracialized McHarris candidate; and the "Jackson" column compares only the racialized and deracialized Jackson candidate. Positive scores indicate that the racialized candidate received more support than the deracialized candidate when pitted against an opponent.

* $p<0.05$; + $p<0.1$; standard errors in parentheses; significance is based on a two-sample test of means.

TABLE 8.6. Differences in voter enthusiasm (1 = low enthusiasm, 5 = high enthusiasm) if hypothetical candidates Wyatt McHarris and Malik Jackson are presented as racialized or deracialized candidates on the 2020 presidential ballot

Candidate type	Both	*N*	White	*N*	Black	*N*
Deracialized candidate	3.21 (0.18)	67	3.27 (0.27)	33	3.15 (0.24)	34
Racialized candidate	3.75 (0.12)	91	3.81 (0.17)	42	3.69 (0.17)	49
Difference	**−0.54* (0.21)**	**158**	**−0.54+ (0.3)**	**75**	**−0.55+ (0.28)**	**83**

Source: Amazon Mechanical Turk survey.

Note: The "Both" column compares racialized and deracialized candidates of both races; the "McHarris" column compares only the racialized and deracialized McHarris candidate; and the "Jackson" column compares only the racialized and deracialized Jackson candidate. Positive scores indicate that the racialized candidate received more support than the deracialized candidate when pitted against an opponent.

* $p<0.05$; + $p<0.1$; standard errors in parentheses; significance is based on a two-sample test of means.

For the most part, the same null relationships occur between the racialized and deracialized candidates of different races when pitted against either Romney or Trump. The one exception to this is that Latinos displayed a strong and significant preference for the white racialized candidate against Trump compared to the same candidate when he focused on economically liberal issues. No less than 90 percent of Latinos who received the white racially liberal candidate expressed that they would support him over Trump. In comparison, only 71 percent of Latinos who received the deracialized white candidate treatment supported this candidate over Trump. This 19 percent difference in support is statistically significant at 0.05. While for the most part the racial ideology of the candidate intersecting with the race of the candidate does not influence presidential election support, there is some evidence that white candidates who make racial appeals may be able to draw Latino support against the right opponent.

Table 8.6 presents the respondents' average intent to vote in 2020 if the hypothetical candidates who focus on either racial justice or economic justice represented the Democratic Party. The table includes the expressed intent to turn out for deracialized and racialized candidates who are either black or white. The voter turnout enthusiasm scale ranges from 1 (very unlikely to vote) to 5 (very likely to vote). The results demonstrate that Latinos expressed a greater intent to vote when the hypothetical candidates focused on racial justice than when they focused on economic justice. Moreover, this occurs for both white and black candidates. Latinos who were given either the racialized white or racialized black candidate were more than half a point more likely (0.54 for the white candidate and 0.55 for the Latino candidate) to express intent to vote in 2020 than Latinos who were presented with the same-race deracialized candidate. This difference was statistically significant at 0.05 based on a two-sample *t*-test. In contrast to the ANES, the experimental results demonstrate that racial appeals may be an effective way to appeal to and mobilize Latino voters. Moreover, it appears that racial appeals made by both black and white candidates can be effective in inspiring higher levels of Latino turnout in the current political context.

Conclusion

In the 1988 Democratic presidential primaries, Jesse Jackson pinned his hopes of winning the nomination on putting together a coalition of blacks, Latinos, and liberal whites. He worked to win the support of these groups by discussing his plans to address racial inequality and to advance progressive politics. The strategy helped Jackson win the vast majority of the black vote and increased turnout among blacks substantially. Jackson also won twice the number of votes from liberal whites that he received in his 1984 presidential campaign (Stout 2015). In spite of reaching parts of his targeted demographic, Jackson failed to gain the support of Latinos. In California, Michael Dukakis defeated Jackson among Latinos by a 2-to-1 margin (Stout 2015). Similarly, in Texas Jackson only received about 21 percent of the Latino vote.

Almost thirty years following Jackson's defeat, Hillary Clinton ran a campaign that, like Jackson's, was geared at attracting a rainbow coalition of voters. However, she enjoyed more success than her predecessor. Clinton not only did overwhelmingly well among black voters, she was also able to consistently win a majority of Latino voters as well. In states like New York, she won almost two-thirds of Latino voters. In California, Clinton won all ten districts where Latinos make up a majority of voters. Clinton's better performance than Jackson may be attributed to many factors, including the fact that Clinton enjoyed more endorsements from Latino elected officials and that Latinos often display a preference for whites over blacks. McClain et al. (2007), for example, find evidence that in some contexts Latinos view blacks as a racial threat, and this often diminishes their support for blacks and by extension black elected officials (but see Lublin 1997). Nonetheless, one notable factor that may explain her greater success compared to Jackson may be that her focus on racial issues inspired more support and enthusiasm among Latino voters in the current political context.

The growth of the Latino population in the United States makes them a critical player in American politics. Moreover, given the growing levels of polarization and the declining support of white working-class voters for the

Democratic Party in recent years, Latinos are a crucial part of the party's coalition. If Latinos fail to turn out or split their vote between Democratic and Republican candidates, the Democratic Party will face a difficult road in winning elected offices throughout the nation. While Latinos overwhelmingly supported Clinton in 2016, Latino turnout did not improve as many had expected. In spite of increasing mobilization efforts and the polarizing influence of Trump's candidacy, Latino turnout nationwide remained the same as it had been in 2012. In future elections, the Democratic Party and the party's nominee are going to have to find a way to increase Latino turnout if they are to succeed. Having Democratic candidates appearing as more racially progressive to Latinos may be key in this endeavor.

While recent research has demonstrated several ways to increase mobilization through contact with campaign volunteers (Michelson 2003; Valenzuela and Michelson 2016), the results in this chapter suggest that the candidate's message can matter. Latinos in my experiment who were presented with a candidate making racial and ethnic appeals that in part addressed problems facing Latinos were more likely to vote. Campaigns that try to deracialize and focus even on economically liberal policies run the risk of an unenthusiastic Latino electorate.

Additionally, there is some evidence that Latinos are more supportive in primaries when they view the candidate as being racially liberal. Latinos were much more likely to vote for Hillary Clinton when she was perceived as being racially progressive in the 2016 Democratic presidential primaries. This represents a reversal from 2008, when Latinos where more likely to vote against Obama when they perceived him as favoring the black community. This change may signal that the current political context leads Latinos to reward rather than punish racially liberal candidates. Overall, as Latinos make up a growing part of the Democratic electorate, presidential candidates who make racial appeals may benefit from reaching out to this important demographic.

It is important to note that politics is a numbers game. The campaign with the most votes wins the election. So, the question that arises from this and the previous chapters is whether racial appeals or appearing as racially progressive attracts enough supportive voters for candidates to win. If Latinos and blacks make up a small portion of the electorate, then gaining their vote should not matter as much to the Democratic Party. In chapter 9, I will explore whether demographic changes in the United States influence the practicality of engaging in racially liberal rhetoric.

9
Using Racial Appeals to Harness Demographic Change

In their 2004 book *The Emerging Democratic Majority*, John Judis and Ruy Teixeira hypothesized that demographic change in the United States would create a long-standing Democratic majority. They argued that the growing black and Latino populations, the declining population of white working-class voters, and the increasing number of liberal-leaning millennials would provide the Democratic Party with insurmountable majorities. The 2008 and 2012 presidential elections seemed to demonstrate the accuracy of their projections. Barack Obama succeeded with a minority of the white vote in both elections (less than 40% in 2012). Obama was able to overcome receiving the least amount of support from white voters of any winning president with high levels of black, Latino, and Asian American support. Following the 2012 election, many commentators questioned whether the Republican Party could ever be competitive again without winning the votes of the Obama coalition.

In spite of these fears, the 2016 presidential election demonstrated that Republicans can still win at the national level. Not only did Donald Trump's victory appear to demonstrate the ability of the Republican Party to succeed without attracting large-scale support from blacks and Latinos, it also led many to question whether the changing racial demographics of the nation could ever enable the Democratic Party to have insurmountable majorities. As a result, following the 2016 election there were several articles that argued that increasing diversity in America should not influence the political strategies of campaigns.

Many of these articles argued that the Democratic Party had fallen into the trap of relying on demographics. Writing for the think tank the Third Way, Hatalsky and Kessler (2017) argued that "demographic change became viewed as electoral destiny for Democrats. And Democrats who bought into it felt they could pursue a base-only strategy without worrying about persuading a broader swath of voters to support them, including the ones who have delivered big tent victories of the past. But this model for winning elections has failed" (2). Similarly, Geraghty (2017) argued in the *National Review* that

Democrats had not been successful persuading white voters to support their party and instead are relying on demographic change: "Moderating your message can get you some wins in districts and states that aren't usually friendly to your party. Luckily for Republicans, Democrats don't seem any closer to realizing they'll have to make their own destiny" (1). These and other writers maintained that the Democratic Party had become too obsessed with minority voters and had shunned persuadable white voters to their peril.

Those writing on this topic generally make two arguments to demonstrate why demographics don't equal destiny for the Democratic Party. The first argument is that the growth in minority population is not even across the United States. While a focus on identity politics may help the party win nationally, it will be greatly disadvantaged in most state, local, and congressional elections, where a substantial number of offices are selected. The second argument is that voters and coalitions are not static and can change relatively rapidly; black and Latino voters may not always be loyal to the Democratic Party. Thus, the assumption that the increase in the number of blacks and Latinos will lead to more democratic voters may not be true. Along these lines, some argue that if the Democrats continue to focus on racial/ethnic minorities, they may perform even worse among whites who are currently supportive of the party. If these arguments are correct, a focus on racial/ethnic voters may lead to limited returns as this electorate may become more divided.

In this chapter, I explore whether changes in demographic patterns in the United States are making racial appeals more rewarding to the Democratic Party or leading to a backlash among the electorate. To do so, I first describe the changes and projected changes in racial demography in the United States over the next forty years. I will then discuss in more detail why some argue that growing diversity in the United States will not lead to a sustainable majority for the Democratic Party. Following this review, I will explore whether racialization helps or hurts the Democratic Party as the demographics of the nation shift. In particular, I will assess how racially liberal candidates at the top of the ballot influence attitudes about the Democratic Party. The results from my analysis at both the state and national level reveal a positive spillover effect of racially progressive candidates for white Democrats, blacks, and Latinos.

Using these findings and a review of the results of the previous chapters, I argue that demographic changes, while uneven across states, will largely benefit Democrats both in presidential and U.S. House elections in the future. I will also discuss how racial appeals may make whites, blacks, and Latinos more Democratic over time. However, I will also argue that the disproportionate distribution of Republicans in small states will make racial appeals less effective in helping Democrats attain majorities in the U.S. Senate. Thus, racial appeals may further cement the Democrats' coalition, which is projected to grow over the next thirty years, but because of uneven growth across states the use of racial appeals may make it more difficult for the party to win Senate elections. The combination of these results demonstrates both the opportunities to expand representation through racial appeals and some potential pitfalls.

The Changing Face of the Nation

Over the past fifty years, the United States has gone through drastic changes in its racial makeup. In 1960, for example, whites made up 85 percent of the population according to the U.S. Census (Frey, Teixeira, and Griffin 2016). Blacks made up about 11 percent of the population and Asian Americans and Latinos made up less than 5 percent combined. Moreover, racial/ethnic minorities did not make up a plurality of individuals in any state in the continental United States. By 2010, the racial landscape of the nation had changed dramatically. The percentage of the white population in the United States had declined by over 20 percent, and the Latino population grew to be the largest racial/ethnic minority group. At the same time, both blacks and Asian Americans experienced slight increases in their share of the population. During this period, New Mexico, California, Texas, and Nevada joined Hawaii to become majority-minority states (i.e., states where racial/ethnic minorities make up a majority of the population).

While the period between 1960 and 2010 was transformative, the projected demographic changes in next thirty years will have a similarly large impact on the nation. By 2044, for the first time in American history whites will no longer make up a majority of the population in the United States. During that same year, Latinos will make up almost of third of the population and Asian Americans and blacks combined will make up an additional 25 percent of the populace (Frey, Teixeira, and Griffin 2016).

The shift in demographics nationally is also reflected at the state level. While only five states were majority-minority as of 2018, that number will grow to twenty by 2050. Moreover, this change is not evenly spread throughout the nation. Some of the most dramatic demographic shifts are happening in the South and in the Sunbelt. For example, Georgia will become a majority-minority state by 2025, as will Florida in 2028. Moreover, North Carolina, Virginia, Louisiana, and Mississippi will also become minority-white by 2050. With these changes, a majority of the old Confederacy will be majority-minority. States in the Mountain West such as Arizona, Nevada, and Colorado will join New Mexico as majority-minority states by 2050.

In 2017, nonwhites already made up a majority of infants in the United States. However, this majority of infants is far away from influencing elections. While states like Texas and California have been majority-minority states for over ten years, given that younger people are disproportionately racial/ethnic minorities who are ineligible to vote because they are under 18, there is often a lag between when states become majority-minority and when nonwhites make up a majority of the state's electorate. Only in the last few years have California's and Texas's eligible electorate become majority-minority. While states are becoming more diverse, there is certainly a lag between when racial/ethnic minorities become a majority of the population and when they become a majority of the electorate. However, by 2050 about a quarter of states will have electorates where whites make up a minority of voters.

These shifts in the nation's demographics are driven by several factors. First, there has been a sharp decline in white fertility compared to that of other racial/ethnic groups. This is in part driven by the fact that whites tend to be much older on average compared to other groups and are disproportionately from the baby boom generation. Moreover, some demographers suggest that whites were disproportionately of child-rearing age during the great recession (Frey, Teixeira, and Griffin 2016). This economic downturn led many to forgo having children in their prime child-birthing years.

Additionally, whites are dying at a younger age on average now than in the recent past. This is particularly true for whites without a college degree. While advances in technology and medicine have generally led to greater life expectancies, whites between forty-five and fifty-four are seeing a reversal of this trend. This is driven by many unnatural deaths related to suicide, the abuse of prescription drugs, and alcoholic liver disease. In combination, the birth-to-death ratio among whites has dropped significantly from 1999 (1.2 births to 1 death) to 2014 (1.04 births to 1 death). When this number declines below 1, replacement will no longer be occurring. The decline in the ratio of births to deaths among whites has already reached less than 1 in seventeen states, including Florida, Pennsylvania, California, and Virginia. The decline in the white population provides other racial groups the opportunity to gain in relative size.

While birth rates are declining among whites, they have increased slightly among blacks and Latinos. The total fertility rate, which is the number of children per woman who survives through childbearing years, is 2.1 for blacks and 2.4 for Latinos; for whites it is less than 2 (Passel and Cohn 2018). Several things account for greater levels of fertility among Latinos and blacks. First, both groups tend to be much younger than their white counterparts and thus a greater proportion of these groups are of childbearing age. Second, Latino immigrants to the United States tend to have more children than those born here (Passel and Cohn 2018). Given that a large portion of Latinos are born outside of the United States, it is not surprising that their fertility rates would be higher. Latinos' higher level of fertility compared to whites' explains much of their population growth between 2000 and 2010 and projected growth between 2010 and 2050 (Passel and Cohn 2018).

In addition to higher levels of fertility, most immigrants into the United States are from Latin American and Asian countries. Given the slowdown in the number of children the average family is having now as the cost of raising a child increases, much of the population growth in the future will come from changing immigration patterns. Between 1965 and 2010 over half of the population growth in the United States was tied to immigrants, their children, and/or their grandchildren (Passel and Rohal 2015). This trend will continue into the future. By 2065, a record number of residents in the United States, almost 1 in 5 (18%), will be immigrants. Pew Research Center projects that 88 percent of the increase in the U.S. population will come from immigrants who have not yet arrived in the country and their descendants (Passel and Rohal 2015). This is particularly true for Asian Americans, who will experience substantial growth over the next thirty years in spite of low fertility rates. Taken together, the country will look a lot more diverse over the next fifty years.

Will a Majority-Minority Nation Translate into Democratic Dominance?

Donald Trump's success in the 2016 presidential election raised several questions about whether the diversification of the nation really would benefit the Democratic Party. Given that the U.S. electoral system considers geography in the allocation of national representatives, and even in the election of the president, an uneven dispersion of minorities may lead to bigger Democratic victories in some states but not to more Democratic representatives in government. This is in part driven by our winner-take-all system in which winning by 50 percent plus one vote is equally as valuable as winning by 100 percent in terms of gaining an elected office. For example, in California in 2018, it does not matter if Dianne Feinstein (D), the incumbent Democratic Californian U.S. senator, wins by 50 percent and 1 vote or by 99 percent, both outcomes ensure that the U.S. Senate seat will still be held by a Democrat. Thus, even as the country diversifies it may not lead to drastic differences in the partisan makeup of government if much of the diversification is occurring in places where Democrats already do well.

Moreover, given that most growth among minority voters occurs in urban areas, Democrats won't benefit from diversification in even the U.S.

House of Representatives because of the way that boundaries are drawn. Hatalsky and Kessler (2017) argue that while the nation is diversifying, most of these changes are occurring in such a way that minorities will make up large majorities in only a few districts and that this will translate to larger wins in these contexts but won't improve Democrats representation in government. Finally, given that growing racial diversity is occurring in populous states like Texas and California and not in states like Wyoming or the Dakotas, this growth is being diluted because smaller states have a disproportionately larger say in the Electoral College and Congress.

The second critique arguing that greater diversification in the United States will not benefit the Democratic Party is that Latinos will increasingly becoming political independents over time. If this is true, their growth in the electorate is unlikely to benefit any political party. In a March 2017 *Slate* article, Yascha Mounk (2017) notes that Latinos may not always be loyal to the Democratic Party as panethnic identification may recede for Latinos over time. Moreover, Mounk argues that Latinos do not have the same strong levels of group consciousness as blacks and will even support Republicans who may appear to be hostile to Latino interests if the candidate can connect to this panethnic group through other means. Trump did as well with Latinos as John McCain in spite of Trump's more aggressive campaign style toward this group (Mounk 2017).

Along the same lines, others warn that demography may not equal destiny for the Democrats because working-class whites may be more willing to switch parties under the right conditions. Hatalsky and Kessler (2017) note that Hillary Clinton performed much worse than Obama did among whites, and this was particularly true of working-class whites, who made up a large portion of the New Deal coalition. The decline in support of whites may make it difficult for the gains Democrats make with blacks and Latinos to offset these losses. Hatalsky and Kessler (2017) observe that "Clinton's dismal performance among white voters (many of whom had reliably voted Democratic in the past) meant that winning black voters 88% to 8% and winning 65% of both Latino and Asian American voters was simply not enough" (10). Overall, these and other authors provide evidence that increases in the number of blacks and Latinos may not lead to permanent majorities for the Democratic Party.

How Do Racial Appeals Impact the Debate on the "Demography Is Destiny" Debate?

One of the main conclusions drawn from the "demography is *not* destiny" argument is that the Democratic Party has failed in part in recent elections because of its focus on identity politics. In some cases, this argument comes in the form of advocating for a color-blind approach to liberal politics. Lilla (2017), for example, argues that identity politics is driving a wedge between liberal voters: "We need a post-identity liberalism, and it should draw from the past successes of pre-identity liberalism. Such a liberalism would concentrate on widening its base by appealing to Americans as Americans and emphasizing the issues that affect a vast majority of them" (1). Mounk (2017), meanwhile, maintains that Democrats need to moderate their messages around minorities to appeal to whites and moderates: "Democrats still need to earn the votes of lots of moderates and whites to oust Donald Trump from the White House. Refusing to recognize this is not going to help" (1). If black and Latino voters are not as crucial for the Democrats as white voters, who may be turned off by racial appeals, then a focus on underrepresented racial groups will more than likely lead to defeat for the foreseeable future.

However, as I will argue in the following section, the analysis in this book provides evidence that racial appeals in combination with changes in demography may make a racialized strategy a more potent campaign approach than is argued by political pundits and scholars. To demonstrate this, I will examine each of the main critiques against the "demography is destiny" idea—noneven distribution of demographic change and shifting political coalitions—in turn, with a focus on how racial appeals may remedy these concerns.

The Uneven Distribution of Growth among Racial/Ethnic Minorities

The 2016 presidential election is a case study in how the uneven distribution of growing minority populations leads to more support for the Democratic Party without leading to electoral success. For example, the growing black and Latino populations of California led to much greater victories for Hillary Clinton in 2016 than even Barack Obama enjoyed four years earlier. Clinton's margin of victory over Donald Trump was 7 percent greater than Obama's victory over Mitt Romney in California in 2012. Moreover, it was almost 20 percent greater than Al Gore's margin of victory over George W. Bush in the state in 2000. As noted by Hatalsky and Kessler (2017), "A strategy based on appealing to nonwhites and Latinos can succeed only in the places those voters reside. But when those voters are concentrated, it is challenging to create electoral majorities" (6). Thus, winning California by about 10 points as Gore did in 2000 provides roughly the same number of electoral votes as winning California by 30 points, as Clinton did in 2016. Along the same lines, Clinton's better performance than Obama in states with growing Latino populations, such as Texas and Arizona, did not lead to higher levels of Electoral College support. The fact that minority population growth is occurring in many uncompetitive states may make it less appealing for Democrats to target black and Latino voters.

Most polls comparing Clinton's performance among whites in 2016 to Obama's performance among the same electorate in 2012 show a large decrease in support. For example, Clinton received 8 percent less of the white vote than Obama did in 2012 in Ohio. Similarly, Obama performed 8 percent better in Michigan, 6 percent better in Wisconsin, and 2 percent better in Pennsylvania among whites than Clinton did in 2016. One path to victory for Clinton in 2016 would have been to maintain the support of whites that Obama had in 2012. According to an analysis conducted before the 2016 presidential election by Frey, Teixeira, and Griffin (2016), Trump would need as much as a 10 percent swing in the white vote to win the election if blacks and Latinos turned out at the same rates in 2016 as they did in 2012. Nationally, this did not occur as the margin of victory for Trump among whites (21%) was only 1 percent greater than Romney's margin of victory (20%) with the same group. Moreover, in swing states Trump only performed better by 10 percent in Ohio, Michigan, and Iowa. In states like Pennsylvania and North Carolina, Trump either performed equally as well as Romney did in 2012 among whites or worse. As a result, it was not large-scale conversions of white Obama voters to Trump voters that alone tipped the scales.

Another significant part of the puzzle is the decline in minority turnout in 2016 compared to previous years. Frey, Teixeira, and Griffin's (2016) calculations were based on 2012 levels of minority turnout. However, black turnout declined by 7 percent in 2016, and Latino turnout declined nationally by about 0.4 percent. At the same time, white turnout increased by about 1.2 percent (Krogstad and Lopez 2017). This decline in minorities' turnout was also significant in the swing states that ultimately decided the election. For example, in Michigan black turnout decreased by 2 percent and Trump won the state by fewer than twelve thousand votes. Analysis conducted by Fraga, McElwee, Rhodes, and Schaffner (2017) shows that had Clinton maintained Obama's turnout in 2016, she would have won Pennsylvania, Wisconsin, and Michigan and become president of the United States.

So what lessons can be learned from this election that are applicable to arguments in support of making racial appeals? First, an unenthusiastic minority voter base can doom a Democratic candidate. The experimental analysis presented in chapters 6 and 8 demonstrated that Latinos and blacks are more likely to vote when the candidates focus on racial issues. Making racial appeals may therefore improve Democrats' chances nationally in 2020 and beyond. Moreover, as the country becomes more diverse and this increase in diversity occurs in a number of swing states such as Florida and North Carolina, a more active minority electorate may make it even more difficult for the Republican Party to succeed without drawing the support of black and Latino voters.

However, some suggest that the use of racial appeals and growing minority populations will alienate white voters and increase their support for the Republican Party. One way Republicans may improve their standing without reaching out to racial/ethnic minority voters is by increasing their support among whites. As noted above, some argue that the use of racial appeals may make it harder for the Democratic Party to translate demographic changes to higher levels of support because they will lose white voters in the process.

The analysis in this book demonstrates that this concern may be unfounded. Not only did Hillary Clinton *not* lose a significant number of white voters because of perceptions of her being racially liberal, but my experimental analysis demonstrates that neither white liberals nor white moderates were less supportive of two hypothetical candidates who made racial appeals as opposed to economically liberal appeals. In fact, the analysis conducted in chapter 4 demonstrated that many white liberals would be more active if they perceived the Democratic Party's candidate as being more racially liberal. This suggests that racial appeals would be no more damning to the party than liberal economic appeals.

Will Racial Appeals from High-Profile Politicians Hurt Democrats' Chances of Winning Locally?

Of course, the presidency is just one position among a myriad of congressional, state, and local elected offices. As Hamilton (1977) argued, the use of racial appeals should be strategic. It makes little sense to address racial inequality in a district or state that is largely conservative and white. While the results in previous chapters demonstrated that whites were not turned off by racial appeals in most cases, they also demonstrated that conservative whites are not largely supportive of racially progressive policies. As a result, a Democratic U.S. House candidate campaigning in rural Oregon or a Democratic U.S. Senate candidate in West Virginia would not gain much, if anything, by focusing on racial appeals.

However, there may be some concern that even if specific candidates do not focus on racial appeals, they may be tainted by being associated with high-profile copartisan politicians who discuss race in their campaigns. If this is true, there may be some cost for high-profile Democratic leaders who speak about race as this may make it harder for Democrats to win locally. For example, if a Democratic presidential candidate racializes, will unsupportive individuals punish copartisan politicians down ballot? If so, a strategy based on racial appeals may make winning elections in liberal and diverse states easier but make it harder for copartisan politicians to win in contexts that don't have these favorable demographic and partisan features. Such a finding would provide support for the claim that a nationally racially liberal platform is making it harder for Democrats to win locally.

To test whether partisans are tarnished by racially liberal party leaders, I return to my online experiment that compared a set of four candidates based on their campaign issues (see chapters 4, 6, and 8). Respondents were presented one of four conditions. In two of these conditions' respondents are presented with a candidate who advocates for racial justice by supporting voting rights, criminal justice reform, and immigration reform with either a white sounding name or a black sounding name. The other groups of respondents are presented with a campaign webpage that advocates for economic justice in a deracialized manner. Again, one candidate had a white-sounding name and the other a black-sounding name. For this analysis, I disregarded the race of the representative and just compared respondents on whether they received the treatment with the racially liberal candidate or the economically liberal candidate.

In addition to asking about vote choice (see chapters 4, 6, and 8), I also asked respondents to provide their feeling thermometer scores for the Democratic Party. These scores ranged from 0 (feel very negatively toward the party) to 100 (feel very positively about the party). The feeling thermometer score was asked after respondents were told that the candidate was a serious contender for the Democratic Party's nomination in 2020. If a candidate's focus on racial appeals is problematic for candidates down ballot, I expected that this would manifest itself in voters becoming less approving of the party under these circumstances. Moreover, I expected that racialized candidates will be more detrimental to their party in states that are more conservative.

To test this possibility, I compared Democratic Party feeling thermometer scores for whites, blacks, and Latinos by whether they received the candidate with the racialized message (i.e., racial justice) or the candidate with the deracialized message (i.e., economic justice). I also disaggregate these results by whether the state supported Clinton more than Trump in the 2016 presidential election or vice versa. By dividing states I this way, I could assess whether the Democratic Party was disproportionately hurt in left-leaning or right-leaning states for making racial appeals. Along with comparisons of means, I also present the results of a *t*-test comparing the whites, blacks, and

TABLE 9.1. Influence of deracialized and racialized candidates on respondents' Democratic Party feeling thermometer score

States Trump won	Whites	Blacks	Latinos
Deracialized	46.16	65.71	44.9
Racialized	46.66	64.21	56.3
Difference	0.5	−1.5	11.40+
N	219	148	90
States Trump lost	**Whites**	**Blacks**	**Latinos**
Deracialized	49.92	62.04	57.86
Racialized	57.72	53.76	57.95
Difference	7.79	−8.3	−0.08
N	149	87	64

* $p<0.1$; ** $p<0.05$; *** $p<0.01$; standard errors in parentheses; significance is based on a two-sample test of means; + significant at 0.10, * significant at 0.05

Latinos who received either the racialized message from either the white or black candidate or the deracialized message from either the white and black candidate. This analysis is presented in table 9.1.

The results in table 9.1 demonstrate that the nomination of a racialized candidate does not appear to tarnish the party's reputation among whites, blacks, or Latinos, regardless of whether the racial appeal occurs in a liberal or conservative state. For the most part, there were no significant differences between the different racial groups based on whether they received the racial or economic justice message. However, Latinos in states that Trump won were actually more approving of the Democratic Party when they were presented with the candidates who focused on racial appeals. On average, Latinos in these states viewed the Democratic Party as being about 11.5 points more favorably when presented with the racialized candidates than did Latinos in the same state who were presented with the deracialized candidates. The results of this analysis suggest that in states were Trump performed well, a racialized approach may improve the standing of the party with Latinos without losing the support of whites and blacks.

The change in the demographics at the state level along with the ability of racialized candidates at the top of the Democratic Party's ticket to improve perceptions of the party may make racial appeals a smarter strategy in the future. As mentioned in the previous section, much of the change in states' demography is driven by growing Latino populations. Moreover, these populations are not simply in states where Democrats dominate. Much of this growth is occurring in swing states and states in which the Republican Party generally performs well. For example, by 2019 the majority of Texas's voting-eligible population will be nonwhite. Given that Texas holds two Republican Senate seats and a 25-to-11 advantage over Democrats in the House in the 115th Congress, the evening out of these disparities would provide Democrats a large advantage. This, of course, depends on a mobilized and supportive Latino and black electorates—both of which are moved in a positive direction by racial appeals in the current context. Twenty years after Texas becomes majority-minority, Alaska, Arizona, and Georgia will follow. Again, these are states where Republicans hold both Senate seats and large advantages in the House. In summary, as these states become more diverse there are substantial opportunities for the Democratic Party to make gains, and they may be able to do so by using racial appeals.

Do Racial Appeals Challenge Shifting Coalitions?

As many who argue that demography is *not* destiny point out, partisan patterns may shift over time as voters begin to like one party more than the other or feel displaced by their preferred political party. This may happen for whites, who are becoming a more volatile voting bloc as they increasingly move from being partisans to independents. This may also be true for blacks and Latinos as both parties diversify. To explore whether racialization may influence attitudes about political parties over time, I analyzed data from the American National Election Study (ANES). In particular, I examine the difference in respondents' feeling thermometer scores for both the Democratic Party and Republican Party.

From 1980 to 2016, ANES respondents were asked to rate the two parties on a scale that ranges from 0 (strongly dislike the party) to 100 (strongly like the party). To calculate respondents' attitudes relative to the other party, I subtract each respondent's Republican feeling thermometer score from their Democratic Party feeling thermometer score. Thus, scores can range from -100 (indicating the respondent strongly likes the Republican Party and strongly dislikes the Democratic Party) to 100 (indicating the respondent strongly likes the Democratic Party and strongly dislikes for the Republican Party).

To assess whether there is any relationship between the racial liberalism of the Democratic presidential candidate and attitudes about the party as a whole, I divided the respondents into two groups. The first group viewed the Democratic presidential candidate as being more racially liberal (i.e., a score of 3 or less) on a spectrum that ranges from 1 (candidate believes government should aid blacks) to 7 (candidate believes blacks should help themselves). The second group either perceived the Democratic candidate as being in the middle (i.e., a 4 on this seven-point scale) or less racially liberal (i.e. a score of 5 or higher). If perceptions of racial liberalism influence how voters view one party relative to another, then those who viewed the Democratic Party's presidential candidate as appealing to blacks should have either a significantly higher or lower score on the relative party index.

White Respondents

The results in figure 9.1 demonstrate that an individual's partisanship largely influences how their perception of the Democratic presidential candidate's racial ideology shapes their attitudes about the parties. Figure 9.1A presents white Democrats' relative party score by whether they viewed the Democratic presidential candidate in a given year as being more or less racially liberal. As expected, white Democrats rated their party much more highly than Republicans in any given year. This difference has also grown over time as the parties have become more polarized. This increasing support from Democrats for their party over Republicans demonstrates how much harder it will be in the future for the Republican Party to attract the support of these voters. In 2016, there was on average over a 40-point favorability gap between the Democratic and Republican Party among Democratic voters. While political coalitions are never stable, there will have to be large-scale changes in politics for Republicans to draw the support of a substantial number of white Democrats who made up about a third of white voters (30%) in 2016 according to the ANES and 36 percent of voters according to the 2016 National Election Pool exit poll.

However, even if Democrats tend to be much more supportive of the Democratic Party than they are of the Republican Party, the question remains of whether racial appeals will strengthen or soften this support. According to figure 9.1A, white Democrats who viewed the Democratic presidential candidate in any year as being more racially liberal and those who viewed them as less racially liberal tended to have the same relative party scores for most years in the ANES. That all changed in 2016, however. In that year, Democrats who viewed Clinton as being more racially liberal rated the Democratic Party about 11 points higher relative to the Republican Party than Democrats who viewed Clinton as being racially conservative. This difference is significant based on a two-sample *t*-test. This indicates that racialized candidates may actually improve the Democratic Party's standing among copartisans. This may help Democrats retain the support of whites who already belong to the party and make it difficult for the Republican Party to win the same levels of support nationally as they have done in southern states.

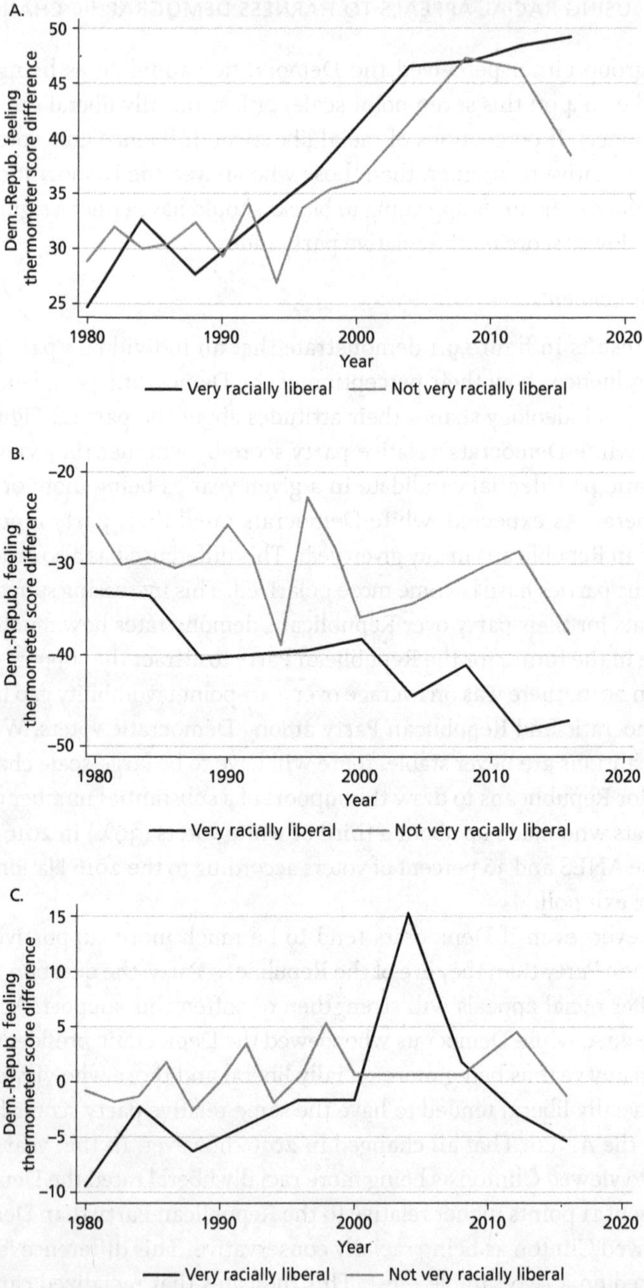

FIGURE 9.1. Whites' perceived Democratic presidential candidate's racial ideology on their Democratic party feeling thermometer score relative to their Republican Party feeling thermometer score: A: white Democrats; B: white Republicans; C: white independents

Source: ANES.

However, there is a possibility that a backlash among non-Democratic whites may offset any gains made by the Democratic Party through the use of racial appeals. Figure 9.1B presents the relative party score for Republicans who viewed the Democratic presidential candidate as being racially liberal and those who viewed them as racially moderate or conservative from 1980 to 2016. Like Democrats, the average Republican Party member has liked their party more relative to Democrats over time. Again like Democrats, the average relative party score for Republicans in 2016 was less than -40, indicating that Republicans disliked the Democratic Party by over 40 points on a 100-point scale. Democrats attracting Republican voters is as unlikely as Republicans attracting Democrats according to this analysis.

Moreover, while Democrats became more supportive of the Democratic Party when the Democratic presidential candidate was perceived as being racially liberal, Republicans had the opposite reaction. In 2016, for example, white Republicans who viewed Hillary Clinton as being more racially liberal rated the Democratic Party as being 10 points worse relative to the Republican Party (a score of -47) than white Republicans who viewed Hillary Clinton as a racial moderate or conservative (a score of -37). This suggests that having a racially liberal Democratic candidate may lead Republicans to become more loyal to their party. In combination with the results for white Democrats, perceptions of high-profile Democratic politicians' racial liberalism may increase partisan political polarization but not lead to drastic differences in the current partisan makeup of white voters.

I now turn to the potential swing vote of whites who identify as political independents. The analysis of their relative support for the Democratic and Republican Party is presented in figure 9.1C. As would be expected among political independents, there does not appear to be a strong preference for either the Republican or Democratic Party. Their support vacillates between parties over time, however. In most years, there is no statistically significant difference in white independents' relative party score. In fact, with the exception of 1980 and 2008, there is no significant difference in relative party scores between white independents who viewed the Democratic presidential candidate as being racially liberal and those who did not. In 2016, for example, white independents who perceived Hillary Clinton as being racially liberal did not feel significantly different about each party to white independents who viewed Clinton as being racially moderate/conservative.

In combination, white independents don't appear to be influenced by how racially liberal a Democratic candidate is perceived to be. Given the fact that the Republican Party needs to win 60–65 percent of white voters to succeed in a more diverse America, the party would have to win over almost all white independents, who don't appear to have strong allegiances to either party. If for some reason such a result does occur in any election cycle, the analysis presented in figure 9.1C demonstrates that it is unlikely to be driven by the Democratic presidential candidate appearing as being racially liberal.

Black Respondents

Figure 9.2A presents black respondents' attitudes about the Democratic Party relative to the Republican Party for those who viewed the Democratic presidential candidate in any year as being racially liberal and those who viewed that candidate as being racially moderate/conservative. As with white Democrats, blacks have become increasingly likely to view the Democratic Party much more favorably than the Republican Party in recent years. This was particularly true in 2008 and 2012, when Obama was the party's nominee for president. On average, blacks rated the Democratic Party 46 points more favorably than the Republican Party in 2016. While the future of the Republican Party's ability to attract blacks is unknown, figure 9.2A demonstrates that this is becoming more rather than less difficult for the party over time.

Moreover, when the Democratic candidate is perceived as being racially liberal, this appears to improve blacks' perceptions of the Democratic Party relative to the Republican Party. For most years in figure 9.2A, blacks who viewed the Democratic presidential candidate as being more racially liberal were also more likely to rate the Democratic Party as being significantly more favorable relative to the Republican Party. The year 2016 was no exception. In that year, blacks who viewed Hillary Clinton as being racially liberal rated the Democratic Party on average 7 points (a statistically significant difference according to a two-sample *t*-test) more favorably relative to the Republican Party than blacks who viewed Clinton as being racially moderate/conservative. In combination, these results suggest that appearing as racially liberal may cement the Democratic Party's support with black voters.

Latino Respondents

Latinos as a group tend to view the Democratic Party as being much more favorable than the Republican Party, and this difference has tended to grow over time. In 2004, when George W. Bush made a strong effort to appeal to Latino voters, Latinos who viewed John Kerry as being racially liberal actually viewed the Republican Party more favorably than the Democratic Party. In 2016, however, Latinos rated the Democratic Party as being 20 points more favorable than the Republican Party, and those who viewed Hillary Clinton as being more racially liberal rated the Democratic Party about 23 points more

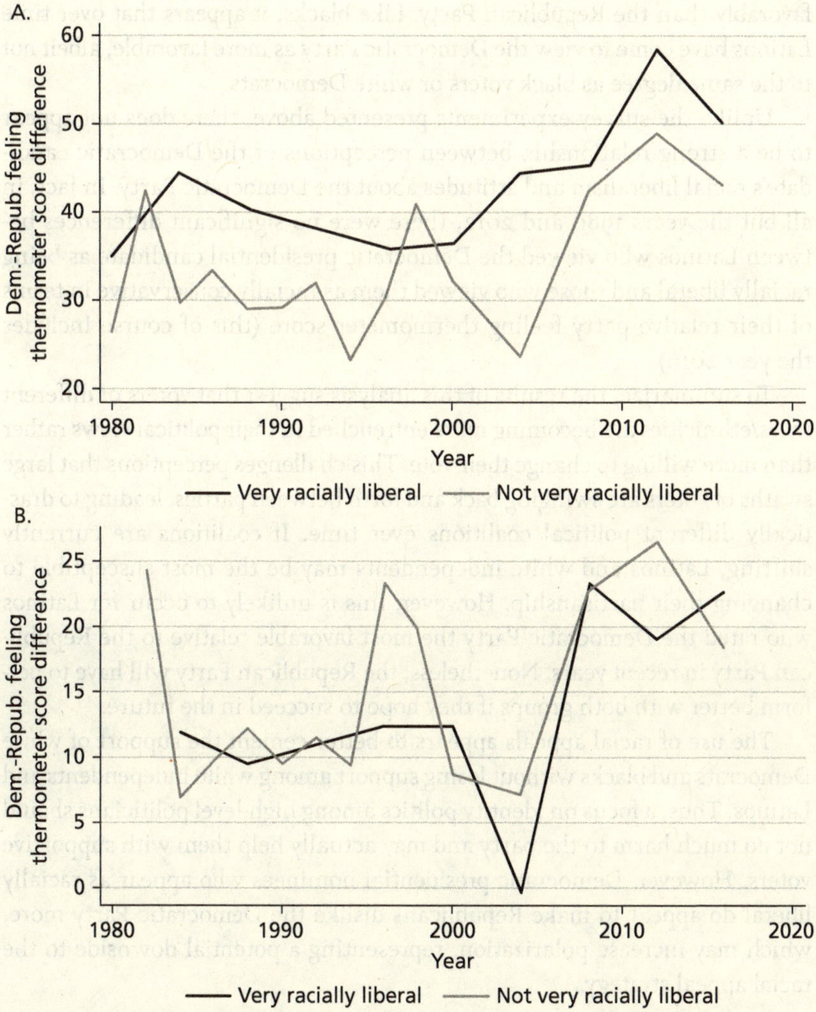

FIGURE 9.2. Blacks' (A) and Latinos' (B) perceived Democratic presidential candidate's racial ideology on their Democratic Party feeling thermometer score relative to their Republican Party feeling thermometer score
Source: ANES.

favorably than the Republican Party. Like blacks, it appears that over time Latinos have come to view the Democratic Party as more favorable, albeit not to the same degree as black voters or white Democrats.

Unlike the survey experiments presented above, there does not appear to be a strong relationship between perceptions of the Democratic candidate's racial liberalism and attitudes about the Democratic Party. In fact, in all but the years 1980 and 2012, there were no significant differences between Latinos who viewed the Democratic presidential candidate as being racially liberal and those who viewed them as racially conservative in terms of their relative party feeling thermometer score (this of course includes the year 2016).

To summarize, the results of this analysis suggest that voters of different races/ethnicities are becoming more entrenched in their political views rather than more willing to change their vote. This challenges perceptions that large swaths of voters are swinging back and forth between parties, leading to drastically different political coalitions over time. If coalitions are currently shifting, Latinos and white independents may be the most susceptible to changing their partisanship. However, this is unlikely to occur for Latinos who rated the Democratic Party the most favorable relative to the Republican Party in recent years. Nonetheless, the Republican Party will have to perform better with both groups if they hope to succeed in the future.

The use of racial appeals appears to better cement the support of white Democrats and blacks without losing support among white independents and Latinos. Thus, a focus on identity politics among high-level politicians should not do much harm to the party and may actually help them with supportive voters. However, Democratic presidential nominees who appear as racially liberal do appear to make Republicans dislike the Democratic Party more, which may increase polarization, representing a potential downside to the racial appeal strategy.

A Potential Downside

While the use of racial appeals may provide significant advantages for the Democratic Party nationally and possibly in the U.S. House, the geographic dispersion of liberals and conservatives across several states may provide a potential problem for Democrats with the U.S. Senate. Every state, regardless of its size, has two U.S. senators. This institutional arrangement was created at the Constitutional Convention of 1787 to ensure that smaller states would not be rendered irrelevant by their small population size in the national legislature. Such a compromise was crucial during a period in which state identities where strong and a national identity was almost nonexistent.

The consequence of this compromise as the population has grown is that individuals within some states are extremely underrepresented in the U.S. Senate. For example, California has the same population as the twenty-two smallest states combined. As a result, two U.S. senators represent the same number of people in California as forty-four other U.S. senators do in those smaller states. This disparity is going to grow over time. By 2040, 70 percent of the U.S. population will live in the largest fifteen states. Thus, 30 percent of the population will elect 70 percent of the U.S. Senate.

In addition to population disparities, there are also significant partisan differences between large and small states. While Democrats make up 55 percent of U.S. senators from the most-populated twenty states, they only make up 40 percent of U.S. senators from the least-populated thirty states. As individuals move to larger states, some predict that the partisan divide between large states and smaller states will become even starker.

What does this mean for the use of racial appeals? If Democrats are going to do better in the U.S. Senate they will have to win in states where there are few Democrats. This requires that they appeal to Republican voters in some places. In the past, candidates like Heidi Heitkamp of North Dakota and Joe Manchin in West Virginia were able to win in such states. However, the results above demonstrate that Republican voters viewed the Democratic Party as being less favorable when they viewed Hillary Clinton as being more racially liberal. As a result, the use of racial appeals may help the Democratic Party win nationally and even in the U.S. House as the black and Latino population grows. However, the institutional makeup of Congress requires that Democrats win some Republican voters to hold unified control of the national legislature. Racial appeals may make this more difficult. In this sense, the use of racial appeals may be a double-edged sword for the Democrats as the country's demographics change. It may help them win some offices but make it difficult for them to get legislation passed, as this requires the help of the U.S. Senate.

Conclusion

Whether changing demographics in the United States will lead to a sustainable coalition that will fuel the Democratic Party into the future is unknown. However, most factors indicate the Democratic Party's position in both national- and state-level governments should improve over the next thirty years. The substantial growth in the number of racial/ethnic minorities, both nationally and within many states, in combination with the fact that many of these minority groups are overwhelmingly and consistently voting with the Democratic Party, provides hope.

However, for the Democratic Party to properly harness these demographic changes it must first strengthen its coalition and second get these individuals out to the polls. As mentioned earlier, if Democrats can replicate Obama's coalition in 2012, Republicans are going to need to make drastic improvements with white voters, many of whom strongly prefer the Democratic Party to the Republican Party. Moreover, according to the analysis by Frey, Teixeira, and Griffin (2016), winning even 70 percent of the white vote may not be enough by the year 2032 at the presidential level if black and Latino turnout remains high. Moreover, given that changing demographics are occurring in states that are considered swing states (i.e., Colorado, Florida, and North Carolina) and Republican-dominated states (i.e., Texas, Missouri, and Georgia), the Democratic Party is also poised to improve its standing at the state and congressional levels due to the diversification of America. This of course assumes that it is able to rebuild the Obama coalition of 2012.

So how can Democrats work toward re-creating the Obama coalition that was missing in 2016? The results of this analysis demonstrate that when Democratic candidates engage in racial appeals or are seen as being racially progressive, they tend to improve perceptions of the party among white Democrats, blacks, and Latinos. For example, Latinos were significantly more approving of the Democratic Party when presented with hypothetical candidates who focused on racially liberal issues than Latinos who were presented with candidates who focused on economically liberal issues. Along the same lines, both white Democrats and blacks who perceived Hillary Clinton as being racially liberal felt significantly more positive about the Democratic Party relative to the Republican Party than their counterparts who viewed her as racially conservative.

It is important to note that racial appeals may not be effective in states that are largely white and more conservative. For example, it would more than likely be ineffective for Democratic candidates in Montana, West Virginia, or Idaho to focus on racial appeals. The party may succeed by strategically using racial appeals in contexts in which the left-leaning electorate prioritizes addressing racial inequality while focusing on other issues in different contexts. Moreover, as discussed above, the use of racial appeals nationally may make it difficult for Democratic candidates to draw the support of Republican voters in these states, which may be necessary to win U.S. Senate seats in states where Republican voters dominate.

Moreover, the effectiveness of these appeals will only matter in contexts where racial/ethnic minorities are not disproportionately barred from participating meaningfully in elections. There are of course examples where majority populations are unable to reward racially progressive candidates because they are prohibited from voting. A good example of this was South Africa during apartheid.

Nonetheless, there do appear to be some advantages for Democrats in engaging in racialized appeals in the current political context. In previous chapters, I demonstrated that blacks, Latinos, and in some cases white Democrats felt better about candidates who were racially liberal. The positive attitudes about these candidates, which may manifest as greater levels of electoral support or turnout, also appear to influence attitudes about their party as a whole. Democratic candidates down ballot of a racialized presidential candidate may benefit from a more enthusiastic and supportive Democratic base, which may matter in swing electorates. In combination with results from previous chapters, the changing demographics of the nation suggest that racial appeals are an important tool that Democrats should use to shore up support and mobilize their base. This may be an increasingly fruitful strategy as the country becomes more diverse.

CONCLUSION

The Path of Least Resistance

The prominent African American abolitionist Frederick Douglass once remarked, "The Republican Party is the deck, all else is the sea" (quoted in Rees 1991). His metaphor illustrates how closely tied the interests of blacks were to the Republican Party during Reconstruction. It had been founded in part as an abolitionist party whose leadership was strongly committed to advancing the political and social rights of blacks. As a result, for blacks wanting to remain safe and become prosperous it was a good idea to align with the Republican Party. In contrast, the Democratic Party was supportive of retaining the institution of slavery during the Civil War and worked hard to restore the racial caste system during Reconstruction. Thus, building coalitions with the Democratic Party would lead blacks to metaphorically drown.

During the period of Reconstruction, the Republican Party dominated American politics. This was in large part driven by African American support in the South and liberal white support in the North. This coalition of voters made it possible for the Republican Party to pass three Amendments to the U.S. Constitution that ended slavery (the Thirteenth), prohibited states from treating blacks differently from whites and expanded citizenship rights to blacks (the Fourteenth), and gave black men the right to vote (the Fifteenth). The Republican Congress was also able to pass the 1875 Civil Rights Act, which provided federal protections for blacks in the South.

The Republican Party's dominance began to fade in the 1870s, however. An economic crash in 1873 led many to question whether Republicans were focusing too much on African Americans at the peril of whites. By 1874, Democrats had regained political control of seven of the eleven states in the former Confederacy. Once in control, the Democratic Party in conjunction with white supremacist groups like the White League, the Red Shirts, and the Ku Klux Klan severely curtailed the rights of African Americans. The final nail in the coffin for black political rights occurred after the 1876 election, in which Republican presidential candidate Rutherford B. Hayes defeated Democrat Samuel Tilden after a highly contested campaign. In a deal to retain control of the presidency, Republicans agreed to remove military oversight in Florida, Louisiana, and South Carolina. The removal of federal troops from the South eliminated protections for blacks and allowed southern whites to systematically disenfranchise African Americans. In return, Republican Rutherford B. Hayes would become president. With these changes, blacks would largely be excluded from participating meaningfully in politics in the South for almost a hundred years.

Given the declining power of the black vote, the Republican Party faced a dilemma. They could either continue to focus on the rights of African Americans or they could try to moderate their racial positions to appeal to southern whites in hopes of bringing them over to their party. The Republicans chose the latter. President Hayes and later the "lily-white" Republicans argued that the party should abandon their focus on advancing black political interests. Moreover, to bring white southerners into the party, they also promised to provide the region with more economic development and patronage for white southern political elites. The strategy proved to be a complete disaster. White southerners took the Republicans' patronage and resources, but they never supported their party. As Heersink and Jenkins (2016) put it, "From a white southerner's perspective, the GOP was the 'Black Party.' . . . 'Respectable' Southern whites could not envision becoming Republican, Hayes's efforts notwithstanding, as the GOP brand was established and invariant" (8). The deracialized Republican Party was never able to gain traction among southern whites, and the Democratic Party dominated southern politics until the civil rights era.

To make matters worse, the Republican Party's abandonment of black voters made them a swing electorate. Over time, blacks became less loyal to the party of Lincoln. In the close election of 1960, blacks' support for John F. Kennedy was one of the main factors in the defeat of Richard Nixon. Moreover, after the civil rights legislation in the 1960s, Nixon's southern strategy in the 1970s, and the growth of racially conservative politicians within the Republican Party, the latter no longer represented the Douglass's deck; they had become the sea.

As several scholars and political pundits have noted, coalitions are not for all time. They can shift under the right circumstances. As illustrated with the example above, the black vote that was once guaranteed for the Republican Party was lost after the party opted to move away from a racially progressive platform. However, given the declining number of black voters due to widespread voter disenfranchisement and Jim Crow laws, the Republican Party could be said to have taken a calculated risk—one that took nearly a hundred years to pay off.

Today, some argue that the Democratic Party should take a similar approach to race as Republicans did at the end of Reconstruction. While the lily-white movement in the Republican Party was fueled in large part by racism—something that is certainly not true of proponents of a deracialized approach within the Democratic Party today—the strategy and aims are similar. By limiting discussions of racial inequality, the Democratic Party may be able to gain the support of racially conservative working-class whites.

The lessons of the Post-Reconstruction era intersect with the analysis in this book to describe the potential limitations of a deracialized campaign strategy. As was true for the Republican Party in the past, Democratic focus on racially conservative whites may not lead to large-scale conversions of these voters. Moreover, if the Democratic Party moves to appease unmovable racially conservative whites at the expense of blacks and Latinos, they may jeopardize their strong support from these underrepresented groups, just as the Republican Party did after Reconstruction. Unlike the dilemma Republicans faced in the past with regard to the disappearing black electorate, recent demographic changes have increased the significance of the black and Latino electorate, a trend that will continue into the future. In this sense, the decision to deracialize may be even riskier for the Democratic Party now than it was for the Republican Party after Reconstruction.

In this conclusion, I will discuss how the analyses in this book help us understand how contextual factors should influence political parties' use or avoidance of racial appeals. I will first summarize why the current political context improves the efficacy of racial appeals. Second, I will describe why the abandonment of identity politics in an attempt to persuade white racially conservative voters is riskier than a campaign strategy that focuses on mobilizing racial/ethnic minorities. Third, I will argue that a unidimensional racialized campaign approach that ignores other groups, including white working-class voters, will be equally exclusionary and ineffective as a deracialized campaign strategy that subjugates the interests of blacks and Latinos. Finally, I will discuss how Asian Americans respond to racial appeals and how conservative opponents counteract racial appeals, as well as outline directions for future research in this area.

Context Matters: Lessons for Understanding When Candidates Should Focus on Race in Their Campaigns

There has long been a debate about how candidates should focus on race in their campaigns. Following the end of civil rights era, the movement toward a deracialized strategy became popular for candidates of different political parties and races/ethnicities. In Hamilton's (1977) article on deracialization, he argued that such an approach is necessary for left-leaning politicians to succeed given the political context of the United States during the latter part of the twentieth century. Given the significance of white southern voters for the Democratic Party and blacks' willingness to accept a deracialized economic agenda, a compromise that would attract both groups would be for candidates to focus on class-based issues.

Hamilton (1997) powerfully presented the significant incentives for candidates to run deracialized campaigns, but he also argued that no political strategy is set in stone and that how candidates address race in their campaigns must *always be calculated*. Most previous work on deracialization has overlooked the significance of the political context in predicting the efficacy of racial appeals beyond the racial composition of the electorate (see Johnson 2017 for an exception). Much of this research arrives at conflicting results, where in some cases candidates who make racial appeals do well, but in others a deracialized approach is advantageous. This study advances research in this area by demonstrating that the national mood of the country plays a significant role in predicting when racial appeals are most effective. In doing so, this book may better help deracialization scholars understand why previous research in this topic has produced such disparate results.

As demonstrated in chapters 5 and 7, when black and Latino linked fate is low, these groups tend to be less concerned about a progressive racial agenda. As a result, blacks and Latinos are less responsive to racial appeals in periods like the end of the twentieth century and beginning of the twenty-first century, when perceptions of racism were lower. This suggests that even as the country becomes more diverse, a racialized approach may not always be the most effective strategy. There will be times when blacks and Latinos prioritize their racial/ethnic group's interests less and as a result won't respond to racial appeals.

However, in periods when both groups feel that their opportunities are limited due to their race/ethnicity (see chapters 6 and 8), they become more responsive to racialized outreach. As has been shown consistently in this book through empirical analysis, blacks and Latinos were more responsive to a variety of racial appeals in 2016 they had not been receptive to in the past. The rise of social movements around racial/ethnic topics, the increased focus of the media on racial/ethnic inequality, and video recordings and accounts of racial/ethnic minorities being mistreated by law enforcement increased the salience of race/ethnicity in the lives of blacks and Latinos. This change in perspectives about race/ethnicity was then correlated with more support for racially progressive politicians.

In chapter 4, I demonstrated that context also matters for predicting the efficacy of a racialized approach in mobilizing white Democrats. During Obama's second term, which coincided with the rise of the Black Lives Matter movement, white Democrats displayed the most racially progressive attitudes recorded in the past thirty years. In many cases, there were dramatic shifts in this group's racial attitudes between 2012 and 2016. This change in racial attitudes links well with white Democrats feeling more mobilized by racial appeals now than in the past. While many caution that a racialized strategy will always lead politicians to sacrifice white voters, the findings of this book suggest that, under the right circumstances, racialized outreach can actually improve a candidate's standing with white Democrats.

In summary, parties and pundits should always pay attention to the national political context around race when arguing for or against a racialized approach. The recent rise in social movements and public attention toward racial issues may provide the best context for racialized candidates to succeed. The 2016 election, and the years that have followed, appear to have been ripe for racially progressive candidates.

Why a Base Strategy Is the Most Efficient Path Forward

Even as campaigns are bringing in more money than ever before, candidates still have to make difficult choices about how they allocate their resources. One of the major decisions for campaigns is whether to focus on mobilizing the base or to moderate their message in hopes of attracting swing voters. As noted in chapter 4, candidates have focused more on the former strategy in recent years. As the population becomes more polarized, it becomes increasingly difficult to gain the support of those who vote for the other party. The results in chapter 9 demonstrated that Democrats' feeling thermometer scores of the Republican Party relative to their own party has been growing dramatically over the past ten years. The same trend was seen in Republicans' feeling thermometer scores for the Democratic Party relative to the Republican Party. Even in the 2016 presidential election, where both Donald Trump and Hillary Clinton were disliked by members of their respective parties, about 90 percent of Democrats and Republicans supported their party's presidential nominee.

Self-identified independents, too, have become more consistent in their political preferences. Smidt (2011) demonstrated that pure independents in the current political context behave the same way as their strong partisan counterparts did in the past. He notes that there are very few pure swing voters given the current state of political polarization in American politics. Gelman et al. (2016), meanwhile, noted that even the appearance of voters swinging back and forth in a single election cycle can largely be attributed to sampling artifacts. This research suggests that a persuasion-centered campaign is unlikely to be effective. If voters are more likely to have their mind made up before campaigns even begin allocating resources, then persuasion may not be the most efficient use of capital. Kalla and Broockman (2018), through a meta-analysis of forty field experiments, estimated the average campaign persuasion effect to be zero. In other words, when politicians use outreach to persuade voters, they on average have no effect. Such a result may explain why Hillary Clinton's effort to pull away disaffected Republicans in Arizona and Texas in the 2016 presidential election largely failed.

So what does the increasing polarization in society mean for a deracialized approach? Those who argue against identity politics implicitly assume that there are swing or cross-pressured voters who *would* support the other party with the correct message. In the past, this was certainly true. So-called Reagan Democrats could be persuaded to join the Democratic Party if it focused more on an economic message rather than a racial message. However, as was demonstrated in chapter 3, these voters have followed the same path as their more elite counterparts and are equally divided by racial issues in the current political context. As a result, simply deemphasizing racial appeals is unlikely to overcome the perils of polarization and bring a large number of racially conservative whites back into the Democratic Party. Such a strategy would take a significant amount of resources and possibly cost the Democratic Party support from racial/ethnic minorities and liberal whites. Overall, the risk of such action would be high for uncertain returns.

In contrast, most research demonstrates that mobilization efforts are fruitful in turning out one's political base. One of the most consistent findings in political science research is that voters respond to campaign strategies when deciding whether to vote (Blais 2006; Gerber and Green 2000; Michelson, Bedolla, and McConnell 2009; Philpot, Shaw, and McGowen 2009). Moreover, a significant amount of research demonstrates that the messaging of a candidate matters in influencing an individual's likelihood of voting in an election (Abramowitz and Stone 2006; Panagopoulos 2009; Stout 2015). The analyses in chapters 4, 6, and 8 corroborate these findings with regard to turnout. While I found little evidence that voters have altered their voting behavior in general elections based on a racialized approach in recent years, I also found that white Democrats, blacks, and Latinos have become more mobilized and enthusiastic for racially progressive candidates.

The combination of the minimal campaign effects on persuasion and the large effects of mobilization suggests the Democratic Party may get the most from their messaging by discussing racial issues. The path of least resistance for the party would be to focus on remobilizing the Obama coalition of liberal whites, blacks, and Latinos through the use of racial appeals. In contrast, the path of most resistance requires a reshuffling of the party's strategy to deemphasize racial/ethnic topics in hopes of getting voters to make dramatic changes in their partisan preferences during a period of growing polarization.

Using racial appeals to mobilize may become even more effective in the future as demographic changes increase the number of individuals who are supportive of progressive racialized outreach. As discussed in chapter 9, the coalition of white liberals, blacks, and Latinos is expected to grow significantly over the next thirty years. This would provide the Democratic Party a huge advantage nationally if it is able to harness the energy of these voters. One of the most consistent findings in this book is that this can best be done through the use of racial appeals.

Should the Democratic Party Focus Only on Racial Appeals and Ignore Working-Class Interests? NO!

It might be easy for someone reading this book to come to the conclusion that the Democratic Party should only focus on racial/ethnic appeals and ignore the most pressing issues of other groups, including working-class whites, women, the LGBTQ community, and others. This is not my intention at all. Moreover, the empirical analysis conducted in previous chapters does not support such a conclusion. A strategy that ignores large segments of the population is exactly what this book is arguing against.

Grossman and Hopkins (2016) note that the composition of political parties should play a role in how they organize and strategize. The authors argue that Republicans tend to be tied together by their conservative ideology. In comparison, Democrats are a coalition of social groups with distinct interests who coalesce around the ideal of a proactive and engaged federal government. Grossman and Hopkins note that the makeup of the Democratic Party provides some challenges to organization because the party has to appeal to more segments of the population whose interests are not always aligned.

As a result, the Democratic Party must find ways to keep all social groups within their coalition engaged without alienating segments of their alliance. The deracialized strategy provided a solution to this problem in the past, given that blacks and Latinos made up a smaller portion of the electorate and largely remained supportive of the party even when it subjugated their group's specific interests to accommodate the preferences of others. However, as has been detailed extensively in this book, the Democratic Party is no longer able to maximize its support from racial/ethnic minorities by ignoring racial/ethnic issues. Moreover, the party does not have to, given the growing racial liberalism of white Democrats. This allows the party to appeal to multiple social groups within its coalition without sacrificing the support of others.

However, this line of reasoning should not be taken as suggesting Democrats should only focus on racial/ethnic minorities. Any strategy that only focuses on a few groups is bound to alienate otherwise sympathetic voters from other social or racial groups. As blacks and Latinos may be turned off by a campaign strategy that minimizes their group's interests, it is likely that liberal whites may be less enthusiastic about a campaign that *solely* focuses on the interests of racial/ethnic minorities. In my previous book, *Bringing Race Back In: Black Politicians, Deracialization, and Voting Behavior in the Age of Obama*, I found that campaigns that solely focus on African American voters not only lead to lower levels of support among liberal whites, but also to lower levels of support from racial/ethnic minorities (Stout 2015). For the former, I argued that campaigns that uniformly focus on racial issues lead white voters to feel left out of the political conversation. For the latter, I showed that some blacks were hesitant to support unidimensional racialized candidates because they were perceived as being uncompetitive and unempathetic.

Any campaign strategy that focuses on one group at the expense of others is going to limit the full potential of parties like the Democratic Party, which is made up of a diverse set of social groups. Such strategies include running a deracialized campaign that subjugates the interests of racial/ethnic minorities and running a unidimensional racial campaign that dismisses the concerns of white voters. Moreover, given the dramatic ongoing demographic changes in the United States, it appears to be unnecessary for the Democratic Party to ignore any of the members of their coalition. As a result, the best way for the party to move forward is recognize and address the interests of all members in their alliance.

Beyond the Electoral Consequences of Identity Politics

While this book focuses on whether engaging in racial appeals is a useful form of electoral outreach, it is important to also discuss the normative implications of identity politics. There are many arguments against identity politics that are not focused on electoral behavior. Two of the most prominent critics of identity politics are political scientist Francis Fukuyama and psychologist Jordan Peterson. Fukuyama and others argue that the use of identity politics may benefit political parties in the short run but will have long-term deleterious effects on the fabric of U.S. democracy. In his rebuke of identity politics, Fukuyama (2018) states: "The Democratic Party, in particular, has a major choice to make. It can continue to try to win elections by doubling down on the mobilization of the identity groups. . . . [This] strategy might allow it to win elections, but it is a poor formula for governing the country. The Republican Party is becoming the party of white people, and the Democratic Party is becoming the party of minorities. Should that process continue much further, identity will have fully displaced economic ideology as the central cleavage of U.S. politics, which would be an unhealthy outcome for American democracy." Fukuyama argues that a focus on identity politics will lead Americans to become more fragmented around individual identities. The major potential drawback of these growing differences is that they will decrease Americans' likelihood of finding common ground on the most pressing issues facing the country. This argument suggests that when politicians focus on racial issues, liberal voters become more attuned to racial inequality and their levels of group consciousness increase. On the other side, Democrats' focus on racial issues like Black Lives Matter or immigration provides fodder for conservative political pundits and politicians to argue that the party is caring for blacks, Latinos, and Asian Americans at the expense of whites. This feeling that benefits are unfairly being given to racial/ethnic minorities then leads to an increase in white group consciousness. The combination of these factors increases divisions among Americans and makes policy solutions unattainable. In essence, for Fukuyama, identity politics is exacerbating political polarization, the long-term effect of which is gridlock and the inability of government to function.

Peterson (2018) is even more forceful in his opposition to the identity politics of the left. He argues that liberal identity politics has gone too far and may even get worse in the future. Similar to other critics of identity politics, Peterson argues that the focus on individual groups could be endless. We all have multiple identities, and while we are all humans we all also identify as a specific combination of our nationality, race, gender, sexual orientation, age, etc. When we fractionalize our identities enough, we all belong to a different group. One of the problems for Peterson, then, is which groups deserve reparations? How specific should we get in addressing inequalities?

Peterson (2018) argues that the world is simply unfair and that this is a reality that everyone will realize at some point in time. Through this realization, Peterson argues that individuals have to take responsibility for their lives and not blame others. He perceives a focus on identity politics as blaming others for inequality rather than finding ways to take personal responsibility to improve their situation.

While these are just two perspectives about the negative implications of a growing focus on identity politics, they represent some of the most common arguments in opposition to racial outreach, which should be addressed.

First, the critique that identity politics is dividing Americans and causing political polarization is an important concern. Countries that become too divided often dissolve into legislative gridlock and can ultimately experience civil war. As Fukuyama (2018) rightly points out, it is essential for those who win elections to be able to govern. If the use of identity politics mobilizes supporters in the elections but alienates others, it may be spell doom for the U.S. government.

While it is possible that a greater focus on identity politics may be tied to polarization, there is good evidence that it alone is not what is causing the high levels of political polarization we see in America today. Instead, it may largely be a symptom of polarization. This book and others have detailed that political polarization began long before identity-based appeals became a common feature in American politics. In fact, several social scientists identified growing levels of political polarization before Barack Obama was elected president in 2008 (Abramowitz and Saunders 2008; Baldassarri and Gelman 2008; Fiorina and Abrams 2008). Moreover, even in a key period in which individuals were divided based on their views of racial resentment and race between 2008 and 2012, very few politicians were making strong cases to address racial inequality (see chapter 1). Americans were therefore becoming divided before a focus on identity politics intensified with the rise of the Black Lives Matter movement.

However, as I have discussed above, it is likely that this polarization made a focus on racial/ethnic minorities more palatable to left-leaning voters. As social movements pushed politicians for recognition, elected officials may have felt safer to take more liberal positions on racial issues because voters who remained on the left during the Obama years were already racially liberal and those who were more racially conservative had already left the party (see Sides, Tesler, and Vavreck 2019). As politicians considered liberal stances on issues like police brutality, voting rights, and immigration and did not see much change in their levels of support because polarization had already sorted these voters, they may have felt freer to take these positions. As a result, it is likely that the rise of identity politics was caused by polarization rather than identity politics being the sole culprit for growing levels of polarization.

This is not to say that racial appeals may not contribute to growing polarization. I found in chapter 9 that white Democrats, blacks, and Latinos rated the Democratic Party more favorably when Hillary Clinton was perceived as being more racially progressive. White Republicans, meanwhile, viewed the Democratic Party less favorably under the same conditions. The focus on racial appeals may deepen the nation's partisan divide, which is certainly a potential downside to the rise of racialized campaigns.

Even in the absence of racial appeals, it is unlikely that the partisan divide will disappear or not be further exacerbated by some other salient issue like universal health care or abortion. Nonetheless, it is important for politicians to think about ways to unify the country and address racial inequality. Identity politics alone may not be able to accomplish both of these important goals. However, this does not mean that it should be disregarded, given that it is important to address the growing problem of racial inequality.

Instead of giving up on racial appeals, Democrats must find ways to engage in racial outreach without alienating voters. One way that this could be done is by educating voters on the advantages of addressing racial inequality for society in general. For example, research shows that by addressing racial inequality many nonblacks experience a growth in economic mobility (Treuhaft, Scoggins, and Tran 2014). Moreover, racial appeals should focus on alleviating racial disparities without accusing others of racism. As I have shown in previous work, accusations of racism tend to diminish support from voters of all races (Stout 2015). While finding the right message may take some work, it is important that political actors don't ignore racial/ethnic disparities in their outreach to voters.

The current political climate provides some opportunities for achieving the goal of diminishing racial inequality. When identity politics is ignored, it is unlikely that social progress will occur in this area. Though political rhetoric may not immediately alter or produce public policy, Gillion (2016) demonstrates that the "ability of government to address inequality in America starts with politicians' voices" (19). Through an analysis of presidential and congressional speeches, Gillion shows not only that race-conscious speech changes the policy agenda, but also that when federal politicians discuss the concerns of racial and ethnic minorities it leads to a greater number of public policies addressing those concerns. As a result, if communities are interested in alleviating racial/ethnic inequalities, politicians should not be afraid to speak out on racial issues. This is particularly true in the current political climate.

In addition to partisan polarization, Fukuyama (2018) fears that identity politics will exacerbate racial polarization and lead whites to leave the Democratic Party because it is focusing too much on racial issues. As mentioned earlier, the largest shift in whites leaving the Democratic Party occurred after the election of Obama in 2008 (who ran a deracialized campaign) but has not worsened since 2012. In fact, this book found little evidence that more whites will leave the Democratic Party because of racial appeals (see chapter 9). Instead, the gap between white Democrats' and white Republicans' feelings about the opposing political party makes large shifts very unlikely in the future. As a result, a focus on identity politics will probably not lead to the tribalism described by Fukuyama (2018), where variation in partisanship becomes almost completely explained by an individual's racial/ethnic background.

The second argument against identity politics is that in any society there are multiple identities, and even more emerge when we begin to look at the intersection of identities. As Peterson (2018) correctly notes, each of these identities faces varying levels of discrimination that influence inequalities. Critics of identity politics often argue that if the world is unequal for many groups, the focus on inequality for some groups and not others is problematic and unfair. While this argument makes sense, lack of discussion of the alternatives significantly weakens this claim.

Not addressing any group's challenges because one cannot solve all inequality in society is an equally unfair proposition. In essence, this argument suggests that individuals who face systematic barriers should do nothing. Surely, wherever inequality exists individuals should take proactive steps to rectify these disparities rather than being lulled into a sense of paralysis. There are multiple fatal and nonfatal diseases in the world, and more emerge all the time. However, very few would argue that there are so many diseases that we should not try to find cures for any of them because it would be unfair to prioritize some over others. Similarly, if there is a lot of inequality in society, elected officials, organizations, and other political actors should do what they can to solve as many disparities as possible. While addressing *all* inequality, like curing *all* diseases, may be impossible, politicians should not ignore racial inequality if there is any hope to make social progress.

Finally, Peterson (2018) argues that instead of focusing on identity politics, individuals should take more personal responsibility and work to improve themselves. He argues that a focus on identity politics decreases individuals' levels of motivation because its rhetoric makes it easier to attribute personal failures to systematic problems in society. One of the main shortcomings with this argument is that it minimizes the plethora of research that demonstrates that racial/ethnic discrimination does in fact lead to significant differences in outcomes, regardless of effort and ability. Pager (2003), for example, showed that employers were more likely to hire whites with a criminal record than blacks or Latinos who have never been to prison.

Peterson's (2018) claim that a focus on discussing identity politics means shirking one's responsibilities misses the fact that discussing racial inequality in hopes of addressing the problem is the pinnacle of striving to improve one's situation. In this way, a focus on identity politics for those who are systematically disenfranchised is an important step in improving their situation.

While the normative implications of identity politics cannot be fully resolved by this short discussion, there are important arguments to counter the narrative that identity politics is a negative force in contemporary society.

Areas for Future Research

How Do Asian Americans Respond to Racial Appeals?

This book will hopefully spur future research answering questions that were not addressed in this study. The focus of this book has been on how voters of different racial/ethnic groups respond to candidates who make racial appeals targeted at blacks and Latinos. An obvious shortcoming of this study is its omission of Asian Americans. Asian Americans are the fastest-growing racial/ethnic group in the United States and represent a key demographic for the Democratic Party (Hune 2002). In the past, Asian Americans tended to be much more conservative than blacks and Latinos. However, in 2016 about twice as many Asian Americans voted for Hillary Clinton as voted for Donald Trump. This makes Asian Americans key swing voters, which may influence whether there are more advantages or disadvantages to the use of racial appeals.

Regrettably, I was not able to assess how this important racial/ethnic group responded to racially liberal candidates and/or racial appeals. This omission is largely due to the small numbers of Asian American respondents in the surveys that I used in my analyses. While the American National Election Studies (ANES) and the Pew Research Center have made concerted efforts to increase the number of blacks and Latinos in their surveys, these and other organizations have been unable to obtain a large number of Asian American respondents.

The lack of data may preclude a formal analysis, but it does not prevent theorizing on how Asian Americans may respond to racialized campaigns. On the one hand, there is a significant amount of research that demonstrates that Asian Americans are often in conflict with the black community. For example, Kim (1999) found that African Americans and Koreans often faced significant conflict when occupying the same space in many American cities. As a result, Asian Americans may reject any campaign approach focused on advancing black interests. Given that Asian Americans are newcomers to the Democratic Party, their loyalty may be fragile. A racialized approach may lead Democrats to lose this key demographic.

On the other hand, there are certainly reasons to believe that Asian Americans may respond favorably to racial appeals in the current political context. Like other racial/ethnic groups, Asian Americans have expressed a growing concern about racial discrimination in the United States. For example, a 2017 poll conducted by Harvard University and the Robert Wood Johnson Foundation found that 1 out of 5 Asian Americans expressed being personally discriminated against because of their race (Robert Wood Johnson Foundation 2017). Moreover, much of the hostile rhetoric from the Trump campaign was focused on Asian American countries, especially China. Republicans' support for ending opportunities for immigrants in the United States by, for example, suspending the Deferred Action for Childhood Arrivals program would also disproportionately hurt Asian Americans, who are more likely to be immigrants than blacks or whites. As a result of these factors, Asian Americans may become more racially conscious.

In fact, in our analysis of a convenience sample of Asian Americans my coauthors and I demonstrated that their levels of racial linked fate increased significantly after the election of Donald Trump and have continued to grow (Le, Arora, and Stout 2018). We found that Asian Americans often linked their poor treatment after Trump's election to their support for other racial/ethnic groups. This is consistent with previous research that demonstrated Asian Americans with high levels of linked fate tend to be more supportive of racially progressive policies, even when those policies are aimed at addressing inequities for other underrepresented groups (Junn and Masuoka 2008).

In our study of Asian American linked fate, my coauthors and I asked participants in an Amazon Mechanical Turk survey to respond to following statement: "If you have experienced an increase in linked fate after the 2016 presidential election, explain why" (Le, Arora, and Stout 2018). Our qualitative data suggested that the current racial context in the United States is leading some Asian Americans to feel closer to other racial/ethnic groups. One Asian American respondent noted, "A lot of Asian Americans have come together as a community to support each other in an uneasy time with Trump as president. They come together in support of the BLM movement, immigration matters and because of growing racism in the USA today." Another Asian American respondent commented that how Trump's handling of race relations has made them feel a stronger need to build coalitions with other groups: "All the recent events have proven that Trump isn't quite 'experienced,' or doesn't care to be experienced, when it comes to dealing with racial harmony. His controversial actions toward women/minorities and 'unintentional' racial remarks are dividing up this great country. We need to stand united."

This growing sense of commonality between Asian Americans and other racial/ethnic groups can be further seen in Letters for Black Lives, an ongoing project for people to create and translate resources on anti-blackness for their communities in solidarity with the Black Lives Matter movement.

Letters for Black Lives was started by a group of Asian Americans who wrote intergenerational letters to demonstrate to others the common experiences that Asian Americans and blacks face in the United States. Such projects suggest that Asian Americans as a group may see blacks more as allies in the current political climate. As a result, it is possible that Asian Americans may be receptive to racial appeals both because they promise to address many of the problems that they are facing around issues such as immigration and discrimination, and also because such messages address inequalities for other racial/ethnic groups that they may increasingly view as allies.

How Do Republicans Influence Minority Turnout?

This book has not tried to definitively answer the question of why Hillary Clinton's racial appeals did not mobilize enough black and Latino voters for her to win the 2016 presidential election. The disconnect between her large number of racial appeals and lower black and Latino turnouts contradicts many of the arguments made in this study. If candidates who racialize in the current context are rewarded with higher levels of racial/ethnic minority turnout, why was Clinton's racial outreach ineffective?

In part, this may have been driven by the Trump campaign's successful effort to paint her as a racial conservative. Trump contracted with Cambridge Analytica and others who used individuals' Facebook data to tailor advertisements to mobilize some groups and minimize turnout among others. Cambridge Analytica whistleblower Christopher Wylie told Congress that an individual's race could be predicted relatively accurately based on their social media presence (Cadwalladr 2018).

Wylie then told a U.S. Senate Intelligence Committee that Trump campaign manager Steve Bannon worked with Cambridge Analytica to provide information to black voters that led them to believe that most elected officials were racist and did not care about blacks, in order to disempower that electorate. Cambridge Analytica also presented black voters with advertisements reminding them that Hillary Clinton once stated that "gangsters" who committed heinous crimes were super-predators. While Clinton did not mention these individuals as being African American, some argued that the statement dehumanized black youth (Stout and Baker 2019).

The Trump campaign also hired Bruce Carter, an African American former supporter of Bernie Sanders, to either secure black support for Trump or get blacks to abstain from voting. One of the common lines Trump would use when he spoke of African Americans was, "Everybody here is voting for Hillary . . . but let me give you a little history on Hillary. If you understood and saw that Hillary saw young black men as super-predators, would that affect you?" (Etter and Riley 2018). These advertisements and statements by the Trump campaign hoped to persuade enough black voters that both the U.S government and especially Clinton did not care about African Americans in order to limit their enthusiasm to turn out in the 2016 general election.

Trump's ability to paint Hillary Clinton as being unsympathetic was aided by Russia's social media campaign in his support. Russian social media activists created numerous fake webpages and organizations that were tied to Black Lives Matter (Stewart, Arif, and Starbird 2018). Stewart, Arif, and Starbird's analyses of Black Lives Matter found that many of Twitter hashtags and tweets associated with the group during the 2016 campaign originated from Russian bots. Many of the tweets reminded voters that Bill Clinton's support for the 1994 Crime Bill increased the incarceration of blacks. Again, such messages were meant to paint Hillary Clinton and her allies as being racially conservative.

Whether this form of outreach diminished black and/or Latino turnout needs to be further analyzed. According to the analyses in chapters 5 and 7, blacks and Latinos who viewed Hillary Clinton as being racially liberal were more likely to report voting in 2016. While much of this book has focused on the campaign tactics of Democratic candidates, more work needs to be done on how their Republican opponents may be able to counter racial outreach by painting Democrats as being racially conservative. Moreover, future research should assess whether and how Democrats can counteract these attacks. In the past, it was advantageous for Republicans to paint Democrats as being racially liberal (Mendelberg 2001). The current political context may provide the incentive for them to do the exact opposite.

Other Areas for Future Research

More work also needs to be done exploring whether certain segments of the white, black, and Latino populations are more or less receptive to racial appeals. This study did include cross-sections of partisanship for whites, but due to lack of data availability I was not able to assess whether race/ethnicity interacted with partisanship for blacks and Latinos. Thus, as more data become available researchers should examine whether blacks and Latinos with different partisanships respond differently to racial appeals. For example, it would be unlikely for racial/ethnic-minority Republicans to respond to racial appeals at the same levels as black and Latino Democrats. However, even this trend may have shifted over time as a broader swath of blacks and Latinos identify as having a lot of linked fate.

There is a significant amount of work that suggests that black women and Latinas tend to be both more racially conscious and racially liberal than their male counterparts (Bejarano 2013; Brown 2014; Gay and Tate 1998; Simien 2005). Thus, it is possible that black women and Latinas may be particularly responsive to racial appeals by politicians. However, my own cursory analysis of this question using the ANES, Pew surveys, and experimental data does not suggest an interaction effect between race and gender. This again may be due to the relatively small sample size of blacks or Latinas in these surveys. As a result, future research may be better able to test the interactive effects of gender, race, and racial appeals as better data become available.

Additionally, this book has focused on one type of identity politics: racial/ethnic appeals. Its analytical framework, however, could be applied to other underrepresented groups. For example, one of the most dramatic changes in American politics following Trump's election to the White House has been the growth of social movements around women's issues. The Women's March in 2017 was the largest protest event in the history of the United States. Moreover, the high-profile sexual harassment cases of Bill Cosby and Harvey Weinstein increased Americans' recognition of the hurdles women face in numerous professions. The online movement #MeToo has allowed women to share their personal stories to others via social media. Similar to the Black Lives Matter movement, its focus on gender issues may increase support for politicians who are vocal about addressing gender inequality in the United States. Future research should examine this possibility and also examine whether and when appeals to other underrepresented groups, such as the LGBTQ community, are most effective.

Finally, this book has largely focused on racial appeals made by Democratic candidates. More work should be done exploring whether Republicans are rewarded or punished for making racial appeals. Given that white Republicans' racial attitudes have not changed much over time, it seems unlikely that a racially progressive agenda would improve Republicans' chances of success. However, it may be that a racially conservative agenda is more or less effective during certain periods of time. For example, both President Trump and Republican presidential candidate Ben Carson argued for ending political correctness, a social norm that protects underrepresented groups from hostile speech. Are candidates rewarded by conservative voters for taking such a hostile position on racial issues? Does the use of such appeals alienate other would be supportive voters? Is such a conservative racial appeal more effective now than in the past? While this study advances our understanding of the efficacy of racial/ethnic appeals for the Democratic Party over time, more research on this topic is necessary.

Final Thoughts

In December of 2017, the white Democrat Doug Jones shocked the country by winning a U.S. Senate seat in deep red Alabama. The state of Alabama had not voted for a Democrat for statewide office since 2006 and had not voted for a Democratic presidential candidate since Jimmy Carter in 1976. In 2016, just one year earlier, only about a third of Alabamans voted for the Democratic presidential nominee Hillary Clinton. How did Jones complete such an upset? The largest factor was that his opponent, Judge Roy Moore, was a controversial figure in the state and had recently been accused of pedophilia. However, even in these circumstances 91 percent of Republicans voted for Moore. Given that the state is overwhelmingly Republican, a bad opponent would not have been enough to carry Jones to victory.

To win, Jones needed an overwhelmingly large black turnout and strong support from white liberals. He would need blacks to comprise a larger percentage of the electorate than they had when Obama ran for president in 2012. This would be a difficult feat given Obama's race. State representative and chairman of the Legislative Black Caucus John Knight told CNN he was skeptical that this could be done: "I hate to say it but [Jones is] no Barack Obama" (quoted in Bradner and Marquardt 2017).

Jones and his allies worked tirelessly to mobilize black voters. Crucially, he had helped convict two Ku Klux Klan members forty years after the 1963 bombing of the 16th Street Baptist Church in Birmingham, Alabama, which killed four young African American girls. He used billboards and fliers to remind black voters of this feat. Jones campaigned with prominent black politicians, including New Jersey U.S. senator Cory Booker and former Massachusetts governor Deval Patrick. He even had Obama record a robocall supporting his candidacy. In the end, Jones achieved what few thought was possible: blacks comprised a larger percentage of the electorate in 2017 than they had when Obama was on the ballot five years earlier.

The ability of Doug Jones to win in the reliably red state of Alabama epitomizes many of the arguments made in this book. The growth of political polarization means that attracting swing voters is largely unlikely to occur. In Alabama, essentially all Democrats (98%) supported Jones and more than 9 out of 10 Republicans supported their party's nominee, even though he was accused of pedophilia. At a time when the public was largely concerned about growing racial inequality and the growing significance of racism in society, a large segment of whites supported Jones in spite of his overtly racialized campaign. In fact, 30 percent of whites in Alabama supported Jones, which was markedly better than Obama's 15 percent of white just five years earlier. In addition to not repelling all white voters, Jones's use of racial appeals appeared to energize black voters. The combination of high black turnout and support from liberal whites helped Jones succeed in a state that may was unwinnable for Democrats in most circumstances.

Doug Jones's success also demonstrates the need for a more nuanced understanding for when a racialized approach is most effective. It is wrong to assume that candidates will always do better if they distance themselves from the concerns of underrepresented groups. A deracialized approach may help some candidates in some circumstances. For example, had Obama used a racialized campaign in 2008 he may not have been successful. During the time Obama was campaigning for president, perceptions of racial/ethnic discrimination were low, and many minority groups displayed low levels of linked fate.

However, there are circumstances, like the ones described in this book, when a deracialized approach may be disadvantageous. The context in which Jones campaigned for office was one where most voters were very cognizant of racial discrimination, and blacks as a group were more racially conscious. Jones needed to address racial issues head on to maximize his support from black voters. Moreover, given the recognition of racial discrimination from some whites in the electorate, he knew that discussing racial inequality would not repel so many white voters that such outreach would be problematic.

In his seminal work on deracialization, Hamilton (1977) reminded practitioners that no political strategy is set in stone. What worked in the past may no longer work today. He warned that politicians and practitioners need to be forward thinking and to calculate when and where a racialized approach is going to be the most effective. From the analysis in this book, it is clear that the racial context of the nation must be included in any such calculation. This book firmly and consistently demonstrates that identity politics can be an important part of any electoral strategy in the right context.

Notes on the Data

This book uses data from about ten unique data sources, including Google Trends, the U.S. Census, Lexis-Nexis, Access World News, and others. However, much of the analysis is based on three of these sources and three separate online experiments. Each is discussed in more detail below.

American National Election Studies

The American National Election Studies (ANES) have been conducted in every presidential election year since 1948. It is the quintessential survey for studying American political behavior. The sample is nationally representative, but in some years they oversampled strategic populations. The survey contacts individuals over phone and later over the Internet. In each presidential election year, about 2,000 respondents are included in the analysis. However, this varies depending on the year. This survey is useful for my purposes because it specifically asks respondents whether they have voted in any given year, whom they voted for, and questions about their racial attitudes on a variety of topics. Given that this book makes the argument that changes over time influence the efficacy of racial appeals, the fact that the ANES survey asks the same questions over a long period of time is extremely useful. While the survey does not include an objective measure of racial appeals, it does include a subjective measure of perceptions of how racially liberal a candidate is. I used this measure in many of my analyses to assess whether racial liberalism hurts or improves a candidate's opportunity for success and whether this has changed in recent years.

General Social Survey

In 1972, NORC at the University of Chicago began collecting data for the General Social Survey (GSS). The GSS is sampled to be nationally representative but, like the ANES, often oversamples certain populations. The main way in which the GSS collects information from individuals is over the phone. The GSS polls Americans' attitudes on numerous issues including crime and violence, intergroup tolerance, and civil rights. The GSS is one of the premier data sets for exploring trends in public opinion over time. Unlike the ANES, which is more focused on political attitudes, the GSS includes several questions that assess individuals' attitudes about other racial/ethnic groups. This data set was useful because it allowed me to explore whether racial attitudes and attitudes about racial public policy have shifted in the new era of American politics.

Pew Research Center

One of the weaknesses of both the GSS and the ANES is that they are only collected every two and four years respectively. Moreover, they often focus on broader policies that have been in the public eye for a long period of time. As a result, both the GSS and ANES only recently began to ask respondents about their attitudes toward Latinos and immigration on their surveys, and many of these questions are only asked sporadically. To supplement the GSS and the ANES, I utilized several surveys from the Pew Research Center. Pew is a nonpartisan think tank that collects information on Americans' attitudes about different issues and has a branch that focuses on Latino public opinion and public opinion on Latinos. Like the GSS and ANES, Pew tracks Americans' changing attitudes over time with cross-sectional surveys. It also collects surveys monthly, allowing me to better identify causes in changing racial attitudes. This data set was particularly useful in that it allowed me to assess whether high-profile appeals to Latinos are effective in shifting support for politicians.

Experimental Analysis

While the ANES, GSS, and Pew Research Center polls allowed me to measure the influence of racial progressivism on vote choice over time, I also commissioned a separate online experiment to a large sample of white, black, and Latino respondents on Amazon Mechanical Turk (MTurk). The collection of the MTurk data took place over four days from July 6 to July 10, 2017. Respondents were paid 50 cents to complete a survey, which took a median time of nine minutes. I used a selective sampling technique to only include those who initially said their race was black or Latino to collect a sample of 160 Latino respondents and 250 black respondents. I also collected data for 410 white respondents. The data set was not sampled to be nationally representative of either the black or white population.

In both experimental groups, survey respondents were told that they were going to be presented with information for an up-and-coming Democratic U.S.

senator who many say could be the party's nominee for the 2020 presidential election. They were then asked their opinions about this hypothetical presidential candidate. Respondents were presented with a campaign webpages with the candidate's name and one issue highlighted.

The survey randomly presented respondents with one of four experimental condition webpages. Respondents reviewed either a webpage with a hypothetical candidate with a black-sounding name (Malik Jackson) or a white-sounding name (Wyatt McHarris). Respondents were also assigned one of two issues. The first was racial justice, and on these webpages the candidate advocated for addressing voting rights, immigrant rights, and fixing a broken criminal justice system. The second issue was economic justice, and on these webpages the candidate advocated for union rights, workers' rights, and fixing a broken financial system. The text describing both issues was written to emulate the "issue" sections of the websites of Hillary Clinton and Bernie Sanders in the 2016 campaign. The texts for the issues were written to mirror each other in most ways and included much of the same language, which can be seen below.

The issues were selected to emulate the current debate around the direction of the Democratic Party. Much of this discussion centers on whether the party would benefit more from adopting a liberal economic agenda or a liberal racial agenda. I also selected the economic justice issue because much of the deracialization literature suggests that the Democratic Party should focus on class issues rather than race to build a successful coalition (see, e.g., Hamilton 1977; Lilla 2017). I made the race of the candidate either black or white because of data that suggest that Obama was particularly punished for making racial appeals. The inclusion of both black and white candidates in my experiment allowed me to assess whether voters still punish black racialized candidates in the current political climate.

Text from Webpages for Black and White U.S. Senate Candidates (Malik Jackson/Wyatt McHarris): Racialized Representation

Racial Justice

I was raised in a household passionate about Civil Rights. From a young age, I knew that hard work must be done to break down barriers and ensure that every American can live up to their full potential.

Below is a list of goals I hope to achieve if I am elected as U.S. Senator . . .

Strengthen the Voting Rights Act—One of the most important achievements of the Civil Rights Movement is under attack. Americans have a fundamental right to be able to cast their ballots without burdensome restrictions. I will fight for the rights of all Americans to . . . *Read more here.*

Fix our Broken Criminal Justice System—While justice is meant to be blind, in practice it is not. As a U.S. Senator, I will fight to end racial profiling as well as strengthen the bonds of trust between communities of color and the police. I will also work to . . . *Read more here.*

Protect Immigrants' Rights and Advocate for Comprehensive Immigration Reform—As a U.S. Senator, I will work towards comprehensive immigration reform, which will include a full and equal pathway to citizenship. Bringing immigrants and families out of the . . . *Read more here.*

Text from Webpages for Black and White U.S. Senate Candidates (Malik Jackson/Wyatt McHarris): Deracialized Representation
Economic Justice
I was raised in a household passionate about workers' rights. From a young age, I knew that hard work must be done to break down barriers and ensure that every American can live up to their full potential.

Below is a list of goals I hope to achieve if I am elected as U.S. Senator . . .

Strengthen the National Labor Relations Act—One of the most important achievements of the Workers' Rights Movement is under attack. Americans have a fundamental right to be able to negotiate with their employers without burdensome restrictions. I will fight for the rights of all Americans to . . . *Read more here.*

Fix our Broken Financial System—While opportunities for economic success is supposed to be balanced for everyone, in practice it is not. As a Senator, I will fight to end unfair corporate loopholes as well as strengthen the bonds of trust between the average Americans and our financial institutions. I will also work to . . . *Read more here.*

Protect Workers' Rights and Advocate for a Mandatory Living Wage—As a U.S. Senator I will work towards broad labor reforms, which will include support for an increase in the minimum wage. Bringing minimum wage workers and their families out of . . . *Read more here.*

Notes on Regression Analysis

In the main text, I utilize logistic regression with min-max probabilities. Logit regression uses a maximum likelihood estimator to provide an understanding between different independent variables and a dichotomous dependent variable. Based on these logit regression models, I estimated min-max probabilities. Min-max probabilities can be interpreted as how much respondents' likelihood of scoring a 1 on the dependent variable changes when they move from having the lowest score on an independent variable of interest to having the highest score on this variable. For example, in chapter 5 I estimate a logit regression predicting support for the leading Democratic candidate in the presidential primary. Based on this analysis, I estimated min-max probabilities that predict how much an individual's probability of supporting the leading Democratic candidate in the primaries changes from when they perceive the candidate as having the lowest value on the aid to black scale to the highest value on this measure.

Bibliography

Abrajano, Marisa, and Zoltan L. Hajnal. 2015. *White Backlash: Immigration, Race, and American Politics*. Princeton, NJ: Princeton University Press.

Abramowitz, Alan I., and Walter J. Stone. 2006. "The Bush Effect: Polarization, Turnout, and Activism in the 2004 Presidential Election." *Presidential Studies Quarterly* 36, no. 2: 141–54.

Alamillo, Rudy, and Loren Collingwood. 2017. "Chameleon Politics: Social Identity and Racial Cross-Over Appeals." *Politics, Groups, and Identities* 5, no. 4: 533–60.

Allen, Jonathan J. M., and Amie Parnes. 2017. *Shattered: Inside Hillary Clinton's Doomed Campaign*. New York: Crown Publishing Group.

Almeida, Joanna, Katie B. Biello, Francisco Pedraza, Suzanne Wintner, and Edna Viruell-Fuentes. 2016. "The Association between Anti-Immigrant Policies and Perceived Discrimination among Latinos in the US: A Multilevel Analysis." *SSM-Population Health* 2: 897–903.

Ansolabehere, Stephen, and Eitan Hersh. 2012. "Validation: What Big Data Reveal about Survey Misreporting and the Real Electorate." *Political Analysis* 20, no. 4: 437–59.

Ayón, Cecilia. 2017. "Perceived Immigration Policy Effects Scale: Development and Validation of a Scale on the Impact of State-Level Immigration Policies on Latino Immigrant Families." *Hispanic Journal of Behavioral Sciences* 39, no. 1: 19–33.

Bacchi, Carol. 2004. "Policy and Discourse: Challenging the Construction of Affirmative Action as Preferential Treatment." *Journal of European Public Policy* 11, no. 1: 128–46.

Bai, Matt. 2008. "Is Obama the End of Black Politics?" *New York Times Magazine*, October 8.

Baldassarri, Delia, and Andrew Gelman. 2008. "Partisans without Constraint: Political Polarization and Trends in American Public Opinion." *American Journal of Sociology* 114, no. 2: 408–46.

Barnett, Arnold. 2018. "Epic Fail? The Polls and the 2016 Presidential Election." *Chance* 31, no. 4: 4–8.

Barreto, Matt. 2010. *Ethnic Cues: The Role of Shared Ethnicity in Latino Political Participation*. Ann Arbor: University of Michigan Press.

———. 2017. "Impact, Influence, and Indignation: Latinos and the 2016 Election." *Aztlan: A Journal of Chicano Studies* 42, no. 2: 141–45.

Barreto, Matt A., and Stephen A. Nuño. 2011. "The Effectiveness of Coethnic Contact on Latino Political Recruitment." *Political Research Quarterly* 64, no. 1: 448–59.

Bartels, Larry M. 2006. "What's the Matter with What's the Matter with Kansas?" *Quarterly Journal of Political Science* 1, no. 2: 201–26.

Bawn, Kathleen, Martin Cohen, David Karol, Seth Masket, Hans Noel, and John Zaller. 2012. "A Theory of Political Parties: Groups, Policy Demands and Nominations in American Politics." *Perspectives on Politics* 10, no. 3: 571–97.

Bedolla, Lisa Garcia, and Melissa R. Michelson. 2012. *Mobilizing Inclusion: Transforming the Electorate Through Get-Out-The-Vote Campaigns.* New Haven, CT: Yale University Press.

Bejarano, Christina E. 2013. *The Latina Advantage: Gender, Race, and Political Success.* Austin: University of Texas Press.

Bell, Aaron T. 2016. "Diversity and Potential: The Latino Electorate in the 2016 Elections." *Contemporary Readings in Law and Social Justice* 8, no. 2: 243–62.

Biesecker, Barbara A. 2017. "From General History to Philosophy: Black Lives Matter, Late Neoliberal Molecular Biopolitics, and Rhetoric." *Philosophy & Rhetoric* 50, no. 4: 409–30.

Blais, André. 2000. *To Vote or Not to Vote?: The Merits and Limits of Rational Choice Theory.* Pittsburgh: University of Pittsburgh Press.

———. 2006. "What Affects Voter Turnout?" *Annual Review of Political Science* 9: 111–25.

Blake, John. 2016. "This is What 'Whitelash' Looks Like." *CNN*, November 19.

Block, Ray. 2011. "Backing Barack Because He's Black: Racially Motivated Voting in the 2008 Election." *Social Science Quarterly* 92, no. 2: 423–46.

Borquez, Julio. 2005. "Partisan Appraisals of Party Defectors: Looking Back at the Reagan Democrats." *American Review of Politics* 26, no 3: 323–46.

Bositis, David A. 2001. *Diverging Generations: The Transformation of African American Policy Views.* Washington, DC: Joint Center for Political and Economic Studies.

Bradner, Eric, and Alex Marquardt. 2017. "Doug Jones Seeks Obama-Level Black Turnout in Alabama Senate Race." *CNN*, December 6.

Brady, David W., Hahrie Han, and Jeremy C. Pope. 2007. "Primary Elections and Candidate Ideology: Out of Step with the Primary Electorate?" *Legislative Studies Quarterly* 32, no. 1: 79–105.

Brown, Nadia E. 2014. *Sisters in the Statehouse: Black Women and Legislative Decision Making.* New York: Oxford University Press.

Cadwalladr, Carole. 2018. "'I Created Steve Bannon's Psychological Warfare Tool': Meet the Data War Whistleblower." *The Guardian*, March 17.

Campbell, David E., and J. Quin Monson. 2008. "The Religion Card: Gay Marriage and the 2004 Presidential Election." *Public Opinion Quarterly* 72, no. 3: 399–419.

Canon, David T., Matthew M. Schousen, and Patrick J. Sellers. 1996. "The Supply Side of Congressional Redistricting: Race and Strategic Politicians, 1972–1992." *Journal of Politics* 58, no. 3: 846–62.

Carneiro, Herman Anthony, and Eleftherios Mylonakis. 2009. "Google Trends: A Web-Based Tool for Real-Time Surveillance of Disease Outbreaks." *Clinical Infectious Diseases* 49, no. 10: 1557–64.

Casellas, Jason P. 2009. "Coalitions in the House?" *Political Research Quarterly* 62, no. 1: 120–31.

Casellas, Jason P., and Sophia J. Wallace. 2015. "The Role of Race, Ethnicity, and Party on Attitudes toward Descriptive Representation." *American Politics Research* 43, no. 1: 144–69.

Casey, Miranda. 2017. "The End of Identity Politics." *Daily KOS*, March 20.

Casteel, Kathryn. 2017. "How Do Americans Feel about the NFL Protests? It Depends on How You Ask." *FiveThirtyEight*, October 9.

Chudy, Jennifer. 2017. "Racial Sympathy in American Politics." PhD diss., University of Michigan.

Clinton, Hillary (@HillaryClinton). 2016. "We are going to respect each other, lift each other up, and celebrate our diversity. #Debate #StrongerTogether http://snappytv.com/tc/2978488." Twitter, October 9. https://twitter.com/hillaryclinton/status/785286087476449280.

Cisneros, Angel Saavedra. 2017. *Latino Identity and Political Attitudes: Why Are Latinos Not Republican?* Cham, Switzerland: Palgrave Macmillan.

Citrin, Jack, Beth Reingold, and Donald P. Green. 1990. "American Identity and the Politics of Ethnic Change." *Journal of Politics* 52, no. 4: 1124–54.

Collingwood, Loren, Matt A. Barreto, and Sergio I. Garcia-Rios. 2014. "Revisiting Latino Voting: Cross-Racial Mobilization in the 2012 Election." *Political Research Quarterly* 67, no. 3: 632–45.

Collingwood, Loren, and Benjamin Gonzalez O'Brien. 2019. *Sanctuary Cities: The Politics of Refuge.* New York: Oxford University Press.

Collingwood, Loren, Francisco Pedraza, and Tye Rush. 2016. "Relieving the Conscience: White Guilt and Candidate Evaluation." Paper presented at Politics of Race, Immigration, and Ethnicity Consortium, University of California, Irvine, CA, March 24.

Cose, Ellis. 2011. *The End of Anger: A New Generation's Take on Race and Rage.* New York: HarperCollins.

Craig, Maureen A., and Jennifer A. Richeson. 2014. "On the Precipice of a 'Majority-Minority' America: Perceived Status Threat from the Racial Demographic Shift Affects White Americans' Political Ideology." *Psychological Science* 25, no. 6: 1189–97.

Dawson, Michael C. 1994. *Behind the Mule: Race and Class in African American Politics.* Princeton, NJ: Princeton University Press.

Defrancesco, Soto, Victoria M. and Jennifer L. Merolla. 2006. "Vota Por Tu Futuro: Partisan Mobilization of Latino Voters in the 2000 Presidential Election." *Political Behavior* 28, no. 4: 285–304.

DeSipio, Louis. 1998. *Counting on the Latino Vote: Latinos as a New Electorate*. Charlottesville: University of Virginia Press.

Desmond-Harris, Jenee. 2016. "A Pollster on the Racial Panic Obama's Presidency Triggered—and What Democrats Must Do Now." *Vox*, December 12.

Dimock, Michael. 2017. "How America Changed during Barack Obama's Presidency." *Pew Research Center*, January 10.

Dittmer, John. 1980. *Black Georgia in the Progressive Era, 1900–1920*. Urbana: University of Illinois Press.

Dovere, Edward-Isaac. 2016. "How Clinton Lost Michigan—and Blew the Election." Politico.com, December 14.

Downs, Antony. 1957. "An Economic Theory of Political Action in a Democracy." *Journal of Political Economy* 65, no. 2: 135–50.

Du Bois, W. E. Burghardt. 1935. "Does the Negro Need Separate Schools?" *Journal of Negro Education* 4(July): 328–35.

Dyson, Michael Eric. 2016. *The Black Presidency: Barack Obama and the Politics of Race in America*. New York: Houghton Mifflin Harcourt.

Egan, Patrick J., and Megan Mullin. 2012. "Turning Personal Experience into Political Attitudes: The Effect of Local Weather on Americans' Perceptions about Global Warming." *Journal of Politics* 74, no. 3: 796–809.

Elder, Laurel, Brian Frederick, and Barbara Burrell. 2018. *American Presidential Candidate Spouses*. Cham, Switzerland: Palgrave Macmillan.

Enten, Harry. 2016. "Americans' Distaste for Both Trump and Clinton Is Record-breaking." *FiveThirtyEight*, May 5.

Etter, Lauren, and Michael Riley. 2018. "Inside the Pro-Trump Effort to Keep Black Voters from the Polls." *Bloomberg Businessweek*, May 29.

Fiorina, Morris P., and Samuel J. Abrams. 2008. "Political Polarization in the American Public." *Annual Review of Political Science* 11: 563–88.

Ford, Pearl K., Tekla A. Johnson, and Angie Maxwell. 2010. "'Yes We Can' or 'Yes We Did'? Prospective and Retrospective Change in the Obama Presidency." *Journal of Black Studies* 40, no. 3: 462–83.

Fraga, Bernard L., Sean McElwee, Jesse Rhodes, and Brian Schaffner. 2017. "Why Did Trump Win? More Whites—and Fewer Blacks—Actually Voted." *Washington Post*, May 8.

Frank, Thomas. 2004. *What's the Matter with Kansas? How Conservatives Won the Heart of America*. New York: Henry Holt.

Frederick, Kristofer A., and Judson L. Jeffries. 2009. "A Study in African American Candidates for High-Profile Statewide Office." *Journal of Black Studies* 39, no. 5: 689–718.

Freelon, Deen, Charlton D. McIlwain, and Meredith Clark. 2016. *Beyond the Hashtags: #Ferguson, #Blacklivesmatter, and the Online Struggle for Offline Justice*. Washington, DC: Center for Media & Social Impact, American University.

Frey, William H., Ruy Teixeira, and Robert Griffin. 2016. "America's Electoral Future: How Changing Demographics Could Impact Presidential Elections from 2016 to 2032." *AEI Paper & Studies*.

Friesema, H. Paul. 1969. "Black Control of Central Cities: The Hollow Prize." *Journal of the American Institute of Planners* 35, no. 2: 75–79.

Frymer, Paul. 1999. *Uneasy Alliances: Race and Party Competition in America*. Princeton, NJ: Princeton University Press.

Fukuyama, Francis. 2018. "Against Identity Politics: The New Tribalism and the Crisis of Democracy." *Foreign Affairs* 97: 90–114.

Gallup. 2012. Presidential Approval Poll.

Garcia, Jennifer R., and Christopher T. Stout. 2018. "Responding to Racial Resentment: How Racial Resentment Shapes the Rhetoric of Members of Congress." Paper presented at the Western Political Science Association Meeting, San Francisco, CA, March.

Gay, Claudine, and Katherine Tate. 1998. "Doubly Bound: The Impact of Gender and Race on the Politics of Black Women." *Political Psychology* 19, no. 1: 169–84.

Gelman, Andrew, Sharad Goel, Douglas Rivers, and David Rothschild. 2016. "The Mythical Swing Voter." *Quarterly Journal of Political Science* 11, no. 1: 103–30.

Geraghty, Jim. 2017. "Demography Isn't Destiny, After All." *National Review*, February 28.

Gerber, Alan S., and Donald P. Green. 2000. "The Effects of Canvassing, Telephone Calls, and Direct Mail on Voter Turnout: A Field Experiment." *American Political Science Review* 94, no. 3: 653–63.

Gerber, Alan S., Donald P. Green, and Christopher W. Larimer. 2010. "An Experiment Testing the Relative Effectiveness of Encouraging Voter Participation by Inducing Feelings of Pride or Shame." *Political Behavior* 32, no. 3: 409–22.

Gilens, Martin. 1999. *Why Americans Hate Welfare: Race, Media, and the Politics of Antipoverty Policy*. Chicago: University of Chicago Press.

———. 2001. "Political Ignorance and Collective Policy Preferences." *American Political Science Review* 95, no. 2: 379–96.

Gillespie, Andra. 2010. "Meet the New Class: Theorizing Young Black Leadership in a "Post-Racial" Era." In *Whose Black Politics?: Cases in Post-Racial Black Leadership*, edited by Andra Gillespie, 23–56. New York: Routledge.

———. 2012. *The New Black Politician: Cory Booker, Newark, and Post-Racial America*. New York: NYU Press.

Gillion, Daniel Q. 2016. *Governing with Words: The Political Dialogue on Race, Public Policy, and Inequality in America*. New York: Cambridge University Press.

Goldstein, Kenneth M., and Travis N. Ridout. 2002. "The Politics of Participation: Mobilization and Turnout over Time." *Political Behavior* 24, no. 1: 3–29.

Gómez, Laura E. 2018. "Manifest Destinies: The Making of the Mexican American Race." New York: NYU Press.

Gonzalez Juenke, Eric, and Anna Christina Sampaio. 2010. "Deracialization and Latino Politics: The Case of the Salazar Brothers in Colorado." *Political Research Quarterly* 63, no. 1: 43–54.

Griffin, Rob, William H. Frey, and Ruy Teixeira. 2016. "Interactive: The Demographic Evolution of the American Electorate, 1980–2060." Center for American Progress, February 24, 2016.

Grossmann, Matt, and David A. Hopkins. 2016. *Asymmetric Politics: Ideological Republicans and Group Interest Democrats*. New York: Oxford University Press.

Guillory, J. Ferrel. 2012. *The South in Red and Purple: Southernized Republicans, Diverse Democrats*. Chapel Hill: University of North Carolina Press.

Gulasekaram, Pratheepan, and S. Karthick Ramakrishnan. 2015. *The New Immigration Federalism*. New York: Cambridge University Press.

Hajnal, Zoltan L. 2006. *Changing White Attitudes toward Black Political Leadership*. New York: Cambridge University Press.

Hajnal, Zoltan, Nazita Lajevardi, and Lindsay Nielson. 2017. "Voter Identification Laws and the Suppression of Minority Votes." *Journal of Politics* 79, no. 2: 363–79.

Hajnal, Zoltan L., and Taeku Lee. 2011. *Why Americans Don't Join the Party: Race, Immigration, and the Failure (of Political Parties) to Engage the Electorate*. Princeton, NJ: Princeton University Press.

Hamilton, Charles V. 1977. "Deracialization: Examination of a Political Strategy." *First World* 1, no. 2: 3–5.

Hanson, Victor. 2017. "The End of Identity Politics." *RealClearPolitics*, February 20.

Harris, Fredrick C. 2012. *The Price of the Ticket: Barack Obama and Rise and Decline of Black Politics*. New York: Oxford University Press.

Harris, Fredrick C., Valeria Sinclair-Chapman, and Brian D. McKenzie. 2005. *Countervailing Forces in African-American Civic Activism, 1973–1994*. New York: Cambridge University Press.

Harrop, Froma. 2016. "Democrats Must Drop Identity Politics" *Denver Post*, November 15.

Hatalsky, Lanae Erickson, and Jim Kessler. 2017. "Why Demography Does Not Equal Destiny." *Third Way*, February 22. https://www.thirdway.org/report/why-demography-does-not-equal-destiny.

Hayden, Sara. 2017. "Michelle Obama, Mom-in-Chief: The Racialized Rhetorical Contexts of Maternity." *Women's Studies in Communication* 40, no. 1: 11–28.

Haynes, Chris, Jennifer Merolla, and S. Karthick Ramakrishnan. 2016. *Framing Immigrants: News Coverage, Public Opinion, and Policy*. New York: Russell Sage Foundation.

Heersink, Boris, and Jeffery A. Jenkins. 2016. "Black-And-Tans Vs. Lily-Whites: Race and Republican Party Organization in the South After Reconstruction, 1868–1952." Paper presented at the Annual Meeting of the American Political Science Association, Philadelphia, PA, September 1–4.

Hero, Rodney E., and Robert R. Preuhs. 2009. "Beyond (the Scope of) Conflict: National Black and Latino Advocacy Group Relations in the Congressional and Legal Arenas." *Perspectives on Politics* 7, no. 3: 501–17.

Hillygus, D. Sunshine, and Todd G. Shields. 2005. "Moral Issues and Voter Decision Making in the 2004 Presidential Election." *PS: Political Science & Politics* 38, no. 2: 201–9.

Hinrichs, Peter. 2012. "The Effects of Affirmative Action Bans on College Enrollment, Educational Attainment, and the Demographic Composition of Universities." *Review of Economics and Statistics* 94, no. 3: 712–22.

Hopkins, Daniel J. 2009. "The Diversity Discount: When Increasing Ethnic and Racial Diversity Prevents Tax Increases." *Journal of Politics* 71, no. 1: 160–77.

Horowitz, Juliana Menasce, and Gretchen Livingston. 2016. "How Americans View the Black Lives Matter Movement." *Pew Research Center*, July 8.

Hsu, Hua. 2009. "The End of White America?" *The Atlantic* (January/February): 46–55.

Huber, Lindsay Perez. 2016. "Make America Great Again: Donald Trump, Racist Nativism and the Virulent Adherence to White Supremacy amid US Demographic Change." *Charleston Law Review* 10, no. 1: 215–44.

Huff, Connor, and Dustin Tingley. 2015. ""Who Are These People?" Evaluating the Demographic Characteristics and Political Preferences of MTurk Survey Respondents." *Research & Politics* 2, no. 3: 1–12.

Hune, Shirley. 2002. "Demographics and Diversity of Asian American College Students." *New Directions for Student Services* 97, no. 1: 11–20.

Hunter, Margaret. 2007. "The Persistent Problem of Colorism: Skin Tone, Status, and Inequality." *Sociology Compass* 1, no. 1: 237–54.

Huntington, Samuel P. 2004. *Who Are We? The Challenges to America's National Identity*. London: Simon and Schuster.

Hurwitz, Jon, Mark Peffley, and Jeffery Mondak. 2015. "Linked Fate and Outgroup Perceptions: Blacks, Latinos, and the US Criminal Justice System." *Political Research Quarterly* 68, no. 3: 505–20.

Ingraham, Christopher. 2016. "The 'Smoking Gun' Proving North Carolina Republicans Tried to Disenfranchise Black Voters." *Washington Post*, July 29.

Issenberg, Sasha. 2012. *The Victory Lab: The Secret Science of Winning Campaigns*. New York: Broadway Books.

Iwama, Janice A. 2018. "Understanding Hate Crimes against Immigrants: Considerations for Future Research." *Sociology Compass* 12, no. 3: 125–65.

Iyengar, Shanto, and Jennifer McGrady. 2007. *Media Politics: A Citizen's Guide*. New York: W. W. Norton.

Jardina, Ashley. 2019. *White Identity Politics*. New York: Cambridge University Press.

Jeffries, Judson L. 1999. "US Senator Edward W. Brooke and Governor L. Douglas Wilder Tell Political Scientists How Blacks Can Win High-Profile Statewide Office." *PS: Political Science & Politics* 32, no. 3: 583–88.

Johnson, Richard. 2015. "Racial Campaign Strategies of Black Candidates in Majority-White Jurisdictions: Decentering Deracialisation." Paper presented at the Conference on Black Politics in a Colour Blind Era, Nuffield College, Oxford University, UK, December 11.

———. 2017. "Hamilton's Deracialization: Barack Obama's Racial Politics in Context." *Du Bois Review: Social Science Research on Race* 14, no. 2: 621–38.

Judis, John B., and Ruy Teixeira. 2004. *The Emerging Democratic Majority.* New York: Simon and Schuster.

Junn, Jane, and Natalie Masuoka. 2008. "Asian American Identity: Shared Racial Status and Political Context." *Perspectives on Politics* 6, no. 4: 729–40.

Kalla, Joshua L., and David E. Broockman. 2018. "The Minimal Persuasive Effects of Campaign Contact in General Elections: Evidence from 49 Field Experiments." *American Political Science Review* 112, no. 1: 148–66.

Kam, Cindy D., and Donald R. Kinder. 2012. "Ethnocentrism as a Short-Term Force in the 2008 American Presidential Election." *American Journal of Political Science* 56, no. 2: 326–40.

Kaufmann, Karen M. 2004. *The Urban Voter: Group Conflict and Mayoral Voting Behavior in American Cities.* Ann Arbor: University of Michigan Press.

Keele, Luke J., Paru R. Shah, Ismail White, and Kristine Kay. 2017. "Black Candidates and Black Turnout: A Study of Viability in Louisiana Mayoral Elections." *Journal of Politics* 79, no. 3: 780–91.

Kerbel, Matthew Robert. 2000. *If It Bleeds, It Leads: An Anatomy of Television News.* New York: Routledge.

Key, Valdimer O., Jr. 1949. *Southern Politics.* Knoxville: University of Tennessee Press.

Kim, Claire Jean. 1999. "The Racial Triangulation of Asian Americans." *Politics & Society* 27, no. 1: 105–38.

———. 2002. "Managing the Racial Breach: Clinton, Black-White Polarization, and the Race Initiative." *Political Science Quarterly* 117, no. 1: 55–80.

Kinder, Donald R., and Allison Dale-Riddle. 2012. *The End of Race?: Obama, 2008, and Racial Politics in America.* New Haven, CT: Yale University Press.

Kinder, Donald R., and D. Roderick Kiewiet. 1979. "Economic Discontent and Political Behavior: The Role of Personal Grievances and Collective Economic Judgments in Congressional Voting." *American Journal of Political Science* 23 no. 3: 495–27.

Kinder, Donald R., and Lynn M. Sanders. 1996. *Divided by Color: Racial Politics and Democratic Ideals.* Chicago: University of Chicago Press.

King, Bridgett A. 2017. "Policy and Precinct: Citizen Evaluations and Electoral Confidence." *Social Science Quarterly* 98, no. 2: 672–89.

Klar, Samara, and Yanna Krupnikov. 2016. *Independent politics.* New York, NY: Cambridge University Press.

Klar, Samara, Yanna Krupnikov, and John Barry Ryan. 2018. "Affective Polarization or Partisan Disdain? Untangling a Dislike for the Opposing Party from a Dislike of Partisanship." *Public Opinion Quarterly* 82, no. 2: 379–90.

Kohut, Andrew. 2015. "Despite Mixed Views on Civil Rights in 1965, Americans Largely Supported Selma Marchers." PBSNewshour.com, March 5.

Krishna, Sankaran. 2019. "Manhunt Presidency: Obama, Race, and the Third World." *Third World Quarterly* 40 no. 2: 284–97.

Le, Danvy, Maneesh Arora, Christopher T. Stout. 2018. "Asian American Identity in the Trump Era." Paper presented at the Midwestern Political Science Association Meeting in Chicago, IL, April 5–8, 2018.

Lee, Frances E. 2016. *Insecure Majorities: Congress and the Perpetual Campaign*. Chicago: University of Chicago Press.

Lefkofridi, Zoe, Nathalie Giger, and Aina Gallego. 2014. "Electoral Participation in Pursuit of Policy Representation: Ideological Congruence and Voter Turnout." *Journal of Elections, Public Opinion and Parties* 24, no. 3: 291–311.

Leighley, Jan E., and Jonathan Nagler. 2013. *Who Votes Now?: Demographics, Issues, Inequality, and Turnout in the United States*. Princeton, NJ: Princeton University Press.

Lenz, Gabriel S. 2009. "Learning and Opinion Change, Not Priming: Reconsidering the Priming Hypothesis." *American Journal of Political Science* 53, no. 4: 821–37.

Levay, Kevin E., Jeremy Freese, and James N. Druckman. 2016. "The Demographic and Political Composition of Mechanical Turk Samples." *Sage Open* 6, no. 1: 1–17.

Levendusky, Matthew. 2009. *The Partisan Sort: How Liberals Became Democrats and Conservatives Became Republicans*. Chicago: University of Chicago Press.

———. 2010. "Clearer Cues, More Consistent Voters: A Benefit of Elite Polarization." *Political Behavior* 32, no. 1: 111–31.

———. 2013. "Why Do Partisan Media Polarize Viewers?" *American Journal of Political Science* 57, no. 3: 611–23.

Lewis, Angela K., Pearl K. Ford Dowe, and Sekou M. Franklin. 2012. "African Americans and Obama's Domestic Policy Agenda: A Closer Look at Deracialization, the Federal Stimulus Bill, and the Affordable Care Act." *Polity* 45, no. 1: 127–52.

Lewis-Beck, Michael S., and Richard Nadeau. 2009. "Obama and the Economy in 2008." *PS: Political Science & Politics* 42, no. 3: 479–83.

Lilla, Mark. 2016. "The End of Identity Liberalism." *New York Times*. November 18.

———. 2017. *The Once and Future Liberal: After Identity Politics*. New York: HarperCollins.

Liu, Baodong. 2003. "Deracialization and Urban Racial Contexts." *Urban Affairs Review* 38, no. 4: 572–91.

Lublin, David. 1997. "The Election of African Americans and Latinos to the US House of Representatives, 1972–1994." *American Politics Quarterly* 25, no. 3: 269–86.

Mack, Brianna. 2011. "Where Did the Mule Go? Analyzing Linked Fate Trends within the 40-and-Under Black Population." Paper presented at the Annual Meeting of the American Political Science Association, Seattle, WA, August 2011.

Mann, Thomas E., and Norman J. Ornstein. 2016. *It's Even Worse Than It Looks: How the American Constitutional System Collided with the New Politics of Extremism*. New York: Basic Books.

Marcus, George E., and Michael B. MacKuen. 1993. "Anxiety, Enthusiasm, and the Vote: The Emotional Underpinnings of Learning and Involvement during Presidential Campaigns." *American Political Science Review* 87, no. 3: 672–85.

Marschall, Melissa J. 2004. "Citizen Participation and the Neighborhood Context: A New Look at the Coproduction of Local Public Goods." *Political Research Quarterly* 57, no. 2: 231–44.

Masuoka, Natalie. 2006. "Together They Become One: Examining the Predictors of Panethnic Group Consciousness among Asian Americans and Latinos." *Social Science Quarterly* 87, no. 5: 993–1011.

McAdam, Doug. 1999. *Political Process and the Development of Black Insurgency, 1930–1970*. Chicago: University of Chicago Press.

McCarty, Nolan, Keith T. Poole, and Howard Rosenthal. 2009. "Does Gerrymandering Cause Polarization?" *American Journal of Political Science* 53, no. 3: 666–80.

———. 2016. *Polarized America: The Dance of Ideology and Unequal Riches*. Cambridge, MA: MIT Press.

McCaskill, Nolan D. 2016. "Trump Tells Wisconsin: Victory Was a Surprise." Politico.com, December 13.

McClain, Paula D., Niambi M. Carter, Victoria M. Defrancesco Soto, Monique L. Lyle, Jeffrey D. Grynaviski, Shayla C. Nunnally, Thomas J. Scotto, J. Alan Kendrick, Gerald F. Lackey, and Kendra Davenport Cotton. 2006. "Racial Distancing in a Southern City: Latino Immigrants' Views of Black Americans." *Journal of Politics* 68, no. 3: 571–84.

McClain, Paula D., Monique L. Lyle, Niambi M. Carter, Victoria M. DeFrancesco Soto, Gerald F. Lackey, Kendra Davenport Cotton, Shayla C. Nunnally, Thomas J. Scotto, Jeffrey D. Grynaviski, and J. Alan Kendrick. 2007. "Black Americans and Latino Immigrants in a Southern City: Friendly Neighbors or Economic Competitors?" *Du Bois Review: Social Science Research on Race* 4, no. 1: 97–117.

McCluskey, Michael. 2019. "Profanity and the President: News Use of Trump's Shithole Comment." *Newspaper Research Journal* 40, no. 4: 415–30.

McCombs, Maxwell E., and Donald L. Shaw. 1972. "The Agenda-Setting Function of Mass Media." *Public Opinion Quarterly* 36, no. 2: 176–87.

McConahay, John B., and Joseph C. Hough. 1976. "Symbolic Racism." *Journal of Social Issues* 32, no. 2: 23–45.

McConnaughy, Corrine M., Ismail K. White, David L. Leal, and Jason P. Casellas. 2010. "A Latino on the Ballot: Explaining Coethnic Voting among Latinos and the Response of White Americans." *Journal of Politics* 72, no. 4: 1199–211.

McCormick, Joseph, and Charles E. Jones. 1993. "The Conceptualization of Deracialization: Thinking Through the Dilemma." in *Dilemmas of Black Politics: Issues of Leadership and Strategy*, edited by Georgia A. Persons, 66–84. New York: HarperCollins.

McIlwain, Charlton, and Stephen M. Caliendo. 2011. *Race Appeal: How Candidates Invoke Race in US Political Campaigns*. Philadelphia: Temple University Press.

Meier, Kenneth J., and Joseph Stewart Jr. 1991. "Cooperation and Conflict in Multiracial School Districts." *Journal of Politics* 53, no. 4: 1123–33.

Memoli, Michael. 2016. "Black Lives Matter Playing a Prominent Role at Democratic Convention." *Los Angeles Times*, July 26.

Mendelberg, Tali. 2001. *The Race Card: Campaign Strategy, Implicit Messages, and the Norm of Equality*. Princeton, NJ: Princeton University Press.

Michelson, Melissa R. 2003. "The Corrosive Effect of Acculturation: How Mexican Americans Lose Political Trust." *Social Science Quarterly* 84, no. 4: 918–33.

Michelson, Melissa R., Lisa García Bedolla, and Margaret A. McConnell. 2009. "Heeding the Call: The Effect of Targeted Two-Round Phone Banks on Voter Turnout." *Journal of Politics* 71, no. 4: 1549–63.

Miller, Arthur H., Patricia Gurin, Gerald Gurin, and Oksana Malanchuk. 1981. "Group Consciousness and Political Participation." *American Journal of Political Science* 25 no. 3: 494–511.

Mohl, Raymond A. 2016. "The Politics of Expulsion: A Short History of Alabama's Anti-Immigrant Law, HB 56." *Journal of American Ethnic History* 35, no. 3: 42–67.

Montagne, Renee. 2008. "Obama's Triumph: A Turning Point for America?" npr.org, June 5.

Mounk, Yascha. 2017. "The Coming Democratic Majority? Not So Fast." *Slate*, March 6.

Mullinix, Kevin J., Thomas J. Leeper, James N. Druckman, and Jeremy Freese. 2015. "The Generalizability of Survey Experiments." *Journal of Experimental Political Science* 2, no. 2: 109–38.

Needham, Catherine. 2005. "Brand Leaders: Clinton, Blair and the Limitations of the Permanent Campaign." *Political Studies* 53, no. 2: 343–61.

Nelson, Thomas E., Kira Sanbonmatsu, and Harwood K. McClerking. 2007. "Playing a Different Race Card: Examining the Limits of Elite Influence on Perceptions of Racism." *Journal of Politics* 69, no. 2: 416–29.

Newman, Benjamin J., Sono Shah, and Loren Collingwood. 2018. "Race, Place, and Building a Base: Latino Population Growth and the Nascent Trump Campaign for President." *Public Opinion Quarterly* 82, no. 1: 122–34.

Newport, Frank. 2012. "Blacks, Nonblacks Hold Sharply Different Views of Martin Case: Blacks More Likely to Believe Race Is a Major Factor." *Gallup Politics*, April 5.

Nteta, Tatishe M., and Melinda R. Tarsi. 2016. "Self-Selection versus Socialization Revisited: Military Service, Racial Resentment, and Generational Membership." *Armed Forces & Society* 42, no. 2: 362–85.

Nuño, Stephen A. 2007. "Latino Mobilization and Vote Choice in the 2000 Presidential Election." *American Politics Research* 35, no. 2: 273–93.

Ojalvo, Holly E. 2012. "What Is Your Reaction to the Trayvon Martin Case?" *New York Times*, March 23.

Orey, Byron D'Andra. 2006. "Deracialization or Racialization: The Making of a Black Mayor in Jackson, Mississippi." *Politics & Policy* 34, no. 4: 814–36.

Orey, Byron D'Andra, and Boris E. Ricks. 2007. "A Systematic Analysis of the Deracialization Concept." *National Political Science Review* 11: 325–34.

Outten, H. Robert, Michael T. Schmitt, Daniel A. Miller, and Amber L. Garcia. 2012. "Feeling Threatened about the Future: Whites' Emotional Reactions to Anticipated Ethnic Demographic Changes." *Personality and Social Psychology Bulletin* 38, no. 1: 14–25.

Ovink, Sarah M., and Demetra Kalogrides. 2015. "No Place like Home? Familism and Latino/a–White Differences in College Pathways." *Social Science Research* 52, no. 2: 219–35.

Owens, Michael Leo, and Jacob Robert Brown. 2014. "Weakening Strong Black Political Empowerment: Implications from Atlanta's 2009 Mayoral Election." *Journal of Urban Affairs* 36, no. 4: 663–81.

Packer, George. 2016. "Head of the Class: How Donald Trump Is Winning Over the White Working Class." *New Yorker*, May 16, 2016.

Padilla, Felix M. 1985. *Latino Ethnic Consciousness: The Case of Mexican Americans and Puerto Ricans in Chicago*. Notre Dame, IN: University of Notre Dame Press.

Pager, Devah. 2003. "The Mark of a Criminal Record." *American Journal of Sociology* 108, no. 5: 937–75.

Panagopoulos, Costas. 2009. "Partisan and Nonpartisan Message Content and Voter Mobilization: Field Experimental Evidence." *Political Research Quarterly* 62, no. 1: 70–76.

———. 2016. "All about That Base: Changing Campaign Strategies in US Presidential Elections." *Party Politics* 22, no. 2: 179–90.

Parker, Christopher Sebastian. 2017. "A History of American Reactionary Movements: From the Klan to Donald Trump." *ZPB Zeitschrift Für Politikberatung* 8, no. 1: 38–48.

Parker, Christopher S., and Matt A. Barreto. 2013. *Change They Can't Believe In: The Tea Party and Reactionary Politics in America*. Princeton, NJ: Princeton University Press.

Passel, Jeffrey S., and David Cohn. 2018. "US Unauthorized Immigrant Total Dips to Lowest Level in a Decade." *Pew Research Center.*

Penn, Mark, and Andrew Stein. 2017. "Back to the Center, Democrats." *New York Times*, July 6.

Perry, Huey L. 1991. "Deracialization as an Analytical Construct in American Urban Politics." *Urban Affairs Quarterly* 27, no. 2: 181–91.

Perry, Ravi K. 2011. "Kindred Political Rhetoric: Black Mayors, President Obama, and the Universalizing of Black Interests." *Journal of Urban Affairs* 33, no. 5: 567–90.

Perry, Samuel. 2018. "President Trump and Charlottesville: Uncivil Mourning and White Supremacy." *Journal of Contemporary Rhetoric* 8, no 1/2: 57–71.

Peterson, Jordan B. 2018. *12 Rules for Life: An Antidote to Chaos*. Toronto: Random House Canada.

Pettigrew, Thomas F., and Denise A. Alston. 1988. *Tom Bradley's Campaign for Governor: The Dilemma of Race and Political Strategies*. Washington, DC: Joint Center for Political Studies.

Philpot, Tasha. 2009. *Race, Republicans, and the Return of the Party of Lincoln*. Ann Arbor: University of Michigan Press.

———. 2017. *Conservative but Not Republican*. New York: Cambridge University Press.

Philpot, Tasha S., Daron R. Shaw, and Ernest B. McGowen. 2009. "Winning the Race: Black Voter Turnout in the 2008 Presidential Election." *Public Opinion Quarterly* 73, no. 5: 995–1022.

Pierannunzi, Carol A., and John D. Hutcheson Jr. 1991. "Deracialization in the Deep South: Mayoral Politics in Atlanta." *Urban Affairs Quarterly* 27, no. 2: 192–201.

———. 1996. "The Rise and Fall of Deracialization: Andrew Young as Mayor and Gubernatorial Candidate." *Race Politics, and Governance in the United States*: 96–106.

Piston, Spencer. 2010. "How Explicit Racial Prejudice Hurt Obama in the 2008 Election." *Political Behavior* 32, no. 4: 431–51.

Pittman, Coretta. 2006. "Black Women Writers and the Trouble with Ethos: Harriet Jacobs, Billie Holiday, and Sister Souljah." *Rhetoric Society Quarterly* 37, no. 1: 43–70.

Piven, Frances Fox, and Richard A. Cloward. 1982. *The New Class War: Reagan's Attack on the Welfare State and Its Consequences*. New York: Pantheon.

Price, Melanye T. 2016. *The Race Whisperer: Barack Obama and the Political Uses of Race*. New York: NYU Press.

Rees, Matthew. 1991. *From the Deck to the Sea: Blacks and the Republican Party*. New York: Longwood Press.

Reeves, Keith. 1997. *Voting Hopes or Fears? White Voters, Black Candidates & Racial Politics in America*. New York: Oxford University Press.

Reich, Michael. 2017. *Racial Inequality: A Political-Economic Analysis*. Princeton, NJ: Princeton University Press.

Reed, Adolph Jr. 2013. "Marx, Race, and Neoliberalism." *New Labor Forum* 22, no. 1: 49–57.

Remnick, David. 2014. "Going the Distance: On and off the Road with Barack Obama." *The New Yorker*, January 20.

Rickford, Russell. 2016. "Black Lives Matter: Toward a Modern Practice of Mass Struggle." *New Labor Forum* 25, no. 1: 1–25.

Roberts, Sam. 2008. "In a Generation, Minorities May Be the US Majority." *New York Times*, August 14.

Robert Wood Johnson Foundation. 2017. *Discrimination in America: Experiences and Views of Asian Americans*.

Sanchez, Gabriel R. 2006. "The Role of Group Consciousness in Latino Public Opinion." *Political Research Quarterly* 59, no. 3: 435–46.

Sanchez, Gabriel R., and Barbara Gomez-Aguinaga. 2017. "Latino Rejection of the Trump Campaign: How Trump's Racialized Rhetoric Mobilized the Latino Electorate as Never Before." *Aztlan: A Journal of Chicano Studies* 42, no. 2: 165–81.

Sanchez, Gabriel R., and Natalie Masuoka. 2010. "Brown-Utility Heuristic? The Presence and Contributing Factors of Latino Linked Fate." *Hispanic Journal of Behavioral Sciences* 32, no. 4: 519–31.

Sanchez, Liliana. 2015. "Crosslinguistic Influences in the Mapping of Functional Features in Quechua-Spanish Bilingualism." In *The Acquisition of Spanish in Understudied Language Pairings*, edited by Tiffany Judy and Silvia Perpiñán, 21–48. Amsterdam: John Benjamins.

Scala, Dante J., Kenneth M. Johnson, and Luke T. Rogers. 2015. "Red Rural, Blue Rural? Presidential Voting Patterns in a Changing Rural America." *Political Geography* 48, no. 1: 108–18.

Schaffner, Brian F. 2011. "Racial Salience and the Obama Vote." *Political Psychology* 32, no. 6: 963–88.

Schmidt, Samuel, Evan. L. Frederick, Ann Pegoraro, and Tyler C. Spencer. 2019. "An Analysis of Colin Kaepernick, Megan Rapinoe, and the National Anthem Protests." *Communication and Sport* 7, no. 5: 653–77.

Sears, David O. 1988. "Symbolic Racism." In *Eliminating Racism: Perspectives in Social Psychology*, edited by P. A. Katz and D. A. Taylor, 53–84. Boston: Springer.

Shaw, Todd, Louis DeSipio, Dianne Pinderhughes, and Toni-Michelle C. Travis. 2014. *Uneven Roads: An Introduction to US Racial and Ethnic Politics.* Washington, DC: CQ Press.

Sides, John, Michael Tesler, and Lynn Vavreck. 2017. "How Trump Lost and Won." *Journal of Democracy* 28, no. 2: 34–44.

———. 2019. *Identity Crisis: The 2016 Presidential Campaign and the Battle for the Meaning of America*. Princeton, NJ: Princeton University Press.

Sigelman, Carol K., Lee Sigelman, Barbara J. Walkosz, and Michael Nitz. 1995. "Black Candidates, White Voters: Understanding Racial Bias in Political Perceptions." *American Journal of Political Science* 39, no. 1: 243–65.

Silver, Brian D., Barbara A. Anderson, and Paul R. Abramson. 1986. "Who Overreports Voting?" *American Political Science Review* 80, no. 2: 613–24.

Simien, Evelyn M. 2005. "Race, Gender, and Linked Fate." *Journal of Black Studies* 35, no. 5: 529–50.

Sinclair-Chapman, Valeria, and Melanye Price. 2008. "Black Politics, the 2008 Election, and the (Im)Possibility of Race Transcendence." *PS: Political Science & Politics* 41, no. 4: 739–45.

Smidt, Corwin D. 2017. "Polarization and the Decline of the American Floating Voter." *American Journal of Political Science* 61, no. 2: 365–81.

Smith, Candis Watts. 2014. *Black Mosaic: The Politics of Black Pan-Ethnic Diversity.* New York: NYU Press.

Smith, Daniel A., Matthew Desantis, and Jason Kassel. 2006. "Same-Sex Marriage Ballot Measures and the 2004 Presidential Election." *State and Local Government Review* 38, no. 2: 78–91.

Smith, Robert C. 1990. "Recent Elections and Black Politics: The Maturation or Death of Black Politics?" *PS: Political Science and Politics* 23, no. 2: 160–62.

Soto, Victoria M. DeFrancesco, and Jennifer L. Merolla. 2006. "Vota por tu Futuro: Partisan Mobilization of Latino Voters in the 2000 Presidential Election." *Political Behavior* 28, no. 4: 285–304.

Spence, Lester K., and Harwood McClerking. 2010. "Context, Black Empowerment, and African American Political Participation." *American Politics Research* 38, no. 5: 909–30.

Stephens-Davidowitz, Seth. 2014. "The Cost of Racial Animus on a Black Candidate: Evidence Using Google Search Data." *Journal of Public Economics* 118: 26–40.

Stephens-Dougan, Lafleur. 2016. "Priming Racial Resentment without Stereotypic Cues." *Journal of Politics* 78, no. 3: 687–704.

Stewart, Charles III. 2012. "Waiting to Vote in 2012." *JL & Pol.* 28, no. 1: 439–54.

Stewart, Leo G., Ahmer Arif, and Kate Starbird. 2018. "Examining Trolls and Polarization with a Retweet Network." In *Proceedings of WSDM workshop on Misinformation and Misbehavior Mining on the Web (MIS2)*, 1–9. New York: ACM.

Stokes, Atiya Kai. 2003. "Latino Group Consciousness and Political Participation." *American Politics Research* 31, no. 4: 361–78.

Stout, Christopher T. 2015. *Bringing Race Back In: Black Politicians, Deracialization, and Voting Behavior in the Age of Obama*. Charlottesville: University of Virginia Press.

———. 2018. "Obamacares: Candidate Empathy, Descriptive Representation, and Black Empowerment." *Journal of Racial and Ethnic Politics* 3, no. 2: 356–80.

Stout, Christopher T., and Keith Baker. 2019. "The Super Predator Effect." Paper presented at the American Political Science Association Meeting in Boston, MA, September 4–8.

Stout, Christopher T., and Jennifer R. Garcia. 2015. "The Big Tent Effect: Descriptive Candidates and Black and Latino Political Partisanship." *American Politics Research* 43, no. 2: 205–31.

Stout, Christopher T., and Danvy Le. 2012. "Living the Dream: Barack Obama and Blacks' Changing Perceptions of the American Dream." *Social Science Quarterly* 93, no. 5: 1338–59.

Swim, Janet K., and Deborah L. Miller. 1999. "White Guilt: Its Antecedents and Consequences for Attitudes toward Affirmative Action." *Personality and Social Psychology Bulletin* 25, no. 4 (1999): 500–514.

Taber, Charles S., and Milton Lodge. 2006. "Motivated Skepticism in the Evaluation of Political Beliefs." *American Journal of Political Science* 50, no. 3: 755–69.

Tate, Katherine. 1991. "Black Political Participation in the 1984 and 1988 Presidential Elections." *American Political Science Review* 85, no. 4: 1159–176.

———. 2003. *From Protest to Politics: The New Black Voters in American Elections*. Cambridge, MA: Harvard University Press.

———. 2004. *Black Faces in the Mirror: African Americans and Their Representatives in the US Congress*. Princeton, NJ: Princeton University Press.

———. 2010. *What's Going On?: Political Incorporation and the Transformation of Black Public Opinion*. Washington, DC: Georgetown University Press.

Teixeira, Ruy, and Joel Rogers. 2001. *America's Forgotten Majority: Why the White Working Class Still Matters*. New York: Basic Books.

Tesler, Michael. 2012. "The Spillover of Racialization into Health Care: How President Obama Polarized Public Opinion by Racial Attitudes and Race." *American Journal of Political Science* 56, no. 3: 690–704.

———. 2013. "'Who Cares about Budget Deficits?" *Monkey Cage* (blog), February 27, 2013. https://themonkeycage.org/2013/02/who-cares-about-budget-deficits/.

———. 2016. *Post-Racial or Most-Racial?: Race and Politics in the Obama Era*. University of Chicago Press.

Tesler, Michael, and David O. Sears. 2010. *Obama's Race: The 2008 Election and the Dream of a Post-Racial America*. Chicago: University of Chicago Press.

Thompson, Krissah, and Jon Cohen. 2012. "Trayvon Martin Case: Poll Finds Stark Racial Divide." *Washington Post*, April 10.

Toomey, Russell B., Adriana J. Umaña-Taylor, David R. Williams, Elizabeth Harvey-Mendoza, Laudan B. Jahromi, and Kimberly A. Updegraff. 2014. "Impact of Arizona's SB 1070 Immigration Law on Utilization of Health Care and Public Assistance among Mexican-Origin Adolescent Mothers and Their Mother Figures." *American Journal of Public Health* 104, no. S1: S28–S34.

Tran, Van C., and Nicol M. Valdez. 2017. "Second-Generation Decline or Advantage? Latino Assimilation in the Aftermath of the Great Recession." *International Migration Review* 51, no. 1: 155–90.

Treuhaft, Sarah, Justin Scoggins, and Jennifer Tran. 2014. *The Equity Solution: Racial Inclusion Is Key to Growing a Strong New Economy*. Oakland, CA: PolicyLink.

Valentino, Nicholas A., Fabian G. Neuner, and L. Matthew Vandenbroek. 2018. "The Changing Norms of Racial Political Rhetoric and the End of Racial Priming." *Journal of Politics* 80, no. 3: 757–71.

Valenzuela, Ali A., and Melissa R. Michelson. 2016. "Turnout, Status, and Identity: Mobilizing Latinos to Vote with Group Appeals." *American Political Science Review* 110, no. 4: 615–30.

Vargas, Edward D., Gabriel R. Sanchez, and Juan A. Valdez. 2017. "Immigration Policies and Group Identity: How Immigrant Laws Affect Linked Fate among US Latino Populations." *Journal of Race, Ethnicity and Politics* 2, no. 1: 35–62.

Waldman, Paul. 2014. "Yes, Opposition to Obamacare Is Tied Up with Race." *Washington Post*, March 23.

———. 2016. "What Hillary Clinton's Latest Slogan—'We're Stronger Together'—Really Says about Her Candidacy." *Washington Post*, May 23.

Walters, Ron. "Barack Obama and the Politics of Blackness." 2007. *Journal of Black Studies* 38, no. 1: 7–29.

Wattenberg, Martin P. 2002. *Where Have All the Voters Gone?* Cambridge, MA: Harvard University Press.

———. 2008. *Is Voting for Young People?* New York: Routledge.

———. 2009. *The Decline of American Political Parties, 1952–1996*. Cambridge, MA: Harvard University Press.

Weir, Kirsten. 2017. "The Men America Left Behind." *Monitor on Psychology* 48, no. 2: 34–47.

Wickham, Dewayne. 2004. *Bill Clinton and Black America*. New York: One World/Ballantine.

Wilcox, Clyde, Lee Sigelman, and Elizabeth Cook. 1989. "Some Like It Hot: Individual Differences in Responses to Group Feeling Thermometers." *Public Opinion Quarterly* 53, no. 2: 246–57.

Williamson, Kevin. 2016. "An End of Identity Liberalism." *National Review*, November 27.

Williamson, Vanessa, Theda Skocpol, and John Coggin. 2011. "The Tea Party and the Remaking of Republican Conservatism." *Perspectives on Politics* 9, no. 1: 25–43.

Wilson, John K. 2019. *President Barack Obama: A More Perfect Union*. New York: Routledge Press.

Wilson, William Julius. 1980. *The Declining Significance of Race: African Americans and Changing American Institutions*. Chicago: University of Chicago Press.

———. 1987. *The Truly Disadvantaged: The Inner City, the Underclass, and Public Policy*. Chicago: University of Chicago Press.

Wolfinger, Raymond E., and Steven J. Rosenstone. 1980. *Who Votes?* New Haven, CT: Yale University Press.

Wright Austin, Sharon D., and Richard T. Middleton IV. 2004. "The Limitations of the Deracialization Concept in the 2001 Los Angeles Mayoral Election." *Political Research Quarterly* 57, no. 2: 283–93.

Zhang, Yinjunjie, Marco A. Palma, and Zhicheng Phil Xu. 2016. "Unintended Effects of the Alabama HB 56 Immigration Law on Crime: A Preliminary Analysis." *Economics Letters* 147: 68–71.

Index

Recent Books in the Series
RACE, ETHNICITY, AND POLITICS

The Case for Identity Politics: Polarization, Demographic Change, and Racial Appeals
Christopher T. Stout

Handcuffs and Chain Link: Criminalizing the Undocumented in America
Benjamin Gonzalez O'Brien

Partners or Rivals? Power and Latino, Black, and White Relations in the Twenty-First Century
Betina Cutaia Wilkinson

Bringing Race Back In: Black Politicians, Deracialization, and Voting Behavior in the Age of Obama
Christopher T. Stout

Ambivalent Miracles: Evangelicals and the Politics of Racial Healing
Nancy D. Wadsworth

Mobilizing Opportunities: The Evolving Latino Electorate and the Future of American Politics
Ricardo Ramírez

The Color of Power: Racial Coalitions and Political Power in Oakland
Frédérick Douzet

Faith and Race in American Political Life
Robin Dale Jacobson and Nancy Wadsworth, editors

Latino Politics: Identity, Mobilization, and Representation
Rodolfo Espino, David L. Leal, and Kenneth J. Meier, editors

Lessons in Integration: Realizing the Promise of Racial Diversity in American Schools
Erica Frankenberg and Gary Orfield, editors